Blender 3D Printing by Example

Learn to use Blender's modeling tools for 3D printing by creating 4 projects

Vicky Somma

BIRMINGHAM - MUMBAI

Blender 3D Printing by Example

First published: December 2017

Production reference: 1191217

Published by Packt Publishing Ltd.
Livery Place
35 Livery Street
Birmingham
B3 2PB, UK.

ISBN 978-1-78839-054-5

www.packtpub.com

Credits

Author
Vicky Somma

Reviewer
Fernando Castilhos Melo

Commissioning Editor
Kunal Chaudhari

Acquisition Editor
Noyonika Das

Content Development Editor
Aditi Gour

Technical Editor
Shweta Jadhav

Copy Editor
Safis Editing

Project Coordinator
Hardik Bhinde

Proofreader
Safis Editing

Indexer
Francy Puthiry

Graphics
Jason Monteiro

Production Coordinator
Aparna Bhagat

About the Author

Vicky Somma started 3D printing her Blender designs in 2014, empowered by the 3D Printing Service Bureau, Shapeways, a full year before owning her own 3D printer. In November 2014, she was named one of the winners of the White House 3D Printed Ornament Design Contest. Her ornament, designed in Blender and inspired by the Library of Congress, hung in the East Wing of the White House and is now part of a Smithsonian Collection. For the 2015 and 2016 Holiday Seasons, she had Blender-designed 3D printed ornaments hanging in the Virginia Executive Mansion.

In addition to Blender, Vicky also designs OpenSCAD. She prints on a MakerGear M2 and a Wanhao Duplicator i3 to make a line of designs that she sells at craft shows and Etsy. She teaches TinkerCad and 3D printing classes for local librarians. She maintains a 3D printing blog and makes regular appearances on the Friday 3D Printing Community Hangouts (#F3DPCH).

Vicky's 3D printed Blender designs have been featured on NBC's TODAY, CBSNews, the Washington Post, Michelle Obama's Instagram, and websites such as 3DPrint, 3DPrintingIndustry, and 3Ders. Her designs have been highlighted by Thingiverse, Simplify3D, and Shapeways.

Acknowledgments

The supportive Shapeways staff and their designer community; "real" designers such as *Ontogenie's* Kimberly Falk, *Universe Becoming's* James Kincaid, *Melange's* Michael Williams, and *Likesyrup's* Scott Denton took the time to offer feedback, share words of encouragement, and answer questions to a brand new, fledgling 3D modeler such as myself.

The YouTubers who work tirelessly to share their knowledge and friendship. Joel Telling from *3D Printing Nerd*, Joe Larson from *3D Printing Professor*, and Tessa Nesci from *SparkyFace5* all taught me skills that immediately improved my workflow. He does not know me or my name, but I will always be grateful to *CG Cookie's* Jonathan Williamson and his impeccable Blender tutorials that got me started.

The embracing maker and 3D printing community, particularly the very first ambassadors who made me feel immediately welcome—Matt Gorton of *Printed Solid* and *3D Central's* Chris Caswell and Andrew Sink.

The educators who are determined to bring 3D printing and design to our public schools and libraries, such as *Design Make Teach's* Josh Ajima and *Fairfax County Public Library's* Margaret Kositch. Their work is inspiring and motivating. They teach me how to teach.

The business owners of Occoquan, Virginia, and their sharing of leads and ideas. The Coordinate Bracelet from chapters 5 to 7 was the suggestion of *The Polka Dot Diva's* Kristyn Gleason.

The friends who encouraged me to take on this intimidating and time-consuming project—Aaron Evans, Ann Bowman Jones, Brian Nenninger, and Mark Duncan.

My boss at my day job at *Management Solutions of Virginia*, Larry Bowman; he endlessly mocks my 3D printing, but I know he is secretly proud of me.

The editing staff at PacktPub who worked just as hard, possibly harder, than me.

My family on the front line. My mother, Anne Sawyer, took on extra chores without complaint or hesitation. My two sons, Sagan and Dyson, not only weathered Mommy's divided focus but patiently posed for pictures again and again and again (and again). My nephew, Lincoln, appears in Chapter 2, *Using a Background Image and Bezier Curves*, thanks to the permission of his parents, Brittany and Chris Neigh.

Finally, my husband, Ryan; from blogging to my embarrassing attempts in college to emulate Kurt Vonnegut—when I write, I write with him in mind.

Photo credits:

Chapter 2, *Using a Background Image and Bezier Curves*, Roy Lichtenstein House 1 Photos by Aaron Evans

Chapter 3, *Converting a Bezier Curve to a Properly Sized 3D Mesh*, Quilt Square photos by Heidi Elliott

About the Reviewer

Fernando Castilhos Melo lives in Toronto, Canada, and works as a software developer. Since 2009, he has worked on 3D modeling using Blender. He has given some lectures about Blender and 3D modeling at several Brazilian free/open source software events. Fernando holds a degree in computer science from UCS (University of Caxias do Sul). This is the third Blender book he has worked on. The other ones were *Blender Cycles: Lighting and Rendering Cookbook* in 2013 and *Blender 3D by Example* in 2015. He developed an integration between Blender and Kinect named "Kinected Blender" to generate a 3D animation. This project is currently in alpha version.

I want to thank my wife, Mauren, my parents, Eloir and Miriam, and all my friends for their support during the review of this book.

www.Packtpub.com

For support files and downloads related to your book, please visit www.PacktPub.com. Did you know that Packt offers eBook versions of every book published, with PDF and ePub files available? You can upgrade to the eBook version at www.PacktPub.com and as a print book customer, you are entitled to a discount on the eBook copy. Get in touch with us at service@packtpub.com for more details.

At www.PacktPub.com, you can also read a collection of free technical articles, sign up for a range of free newsletters and receive exclusive discounts and offers on Packt books and eBooks.

https://www.packtpub.com/mapt

Get the most in-demand software skills with Mapt. Mapt gives you full access to all Packt books and video courses, as well as industry-leading tools to help you plan your personal development and advance your career.

Why subscribe?

- Fully searchable across every book published by Packt
- Copy and paste, print, and bookmark content
- On demand and accessible via a web browser

Customer Feedback

Thanks for purchasing this Packt book. At Packt, quality is at the heart of our editorial process. To help us improve, please leave us an honest review on this book's Amazon page at https://www.amazon.in/dp/1788390547.

If you'd like to join our team of regular reviewers, you can email us at customerreviews@packtpub.com. We award our regular reviewers with free eBooks and videos in exchange for their valuable feedback. Help us be relentless in improving our products!

Table of Contents

Preface   1

Chapter 1: Thinking about Design Requirements   7

  Thinking about printing processes   7

    Home printing – Fused Filament Fabrication (FFF) printers   8

      Overhangs   8

      Detailing   11

        Layer height   11

        Extrusion width   13

      Wall thickness   14

      Other considerations – flat bases   15

    Home printing – Stereolithography (SLA) printers   16

      Overhangs   17

      Detailing   17

      Wall thickness   17

      Other considerations – drain holes   17

    Service Bureaus – Selective Laser Sintering (SLS) and more   17

      Overhangs   18

      Details   19

      Wall thickness   19

      Other considerations – escape holes   20

    Comparing the Requirements   20

  Thinking about size   21

    Sizing for the printer   21

    Sizing for function   22

    Sizing for yourself   22

  Summary   23

Chapter 2: Using a Background Image and Bezier Curves   25

  Getting started   26

  Adding a background image   27

    Finding a good photo   29

    Adding the background image to Blender   29

    Switching to Orthographic View   31

      Perspective View   31

      Orthographic View   32

  Tracing with Bezier curves   33

    Moving the 3D Cursor and adding a new Bezier curve   34

Changing Object Interaction Mode and editing the Bezier curve   35
Moving control points   37
Adjusting the shape of the curve with handles   38
Adding additional control points   39
Changing handle types   41
Checking your work and finalizing your curve   42
Deviating from the photograph   43
Toggling Cyclic to close your curve   44
Summary   44

Chapter 3: Converting a Bezier Curve to a Properly Sized 3D Mesh   45

Converting a Bezier curve into a mesh   45
Selecting vertices and making a new face   49
Extruding to make 3D objects   52
Understanding and viewing face normals   52
Using Extrude Region   54
Scaling and sizing the mesh   56
Converting to the metric system   57
Reading the current dimensions and scale   58
Scaling a model by typing dimensions   59
Fixing proportions by updating scale   61
Summary   63

Chapter 4: Flattening a Torus and Boolean Union   65

Creating and laying out a torus   65
Adding a new torus object   67
Positioning the torus   70
Rotating the torus (for Service Bureau)   72
Giving the torus a flat bottom (for home)   75
Toggling vertex visibility and using border select   76
Using Scale to align vertices   79
Combining objects together with Boolean Union   82
Exporting your work for 3D printing   86
Summary   87

Chapter 5: Building a Base with Standard Meshes and a Mirror   89

Working with a cube and cylinder   90
Resizing the default cube   90
Adding and sizing a cylinder   92
Using Object Origins to line up objects   94
Understanding Object Origin points   94

Moving the cylinder into place	97
Making the base whole	100
Understanding the mirror axis	100
Updating an Object's Origin to a specific vertex	102
Adding a Mirror Modifier	107
Summary	110
Chapter 6: Cutting Half Circle Holes and Modifier Management	111
Duplicating and sizing a cylinder	112
Placing the hole and preserving wall thicknesses	115
Positioning with subtraction	116
Positioning with a reference cube or ruler	118
Mesh modeling to make a half cylinder	121
Using Shift to multiselect	121
Using Ctrl to multiselect	122
Deleting vertices in the cylinder	125
Creating new faces	127
Making a hole with Boolean difference	130
Changing your object with modifier order	132
Summary	135
Chapter 7: Customizing with Text	137
Adding a new text object	137
Changing the text	140
Changing font settings	143
Finding the font filename	144
Picking a new font	146
Adjusting font size and line spacing	148
Converting the text to a 3D mesh	150
Using the text object properties	150
Using the Extrude tool	152
Finalizing the bracelet	153
Summary	155
Chapter 8: Using Empties to Model the Base of the House	157
Using Empties for reference images	158
Adding Empties	158
Rotating the Empties	162
Scaling empties and adjusting for differences in pictures	166
Modeling the base of the house	174

Using Extrude and merging vertices   178
Using Loop Cut and Slide   186
Summary   191

Chapter 9: Mesh Modeling and Positioning the Details   193

Modeling windows   193
Creating a window as a separate object   195
Adding shutters with a multi-cut Loop Cut and Slide   196
Starting window panes with Subdivide   200
Subdividing edges   200
Controlling the number of cuts   201
Finishing window panes with Inset   204
Noting and applying exact thicknesses   205
Raising the details with Extrude   210
Renaming and copying windows   216
Perfecting the positioning with Snap   220
Summary   222

Chapter 10: Making Textures with the Array Modifier and Scalable Vector Graphics   223

Making brickwork with the Array Modifier   224
Adding an Array Modifier   225
Picking the Fit Type   225
Understanding the impact of scale on the Array Modifier   227
Setting the Offset   230
Nesting Array Modifiers   232
Importing a Scalable Vector Graphics file for stonework   237
Using the Outliner and Properties Shelf to find objects   241
Scaling, rotating and converting to 3D mesh   242
Combining with the Array Modifier   245
Summary   247

Chapter 11: Applying Textures with Boolean Intersection   249

Making template shapes   249
Duplicating and separating vertices   252
Joining and separating objects as a shortcut   257
Joining and making new faces   261
Deleting unnecessary faces and edges   262
Adjusting vertex coordinates   265
Creating new edges and filling faces   267
Taking an intersection   272
Adding a Boolean Intersection Modifier   273

Previewing modifiers	274
Switching viewport shading to wireframe	275
Hiding the supporting object	276
Making adjustments	276
Applying and Placing the Intersection	278
Finalizing and exporting the house	281
Summary	282

Chapter 12: Making Organic Shapes with the Subdivision Surface Modifier — 283

Thinking about overhangs and flat bases	283
Making a low-poly hand	286
Adding in reference images	286
Modeling a low-poly hand from a cube	288
Planning ahead for fingers with Loop Cut and Slide	289
Shaping with Extrude and Scale	291
Rotating faces and making manual adjustments	294
Extruding and scaling fingers	297
Modeling a low-poly hand from a plane	299
Adding a Subdivision Surface Modifier	301
Summary	305

Chapter 13: Trial and Error – Topology Edits — 307

Preparing yourself mentally	307
Embracing failure	308
Aiming for quads	308
Adding extra edge loops	310
Controlling rounding	311
Shaping details	312
Flattening the base	313
Flattening with Loop Cut and Slide	314
Flattening with Mean Crease	314
Moving vertices and edge loops	315
Selecting edge loops	315
Sliding edges	317
Rotating around the 3D Cursor	320
Using Proportional Editing	324
Modeling fingernails and wrinkles	329
Using Inset and Extrude for fingernails	329
Using edge loops for wrinkles	333
Summary	336

Chapter 14: Coloring Models with Materials and UV Maps   337
   Using materials   337
      Adding a material to the whole object   338
      Adding a material to specific faces   341
      Reusing existing materials   345
   Coloring with UV Maps   347
      Adding a new panel to Blender   347
      Unwrapping an object into a UV Map   350
      Marking and clearing seams   354
      Preparing to Texture Paint   359
      Painting in Blender   367
         Using the Fill Brush   369
         Painting in the UV/Image Editor   371
      Editing images outside of Blender   374
   Exporting and uploading X3D files   378
      Zipping up the model and image files   379
      Checking the renders for CMYK issues   380
   Summary   381
Chapter 15: Troubleshooting and Repairing Models   383
   Removing duplicate vertices   383
   Flipping face normals   386
   Finding and fixing non-manifold edges   391
      Exploring examples of non-manifold edges 392
         Faces without thickness   392
         Missing faces or holes   392
         Inconsistent face normals   393
         Overlapping and unconnected geometry 394
      Highlighting non-manifold edges   394
      Turning on and using 3D Print Toolbox   396
      Correcting non-manifold edges   400
   Repairing models with 3D Builder   402
   Summary   406
Index   407

Preface

My very first 3D print was a pendant I designed for myself in Blender. It was about a year before I owned my own 3D printer. I uploaded my model to a 3D Printing Service Bureau to do the printing for me. About a week later, I was holding my creation in my hand. My idea had become real. I was no longer bound to buy what someone else decided to mass produce and market. I could design and make what I wanted to make. I was instantly hooked.

With this book, I hope to empower you with the ability to make what you want to make. Blender has served me well. I hope it does the same for you.

What this book covers

Chapter 1, *Thinking About Design Requirements*, gives you a moment to answer some questions about your project. What kind of printing process will be used? Are there any overhang or thickness requirements? How big do you want the piece to be?

Chapter 2, *Using a Background Image and Bezier Curves*, describes how to import in a photograph as a background image and how you can use Bezier curves to trace out a person's profile.

Chapter 3, *Converting a Bezier Curve to a Properly Sized 3D Mesh*, is about turning a 2D curve into a 3D object. You'll learn to set specific dimensions and how to preserve proportion with scale.

Chapter 4, *Flattening a Torus and Boolean Union*, explains how a torus object can serve as a hook for a pendant. You'll learn about rotation. You'll also learn a scaling trick to flatten the back. Finally, you'll learn about the Boolean Union Modifier and how it can combine two objects into a single clean mesh for 3D printing.

Chapter 5, *Building a Base with Standard Meshes and a Mirror*, shows how standard shapes such as cylinders and cubes can be resized and combined to make a new shape. The Mirror Modifier is used to keep the work symmetrical.

Chapter 6, *Cutting Half Circle Holes and Modifier Management,* shows how you can delete specific parts of a standard shape to make a new one. You'll also learn how to use the Boolean Difference Modifier to subtract one object from another to create holes. You'll see firsthand how the order modifiers are applied can impact the final product.

Chapter 7, *Customizing with Text,* illustrates how an embossed message such as coordinates can be added to personalize a piece.

Chapter 8, *Using Empties to Model the Base of the House,* presents another way to add and use reference images in Blender. You'll practice techniques such as extruding and merging vertices as you model the base shape of a house.

Chapter 9, *Mesh Modeling and Positioning the Details,* dives further into mesh modeling techniques as you learn about subdividing and insetting to make windows for a house. Blender's Snap tool is introduced to perfect the placement of those windows.

Chapter 10, *Making Textures with the Array Modifier and Scalable Vector Graphics,* illustrates how you can build textures within Blender with the Array Modifier and outside of Blender by importing in Scalable Vector Graphics (SVG) files.

Chapter 11, *Applying Textures with Boolean Intersection,* introduces you to the power of the Boolean Intersection Modifier. By taking just the overlap of two shapes, you get texture detailing that is the right size and shape for your house.

Chapter 12, *Making Organic Shapes with the Subdivision Surface Modifier,* exposes you to another side of Blender. By adding a Subdivision Surface Modifier, you'll see how a simple structure can become more organic in appearance.

Chapter 13, *Trial and Error - Topology Edits,* arms you with techniques for making topology edits. You'll learn about edge slides, more advanced rotation, and how to use Blender's Proportional Editing tool.

Chapter 14, *Coloring Models with Materials and UV Maps,* explains how you can add color to your models for full color printing services. You'll learn about adding materials to objects or faces. You'll also learn how to unwrap your object into a UV Map for more advanced texture painting.

Chapter 15, *Troubleshooting and Repairing Models,* describes common modeling issues such as flipped face normals and non-manifold edges. You'll learn how to remedy these issues within Blender and outside of Blender with applications such as 3D Builder.

What you need for this book

The only steadfast requirement for this book is to install the free, open-source software Blender. It can be downloaded from `https://www.blender.org/`.

You do not even need a 3D printer to begin. Companies such as Shapeways and Sculpteo can do the printing for you. You may have a nearby library or makerspace with 3D printers available to the public. Finally, you can find local printer in your area with websites such as `3dhubs.com` or `makexyz.com`.

There are two additional tools that are optional, but may be helpful:

- A ruler or calipers to help judge the sizes of your piece
- Image editing software such as Photoshop, GNU Image Manipulation Program (GIMP), or Microsoft Paint may assist with coloring models

Who this book is for

This book is for designers, artists, and crafters who would like to use Blender to make accurate models for 3D printing. Although previous experience with Blender would be helpful, it is by no means required.

Conventions

In this book, you will find a number of text styles that distinguish between different kinds of information. Here are some examples of these styles and an explanation of their meaning.

Code words in text, database table names, folder names, filenames, file extensions, pathnames, dummy URLs, user input, and Twitter handles are shown as follows: "Before converting your curve to a mesh, you may want to make a backup copy of the curve or your entire `.blend` file."

New terms and **important words** are shown in bold. Words that you see on the screen, for example, in menus or dialog boxes, appear in the text like this: "Under **Tools**, click on the **Ruler/Protractor** button."

Warnings or important notes appear in a box like this.

Tips and tricks appear like this.

Reader feedback

Feedback from our readers is always welcome. Let us know what you think about this book-what you liked or disliked. Reader feedback is important for us as it helps us develop titles that you will really get the most out of.

To send us general feedback, simply e-mail `feedback@packtpub.com`, and mention the book's title in the subject of your message.

If there is a topic that you have expertise in and you are interested in either writing or contributing to a book, see our author guide at `www.packtpub.com/authors`.

Customer support

Now that you are the proud owner of a Packt book, we have a number of things to help you to get the most from your purchase.

Downloading the example code

You can download the example code files for this book from your account at `http://www.packtpub.com`. If you purchased this book elsewhere, you can visit `http://www.packtpub.com/support` and register to have the files e-mailed directly to you.

You can download the code files by following these steps:

1. Log in or register to our website using your e-mail address and password.
2. Hover the mouse pointer on the **SUPPORT** tab at the top.
3. Click on **Code Downloads & Errata**.
4. Enter the name of the book in the **Search** box.
5. Select the book for which you're looking to download the code files.
6. Choose from the drop-down menu where you purchased this book from.
7. Click on **Code Download**.

Once the file is downloaded, please make sure that you unzip or extract the folder using the latest version of:

- WinRAR / 7-Zip for Windows
- Zipeg / iZip / UnRarX for Mac
- 7-Zip / PeaZip for Linux

The code bundle for the book is also hosted on GitHub at `https://github.com/PacktPublishing/Blender-3D-printing-by-Example`. We also have other code bundles from our rich catalog of books and videos available at `https://github.com/PacktPublishing/`. Check them out!

Downloading the color images of this book

We also provide you with a PDF file that has color images of the screenshots/diagrams used in this book. The color images will help you better understand the changes in the output. You can download this file from `https://www.packtpub.com/sites/default/files/downloads/Blender3DPrintingbyExample_ColorImages.pdf`.

Errata

Although we have taken every care to ensure the accuracy of our content, mistakes do happen. If you find a mistake in one of our books-maybe a mistake in the text or the code-we would be grateful if you could report this to us. By doing so, you can save other readers from frustration and help us improve subsequent versions of this book. If you find any errata, please report them by visiting http://www.packtpub.com/submit-errata, selecting your book, clicking on the **Errata Submission Form** link, and entering the details of your errata. Once your errata are verified, your submission will be accepted and the errata will be uploaded to our website or added to any list of existing errata under the Errata section of that title.

To view the previously submitted errata, go to https://www.packtpub.com/books/content/support and enter the name of the book in the search field. The required information will appear under the **Errata** section.

Piracy

Piracy of copyrighted material on the Internet is an ongoing problem across all media. At Packt, we take the protection of our copyright and licenses very seriously. If you come across any illegal copies of our works in any form on the Internet, please provide us with the location address or website name immediately so that we can pursue a remedy.

Please contact us at copyright@packtpub.com with a link to the suspected pirated material.

We appreciate your help in protecting our authors and our ability to bring you valuable content.

Questions

If you have a problem with any aspect of this book, you can contact us at questions@packtpub.com, and we will do our best to address the problem.

1
Thinking about Design Requirements

In this book, we will walk through four custom 3D printing projects in Blender. First, we will use Bezier curves to make a custom shape, the silhouette of a child, for a profile pendant. Our second project, a coordinate bracelet, illustrates building with standard shapes and how text can be used to personalize models. You'll get more acquainted with mesh modeling tools and Boolean intersections in our third project, creating a textured house figurine. Finally, you'll learn how Blender can be used for organic shapes as you work on modeling a human hand.

Before you build a house, before you sew a quilt, the process begins with a plan. The same is true with 3D modeling and 3D printing. When you model with your design requirements in mind, every measurement, every angle, every click of the mouse, all work toward your end goal. This chapter will cover some key questions to reflect on before you begin to model:

- What type of printing process will be used to make your design?
- How does that process impact design elements such overhangs, detailing, and wall thicknesses?
- How big do you want the final piece to be?

Thinking about printing processes

Not all 3D printers work in the same manner. The printers at the Service Bureaus, such as Shapeways, Sculpteo, and iMaterialise, use different types of technology than what is typically seen with at-home desktop printers.

All 3D printers will start with your 3D model and use an additional piece of software called a **slicer** to cut your object up into small cross sections, or layers. From there, all the printing processes will create your object one layer at a time. Different types of printing, however, add the material in different manners. Those differences in production processes can impact how you approach your design.

Home printing – Fused Filament Fabrication (FFF) printers

Currently, the most common printers you would find in a home, library, makerspace, or neighborhood 3D Hub are what are called the **Fused Filament Fabrication (FFF)** or **Fused Deposition Modeling (FDM)** printers. I often describe these printers as similar to the hot glue guns you would see used for crafting or electronics projects. A spool of plastic string (**filament**) is fed through a hot end that heats the plastic up to the point where it is malleable and the printer can draw with it. The printer will print one layer of your object directly on a platform called the **built plate**, move up, print the next layer, and so on until your piece is finished.

Overhangs

With the exception of the *Made in Space* printer on the International Space Station, FFF/FDM printers are subject to gravity. Higher portions of your model will need a foundation or support from the lower ones. As a design consideration, you'll want to be conscious of the slopes in your piece, the **overhangs.** The angle of those overhangs impact how far a layer extends over the previous layer one. If a layer extends out too far, the filament could droop or curl up, causing imperfections, or worse, a failed print.

For most FFF/FDM desktop printers, the rule of thumb is 45 degree overhangs. If you keep your slopes and curves to 45 degrees or less, each layer will have a good foundation with the layer underneath. When you look at larger angles, you can see how layers may have trouble supporting their own weight. The following image shows the difference between 45 degrees and the more troublesome 85 degrees:

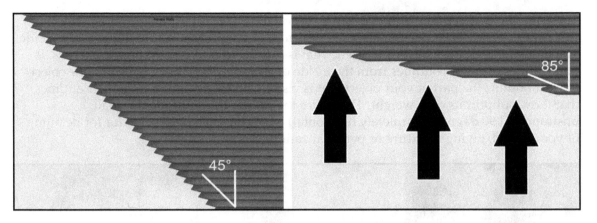

Layers at 45 degrees or less can be reliably printed by FFF/FDM printers. As the angle increases, it becomes harder for the plastic lines to support themselves.

The human hand model later in the book is one where thinking about overhangs will be important. If one of the fingers was angled more than 45 degrees, you can see in the slicer preview how the printer would be drawing lines with nothing underneath it. For other portions of the finger that are more upright, you would see that each layer has good contact with the layer underneath:

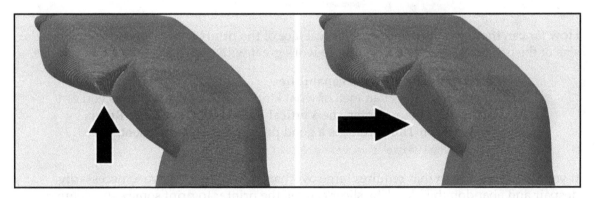

Portions of the tip of the finger will be printing over air with nothing underneath. Earlier sections of the finger are better angled for printing.

Find out your printer's capabilities

If you want to put your particular printer to the test and get an assessment of its overhang capabilities, try the **Massive Overhang Test** by thingster on Thingiverse at `https://www.thingiverse.com/thing:40382`.

There is a lucky exception with overhangs. When the printer starts a layer, it usually starts by printing perimeters, sometimes called **outlines**, of your object before filling in the inside. The molten plastic likes to stick to itself. That is exactly why FFF/FDM printing works. If your printer draws its outlines from the inside of your object to the outside of your object, the last outline, the part of your object that is visible, sticks enough to the earlier outlines that it can support its own weight. That gives the printer the ability to do small, unsupported 90 degree (completely horizontal) overhangs, a handy behavior for detailing of your model, giving it texture or personalization:

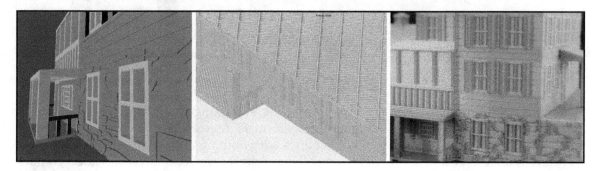

You can put small, completely horizontal overhangs in your design. When the printer works inside out, outer lines can stick to previously printed lines for that same layer, permitting fine detailing for your model.

How far can those details come off a vertical face of the print? It will depend on the nozzle size of the printer. I have found 0.5 mm to work great with both 0.35 and 0.4 mm nozzles.

Find out your printer's capabilities
If you want to get an idea of what kind of unsupported details you can achieve on your printer, the **Vertical Embossed Detailing - Remix** by SpikeUK on Thingiverse is a good print to get an assessment: `https://www.thingiverse.com/thing:2462735`.

If you do have a design that requires large overhangs, you do not have to necessarily despair and abandon the idea. The slicer can tell the printer to print some extra columns called **supports** to assist your object. This is extra work for the printer that will add to your material usage and printing time. In addition, supports can leave markings on your piece, requiring sanding and cleanup to be done afterward. You don't have to avoid large overhangs when modeling, but it makes the printing process a lot cleaner if you do:

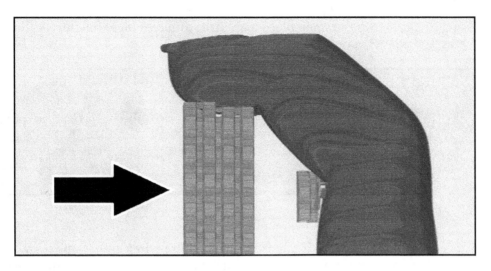

An example of temporary supports the printer can use to assist your object.

Detailing

If you were to crochet with thin embroidery floss, you could achieve a much more intricate level of detail than if you were working with thick yarn. The width of the thread being used plays a key role in what can be achieved in the final product. You can think of FFF/FDM printing as also using a thread, a small thread of plastic. With FFF/FDM printing, there are two dimensions of that thread that impact our detailing.

Layer height

When the slicer is cutting up your file into small cross-sections for 3D printing, the height of those cross sections is called the **layer height**. This can not only vary from printer to printer, but it can also vary from print to print. A smaller layer height would cut your model up into more cross sections. It would be a longer printing process, but at the same time would give your object a greater level of detail and resolution. In my prints, the layer heights tend to be between 0.10 mm-0.25 mm layers.

The following image shows the same piece with three different layer heights. As the layer height increases, the level of detail decreases:

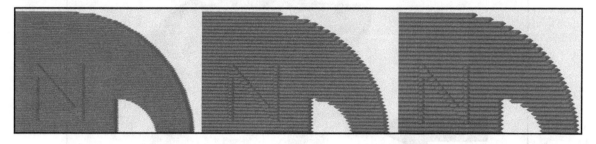

As layer height increases, you will have faster printing times, but less detail.

Thinking ahead about layer height is a worthwhile venture when embarking on a 3D modeling project, particularly if you are planning small detailing. Consider the house figurine that will be highlighted later in the book. If the window panes are shorter than the planned layer height, the slicer (and therefore the printer) will skip that detailing, as shown in the following image:

In this example, a window pane is smaller than the layer height and is skipped by the slicer and printer.

Extrusion width

As your printer lays down lines of malleable plastic to bring your model to life, the hole in the nozzle impacts how wide those lines are. You can also think of it as your **thread width**, how wide the thread of plastic that comes out of your nozzle is. A more technical term is **extrusion width**, how wide the extruded plastic is. That width isn't necessarily equal to your nozzle size. For example, a nozzle with a 0.4 mm hole may be using a 0.42 mm extrusion width.

Find Your Extrusion Width

You may be able to look up your extrusion width in your slicing software. Different slicers use different terminology. Three examples are:

Slicer	Setting
Simplify3D	Extrusion Width
Cura	Line Width
Slic3r	Extrusion Width

If you aren't able to look up your specific extrusion width, start by designing for your printer's nozzle size instead.

Extrusion width is important to consider during design as it can also impact the detailing of your piece, which is most readily visible on the top. Later in the book, we will create a bracelet with custom coordinates on the top. If that piece was printed flat on the bed and portions of text were thinner than the extrusion width (such as part of the number *4* in the following image), that detail could very well get skipped:

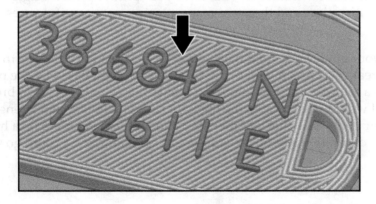

A section of the number four in the coordinates is thinner than the extrusion width, so it is skipped by the slicer and printer.

Layer heights are smaller, sometimes substantially so, than extrusion widths. That means detailing going up vertically can be finer than the horizontal details you have at the top. If we printed that coordinate bracelet on its side, the same number we had trouble with before shows up fine:

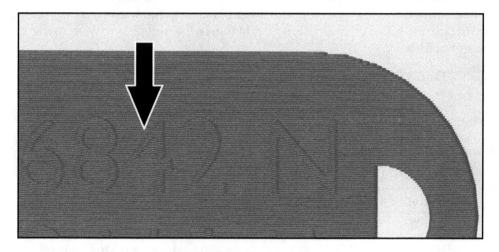

Vertical details can be finer than horizontal ones.

Wall thickness

Wall thickness is simply how thick your printed object is from side to side. Wall thickness directly applies to the strength of that section of the piece. Technically, you could have walls as thin as your extrusion width. You could have your printer print a single line of plastic thread for your entire piece and there are many examples of beautiful vases printed in that manner.

Depending on your application, that may not be the best plan of attack. A thin wall of 0.42 mm is easy to break. Our first model in this book is a pendant based on the profile of one of my sons. This is a sentimental piece. Surely, I would not want the clasp to break during my daily activities. I would want to give the hook for the pendant enough strength to survive the wear and tear of my daily life. On the other hand, railing detailing on a house figurine would be purely decorative and not be subject to the same stress. I could go smaller there.

Another thing to consider is how this section of your print is attached to the rest of the model. If it is a wall connected to other sections on two or more sides, it is considered a **supported wall**. It does not have to have to be as thick as a wall that stands by itself, an **unsupported wall**. The front wall of a house figurine is an example of a supported wall. It is attached to many other sides, the left side of the house, the right side of the house, the roofing. On the other hand, the thickness of a profile pendant, I would consider an unsupported wall:

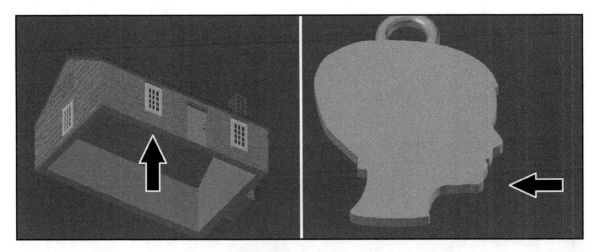

The front wall of a house is a supported wall. The thickness of a profile pendant is an unsupported wall.

It is not a hard and fast rule, and you may fine-tune what works best with your printer. As a starting point for your design requirements, I tend to give supported walls at least 1 mm in thickness and unsupported walls at least 2 mm in thickness. For sections that I feel may need extra strength, I consider sizing those portions up to 3-5 mm.

Other considerations – flat bases

With FFF/FDM printers, the printer starts with one initial layer which, if all goes well, sticks to the print bed for the duration of the print. If you have seen musings about hairspray, glue sticks, painter's tape, those are all measures to assist that important first layer in staying put. When you are designing for an FFF/FDM printer, it is ideal for the design to have a good footprint, a perfectly flat section to print straight on the print bed.

Sometimes a nice flat base isn't going to be possible with the design you have in mind. The slicing software for the printer can assist in those cases. For designs that have small footprints that would not have a lot of contact area on the print bed, the slicer can add a temporary foundation printed underneath your object, a **raft**, to keep that all-important first layer stationary. If we did decide to print the coordinate bracelet on its side to take advantage of better detailing, the base of that print is just a very thin line, not likely to stay secure for the duration of the print. The raft, however, helps give it a sturdy anchor:

The print on the left has little contact with the bed and would be prone to unsticking. A raft assists the print on the right.

Home printing – Stereolithography (SLA) printers

Another printing technology that is becoming more accessible at home is the **Stereolithography** (**SLA**) printer, commonly referred to as *Resin Printers*. Instead of a spool of plastic filament, the raw material for resin printers is a pool of UV-sensitive liquid. The printer works by using a UV light to cure and solidify just the sections that will become your object. Your object is raised slightly out of the liquid pool, a process called **peeling**, and then the printer will solidify the next layer of your object and so on.

Overhangs

SLA printers tend to have a lot more flexibility with overhangs. The design guidelines for one of the most common desktop SLA printers, the Formlabs Form 2, support up to 71 degree overhangs, a substantial improvement over the FFF/FDM printers. SLA printers can also handle those small, completely horizontal overhangs for embossed detailing. The Form 2 Design Requirements refers to those as unsupported overhangs and recommends keeping them at a height of 1 mm or less.

Detailing

The Formlabs Form 2 can work in layer heights as small as 0.025 mm. Its equivalence to extrusion width or nozzle size would be the beam of light that is interacting with the liquid resin. In the case of the Form 2, that is 0.14 mm. Combined, the Form 2 Design Requirements say the printer can support details as small as 0.1 mm.

Wall thickness

Although the light beam is 0.14 mm, the Form 2 Design Requirements do recommend a minimum supported wall thickness of 0.4 mm and unsupported wall thickness of 0.6 mm. Part of the recommendation is due to the peeling process. Smaller walls could warp as your print is pulled out of the pool of resin between layers.

Other considerations – drain holes

If you are hoping for a design to be hollow inside, you will want to include holes in your model to allow excess, uncured, liquid to drain.

Service Bureaus – Selective Laser Sintering (SLS) and more

The 3D Printing Service Bureaus open up a lot of doors in regards to what materials you can have your pieces produced in. You can have your jewelry designs cast in precious metals such as gold and platinum. You can have functional items, such as bottle openers, printed in sturdy stainless steel. You can have your custom designed coffee cup made in food-safe porcelain.

When working with at-home FFF/FDM printers, sometimes you have to put in the investment to learn your printer and its capabilities. At the 3D Printing Service Bureaus, they have already done that assessment for you and have documented design requirements for each material:

Material requirements and design specifications from Shapeways, iMaterialise, and Sculpteo.

Overhangs

It can vary by material, but the printing processes at the large Service Bureaus often free you from the concern of overhangs. The industrial **Selective Laser Sintering** (**SLS**) printers used for Nylon pieces, for example, have an ingenious way to get around the gravity problem. The whole print bed is covered in a layer of nylon powder. A laser will heat up and solidify just the sections of powder that will become the first layer of your object. A fresh layer of powder is laid down on the printer and the laser will solidify the next layer of your object. The printing process finishes with a big block of powder on the printer. Your piece is dug out of the loose powder, much like an archaeologist excavating pottery from soil.

Because the excess powder provides a natural support system, even completely horizontal overhangs are achievable. You also don't have to worry about flat bases and having solid contact with the print bed. The extra powder from previous layers is there to act as a foundation no matter where or how small your object starts.

Details

Depending on the material and the process, the cutting edge printers at the 3D Printing Service Bureaus can offer up a higher level of detailing and resolution than your typical home printer. This will be specific to the material you select. High Definition Acrylate would permit embossed and engraved details as small as 0.1 mm. Porcelain, on the other hand, has very different requirements. Porcelain pieces finish up with a glazing process. Since the glaze adds its own thickness to the piece, it could pool into crevasses and obscure shallow details. As a result, a model geared for porcelain would need to have much deeper engravings, at least 1 mm.

Find the requirements of your material

The section name could vary in the Design Requirements or Material Information Sheets. Examples from three 3D Printing Service Bureaus are shown as follows:

Service Bureau	Section(s)
iMaterialise	Minimum Details
Sculpteo	Minimum width and height details
Shapeways	Minimum Embossed Detail, Minimum Engraved Detail

Wall thickness

The 3D Printing Service Bureaus offer a lot of perks with top-notch quality. Their services are, as expected, more expensive than a print from a desktop FFF/FDM printer. Part of the cost is determined by the amount of material you use. This could be expensive, particularly in the case of pricey cast metals such as platinum or gold. As you design for one of the Service Bureaus, you'll likely want to minimize the amount of material being used to keep your cost low. Suddenly the minimum wall thickness takes on a deeper meaning. To save cost, you may opt to make your object hollow. You may also opt to make your walls as thin as possible.

Find the requirements of your material

How thin can your piece be? Look for sections mentioning "wall thickness." Examples for three 3D Printing Service Bureaus are shown as follows:

Service Bureau	Section(s)
iMaterialise	Minimum Wall Thickness
Sculpteo	Minimum wall thickness (flexible), Minimum wall thickness (rigid)
Shapeways	Min supported wall thickness, Min unsupported wall thickness

Other considerations – escape holes

Since the SLS printing process creates a big block of powder, you will want to keep in mind how that powder will be cleaned out of your piece. If you intend for your piece to be hollow inside, for example, you will need to include an *escape hole* in your piece to allow the technicians to remove excess powder.

Comparing the Requirements

Although there additional printing processes, such as Binder Jetting, we don't have to discuss them all to understand how the process and the material can impact your design. Your decisions about overhangs, detail size, and wall thicknesses all vary with the final material and process. To serve as some starting guidelines, a summary of the three processes we did discuss are:

Design requirement	FFF/FDM (0.4 mm Nozzle)	SLA (Form2 at 0.10 Layers)	SLS (Shapeways Strong & Flexible Plastic)
Minimum supported wall thickness	1 mm	0.4 mm	0.7 mm
Unsupported wall thickness	2 mm	0.6 mm	0.7 mm
Overhangs	45 degrees or less	71 degrees or less	Any

Height of unsupported overhangs	0.5 mm	1 mm	Any
Minimum detail (vertical faces)	Layer height	0.1 mm	0.2 mm
Minimum detail (horizontal faces)	Extrusion width	0.1 mm	0.2 mm
Other	Flat base recommended	Drain holes may be needed	Escape holes may be needed

Even when you decide on how you'll print your design, there are still some questions worth reflecting on. For example, how big do you want your print to be?

Thinking about size

Once you have an idea of which printing process will be used, I recommend thinking about the final size of your piece. We've put some thought into how high we want to emboss detailing as well as our wall thicknesses. If we made our entire model without thinking of the final dimensions, we would have to resize everything accordingly at the end.

If I scaled my piece down, suddenly I may have walls that are too thin to pass the automated checks at one of the 3D Printing Service Bureaus. Or perhaps I scaled my final piece up, making all my vertical detailing too large for an FFF/FDM printer to make without adding extra supports. You always have the ability to edit your model and there is indeed a natural iterative process to design. However, mass changing dimensions can be tedious and time consuming, possibly demoralizing. It is well worth a few moments to get out a tape measure or calipers and reflect on sizing.

Sizing for the printer

Regardless of the type of printer being used, it will have some size limitations. With the home FFF/FDM or SLA printers, you may be mainly concerned about the size of your print bed. With the 3D Printing Service Bureaus, economic forces may have you more concerned by cost. Some 3D Printing Service Bureaus will also have a minimum size requirement as well. If you do wish to push the limits in either direction, the technical specifications of the printer or the Material Design Requirements will guide you accordingly.

Design too big?

If your design is too big, don't abandon it just yet. First off, if it is slightly too big for your print bed, remember that the hypotenuse of a triangle is longer than the other sides. See if placing your object at a diagonal will give you the room you need. Your print bed may only be 200 mm x 200 mm, but the diagonal could accommodate almost 283 mm. If all else fails, you can split your model into parts to be printed separately.

Sizing for function

The function of what you are designing could go a long way to determining the size. This is particularly true if you are combining your print with another part. If I had a lobster claw clasp I wanted to use with a custom designed pendant, I would want to make sure the hook for that pendant was wide enough for the clasp. Once that is decided, aesthetics may kick in. I may size the rest of the piece purely to look proportionate with the hook.

Existing objects also give good direction with sizing. Making a coaster? Measure a coaster you already have. Holiday ornaments, paperweights, bottle openers, magnets, soap dishes, earrings, bookmarks, and business card holders are just the tip of the iceberg. Your house and your office are full of reference objects to guide you with sizing.

Sizing for yourself

Finally, when designing jewelry or accessories, it makes sense to take the tape measure to yourself. Get a feel for what would look good on you and what would look too clunky. Use your own dimensions to guide the dimensions of your 3D model.

You don't have to measure everything

Sometimes online references can help you with jewelry and accessory sizing. For example, if you are making a ring and know the ring size, there are conversion charts to translate the ring size to the inner diameter in millimeters.

Summary

In this chapter, you learned to think about the printing process and how each approach impacts your overhangs, your detail size, and your wall thicknesses. You also learned to think ahead about sizing so you can model your object to the desired size from the very beginning.

In the Chapter 2, *Using a Background Image and Bezier Curves*, you will start to make a custom profile pendant in Blender for 3D printing.

2

Using a Background Image and Bezier Curves

loOne of the advantages of 3D printing is the ability to make custom projects and gifts. A custom gift may entail a unique shape, one that you aren't going to be able to readily drag and drop from standard meshes. In this chapter, you will start to use Blender to make a custom pendant based on the profile of a child. You don't have to be an artist to accomplish this piece. You will learn about a tool called Bezier curves that you can use to trace your desired shape from a background photo. This chapter will cover the following skills:

- Importing a photo to use as a background image in Blender
- Creating and editing Bezier curves to make unique shapes
- Switching view perspectives, projection modes, and object interaction modes to evaluate your work

Getting started

When you first open Blender, your brand new project always starts with three objects—a **camera**, a **lamp**, and a **default cube**. Cameras and lamps are more applicable to modeling for animations and videos than they are for 3D printing, but there is no harm in leaving them in your project. The default cube, however, is not going to be necessary for our pendant and will just clutter up the screen:

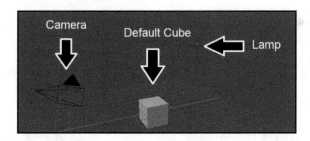

Three default objects for every Blender project—a camera, a cube, and a lamp

The first thing you'll want to do is delete the unnecessary cube with the following steps:

1. Right-click the cube to select it. You will see the cube highlighted in yellow and a trio of axis arrows originating from the center of the cube.
2. Along the left side of your screen is an area called the **Tool Shelf**. If necessary, select the **Tools** tab.
3. Under the **Edit** section, hit the **Delete** button. Alternatively, you can hit the *Delete* key on your keyboard.
4. A popup menu will ask you to confirm. Click **Delete** or hit the *Enter* key:

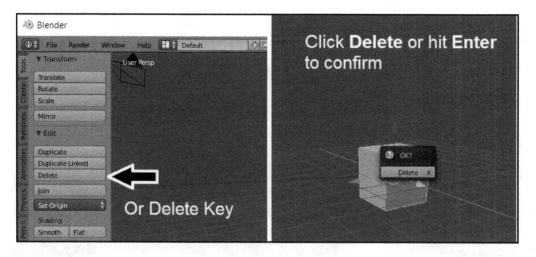

Deleting the default cube

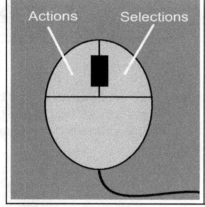

Clicking in Blender
In Blender, one thing that may seem counterintuitive at first is clicking.
You right-click to *select objects*. You use left-click to take an *action* such as moving an object or deleting it. You can think of it in terms of alphabetic order. Left-click for actions. Right-click for selections.

Adding a background image

When working with 3D objects, you don't want just one side to look good, you want the whole object to look good. Therefore, it is beneficial to review your work from varying perspectives. Blender has some preset *viewpoints* already defined to help you navigate from side to side. You can reach those by clicking on the **View** menu at the bottom of the screen.

There, you can change your perspective and view your design from the **Top**, **Bottom**, **Left**, **Right**, **Front**, and **Back**:

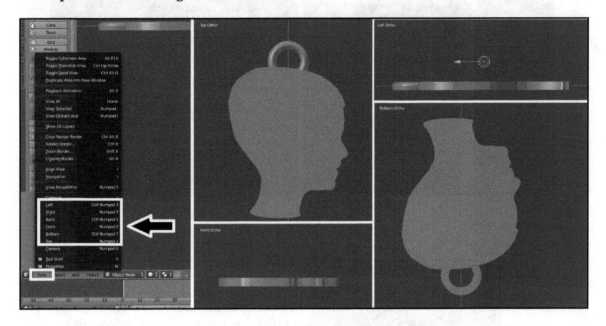

Under the View menu, you can use shortcuts to view your work from various perspectives

For each of those predetermined viewpoints, you can tell Blender to display a background image of your choosing. In this chapter, you'll be adding a background image to the **Top** view; this means when you are looking down on your object from the top, your image will be visible.

Navigating in the 3D View Window

You are not limited to the preset viewpoints. If you click and hold the mouse scroll wheel, you are able to move your perspective around the 3D View Window. Holding down the *Shift* key while doing so will allow you to pan your view. Scrolling up and down with the mouse wheel changes your zoom level. Together, these techniques give you the ability to view your model from any direction and any distance.

Finding a good photo

Before you add a background image, you should decide on what would constitute a good photo. For this project, we are interested in tracing out the profile of our subject. Here are a couple of guidelines when looking for a photo:

- It's okay if the lighting is not optimal. It doesn't matter whether the subject has red eye or is over exposed as long as we can make out the shape of the head.
- The position of the head, on the other hand, is important for our purposes. We would be looking for a shot that catches the full profile of our subject.
- Generally I have found that closed or slightly open mouths make for more recognizable silhouettes. I would recommend avoiding photos with large, gaping mouths.
- Unless you intend to include it, a photo with a hat should be avoided as it would obscure the shape of the head.
- Glasses, however, are okay as you could readily make out the curve of the nose and forehead.

Adding the background image to Blender

With a photo selected, your next step is to import that image into Blender to use as a background image. Your steps would be:

1. In the upper right-hand corner, you will want to click the + icon to display what is known as the **Properties Shelf**. Alternatively, you can type *N* on the keyboard:

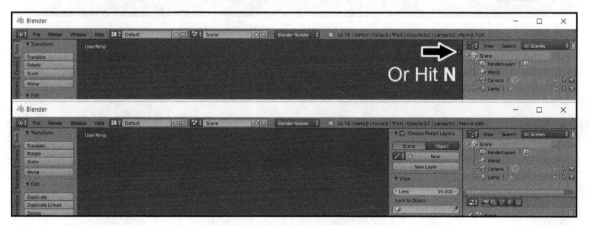

Toggling the display of the Properties Shelf.

2. Scroll down to the **Background Images** section and click the black triangle icon to display it.
3. Check the **Background Images** checkbox. Click the **Add Image** button:

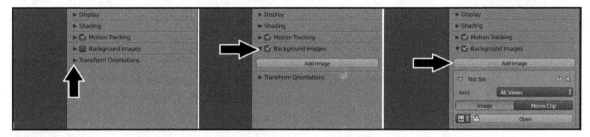

Telling Blender to add a new background image.

4. Click the **Open** button. A popup window allows you to browse the folder structure on your computer.
5. Browse to and select your photo, and click **Open Image**:

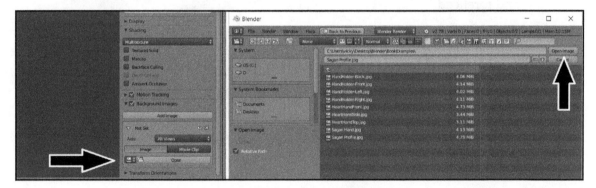

Selecting the desired image from your computer.

6. The **Axis** setting allows us to define which preset viewpoint you would like the image visible for. In our case, set the **Axis** to **Top**. Our background image will only be displayed when we are perfectly looking down on our object from above:

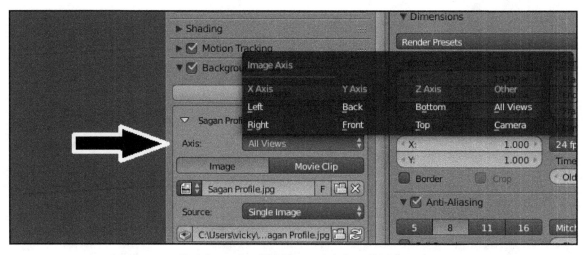

Blender lets you select which Axis you want the background image for.

At this point, the background image has been added. You may be unnerved to see that nothing has changed. This is normal.

Switching to Orthographic View

Not only do you have to be looking at your workspace in the right direction to see your background image, but you have to be in the right viewing projection mode as well. We are making 3D models, but we are previewing them on a 2D computer screen. Blender gives us a couple of options of how it projects, or portrays, 3D objects in 2D.

Perspective View

Sometimes it is advantageous to look at your object as it would appear to your eye. If we were looking at a straight road going to the horizon, due to foreshortening the parallel sides of the road would come together toward the horizon. In Blender, this is called the **Perspective View**. The object is shown in a manner to portray depth and size differences based on distance. This view gives us a good idea of how our object will appear in real life.

Orthographic View

Perspective and foreshortening can be misleading. Optical illusions such as the House 1 sculpture by Roy Lichtenstein are a great illustration of that. The dimensions of the house are very different from how they appear:

House 1 by Roy Lichetnstein illustrates how perspective can be misleading

To combat such illusions, Blender gives us a second way of looking at our 3D objects, called **Orthographic View**. In this view, sizes stay consistent regardless of depth and distance. Parallel lines stay parallel as they reach toward the horizon. This often gives us a truer sense of the sizing and proportions of our object. If we were looking at our road in Perspective View, it would be difficult to ascertain at a glance whether the width of our road at the beginning is the same as the width of our road at the end. In Orthographic View, the same road would be displayed as a simple rectangle, confirming that the width is indeed consistent:

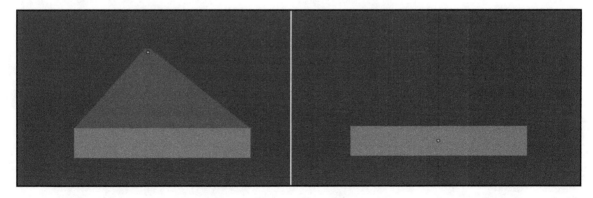

On the left, a road in Perspective View gives a sense of the depth of the object. On the right, Orthographic View gives a sense of the true proportions.

When working with background images, Blender requires you to be in **Orthographic View**. That means the steps to view our new background image are:

1. Click the **View | Top** menu option (or hit 7 on your number pad) so you are specifically viewing from the **Top** viewpoint
2. Click the **View | View Persp/Ortho** menu option (or hit 5 on your number pad) to toggle between Perspective View and Orthographic View

The upper left-hand corner of your 3D View Window will detail what viewpoint and what projection mode you are using. When you are in **Top Ortho**, meaning you are viewing the top of your object in Orthographic View, your background image will be displayed:

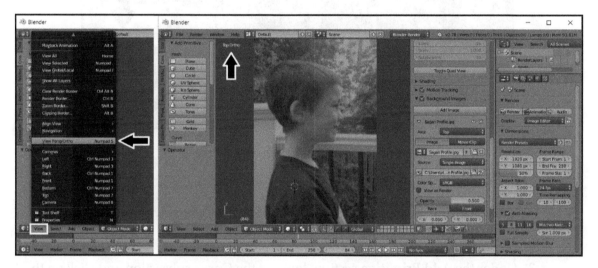

Use View | View Persp/Ortho to switch projection modes. In Top Ortho View, a background image for the Top Axis is visible.

Tracing with Bezier curves

If you don't have an artistic background, you may be intimidated by the idea of drawing someone's head. We aren't drawing—we're simply tracing! The tool we are going to use for this is called **Bezier curves**. Bezier curves can build complex curves out of a series of straight lines.

Moving the 3D Cursor and adding a new Bezier curve

When you are adding new objects to your project, including Bezier curves, they appear at a spot designated by the **3D Cursor**, a small target-like icon in your 3D View Window. Moving that 3D Cursor is considered an action, so use the left mouse button. You simply click where you want the cursor to go in your 3D View Window. You can also key in exact coordinates under the **3D Cursor** section of the **Properties Shelf**:

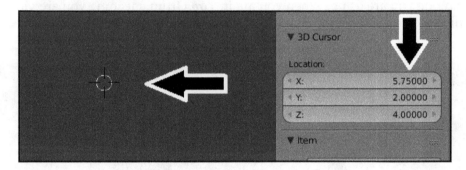

The 3D Cursor can be moved by left-clicking or by entering specific coordinates

The steps to add a new Bezier curve are:

1. Left-click your screen to move the 3D Cursor to where you would like to place your curve
2. If necessary, click the **Create** tab in the **Tool Shelf** on the left side of your screen
3. Under the **Add Primitive** section, look for the **Curve** subsection and click on the **Bezier** button

A new Bezier curve will appear in your 3D View Window where your 3D Cursor is placed:

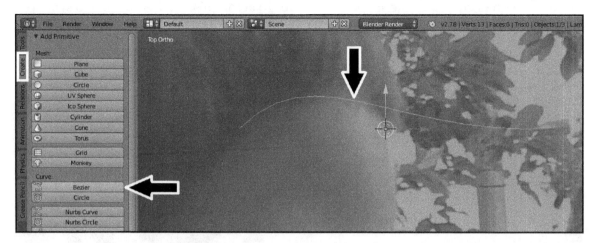

Under Create | Add Primitive | Curves in the Tool Shelf, click the Bezier button

Changing Object Interaction Mode and editing the Bezier curve

Just as there are different ways of viewing your object, there are different ways of interacting with it. This is called **Object Interaction Mode** and there is a dropdown at the bottom of your 3D View Window to allow you to switch back and forth between two options:

- **Object Mode**: In Object Mode, you are interacting with the entire object. You can perform actions such as scaling, rotating, moving, or deleting.
- **Edit Mode**: In Edit Mode, you are able to get down into the nitty gritty details and edit very specific points to change the underlying structure and appearance of your object.

In the case of our Bezier curve, in Object Mode, we can make our curve bigger or smaller, but that doesn't help match the shape of our face. To accomplish that we'll need to switch to **Edit Mode**:

1. At the bottom of your 3D View Window, change the **Object Mode** drop-down to **Edit Mode**. Alternatively, you can hit the *Tab* button to switch back and forth:

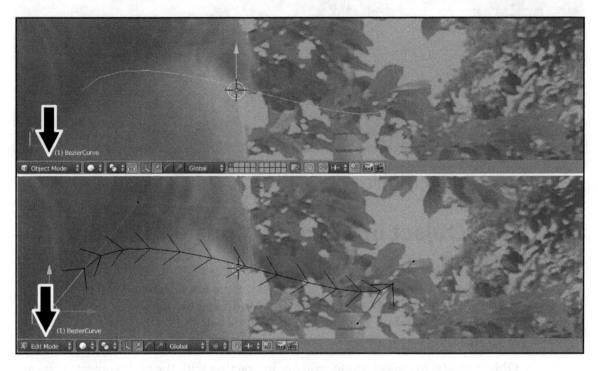

Bezier curve in Object Mode and Edit Mode

With Bezier curves, each section of curve is defined by a combination of points:

*   **Control points**: Control points can be thought of as the starting point and ending point of the curve, where you are coming from and where you are going to.
*   **Handles**: In addition, each curve segment is defined by two handle points. Handles will not necessarily lie on the final curve, but will influence the direction and severity of it:

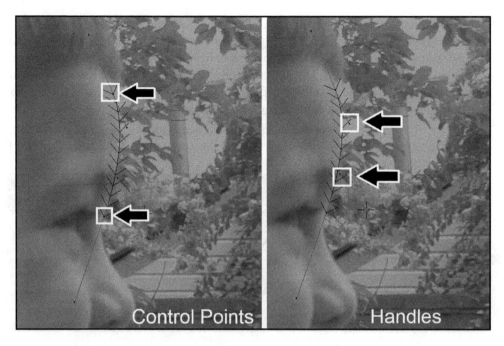

For each control point, there are two handles to control the direction of the curve

Moving control points

Just like in **Object Mode**, you right-click items to select them in **Edit Mode**. We can start by right-clicking on one of the end points, a control point, of our curve. When a point is selected, it will be surrounded by a white circle with axis arrows. Once selected, you have four options for moving that point:

- You can left-click anywhere inside that white circle and drag and drop that point to the desired location. This is quick and fast, but there is a potential downside. Since you are working in 3D space, you may also unknowingly move the point in an unintended direction.
- If you'd like to be more deliberate with your actions, then you can left-click one of the axis arrows. You can also drag and drop the point to a new spot. The difference is your movements are restricted to the direction of that axis. Moving with the arrows is predictable, but does add extra clicks as you can only adjust one direction at a time.

- Sometimes clicking the white circle or axis arrow can be tricky, particularly if you are zoomed out quite far (or trying to work in a bouncy car). Luckily, Blender also gives you a keyboard shortcut. Hit *G* to "grab" the current selection, move the mouse to move the selection, and left-click to apply. You can also restrict the movement to a specific axis by typing in **X**, **Y**, or **Z**. Typing G and then z, for example, would restrict the movements to the **Z** (blue) axis.
- Finally, if you have a specific placement in mind, under the **Transform** section of the **Properties Shelf**, you can key in the exact coordinates of your **Control Point**:

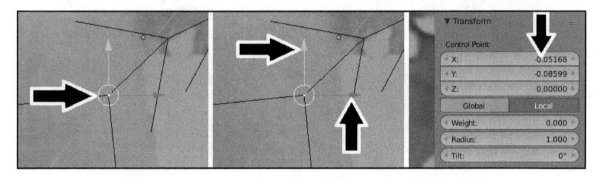

Three ways of moving control points—left-clicking in the white circle, left-clicking one of the axis arrows, and typing specific coordinates in the Properties Shelf

Putting this all together, the steps to move a control point would be:

1. Right-click a control point to select it
2. Left-click and hold either the white circle or one of the axis arrows
3. Drag and drop the control point to the next location and release the left mouse button

In the case of our profile photo, I'm placing one control point at the top of the forehead and another one at the bridge of the nose.

Adjusting the shape of the curve with handles

How a person travels between any two destinations could vary widely. Such is the case with curves. In Blender, we can adjust how the curve moves between one control point and another by changing the positioning of the handles. The curve wants to bend toward those handle points, almost as if they have a gravitational pull.

You can select and move handles the same way you would control points—right-click to select, left-click to move:

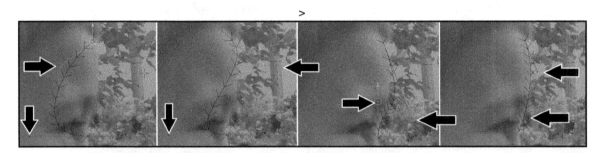

Changing the positioning of the handles changes the shape of the curve.

Your curve may be very small by default. If you are having trouble deciphering the control points from the handles, you can get a better look by scrolling up with the mouse wheel to zoom in close to your work. Another option is to hit *S* for scale and move your mouse away from the curve, to make the section bigger and add extra distance between the control point and the handles. Scaling will be discussed in more detail in Chapter 3, *Converting a Bezier Curve to a Properly Sized 3D Mesh* and Chapter 8, *Using Empties to Model the Base of the House*.

I found it took some practice to get used to handles and their impact on the curve. Don't get discouraged if it seems confusing at first. Permit yourself the time to experiment and explore.

Adding additional control points

At this point, we just have a small curve going down the forehead. The entire profile for our pendant is going to be made up of a series of these little Bezier curves, all with their own control points and handles. We don't have to start from scratch. We can grow the curve we already have. An end point of our existing curve can serve as the starting point for our next one. All we have to do is add a new control point so the new curve segment knows where to go.

The steps for adding a new control point are:

1. Right-click to select the existing control point you want to use as the starting point for the next section of the curve. In this example, I want to grow the curve downwards towards nose, so I right-click the control point by the eye.

Right-click to pick an existing control point.

2. Hold down the *Ctrl* key and left-click where you'd like the new control point:

Ctrl + left-click adds new control points

Changing handle types

As you start adjusting the handles for your new control point, you may notice it is impacting the forehead curve you already defined. This is due to the handle type. In Blender, we have the ability to define how the handles are going to behave:

- **Automatic/Aligned**: The default handle type is Automatic/Aligned, which is going to try to make the smoothest curve possible. This includes making the connections between curve segments seamless so you can't tell where one ends and another begins. As a result, when you move one handle for a control point, it'll automatically adjust the handle on the other side. The line between those two handles is always completely straight.
- **Free**: The Free handle type allows the handles on either side of the control point to move freely and independently of each other. This is particularly useful for places where you want sharp corners. An example is above the forehead at the hairline. With an Automatic or Aligned handle type, I'm mangling my forehead trying to get the hairline right. A Free handle type allows me to keep my forehead curve intact while achieving the direction change I'm looking for.

The steps for changing a handle type to Free are:

1. Right-click the control point to select it
2. In the **Tool Shelf** on the left side of your screen, click on the **Tools** tab

3. Under **Curve Tools**, look for the **Handles** section and click **Free**:

With an Aligned handle type, the handles around a control point are interconnected and the line between them always stays straight. A Free handle type allows the two handles to move independently of each other.

Checking your work and finalizing your curve

As you grow your curve, I recommend using the mouse scroll wheel to zoom in and out to check your work. It is often helpful to switch back to **Object Mode**. When selected, your entire curve will be highlighted yellow, which gives you a good reference to compare against the background image. If you'd like to evaluate your curve without distraction, you can hide the background image by clicking on the eye icon in your **Properties Shelf**:

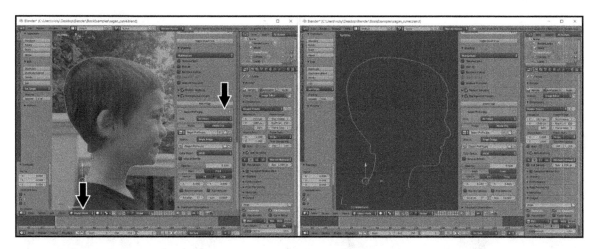

Switching to Object Mode and turning off the background image is a good way to check your work

Deviating from the photograph

You may decide to take some artistic liberties. Although true to the photograph, I am not fond of how the tuft of hair looks at the back of the neck. In this case, I make an aesthetic adjustment that deviates from the photograph. You may also opt to simplify some details, such as skipping erratic hairs, or fill in some details that are missing from the photograph:

The photograph is just a reference. You can skip or simplify details, or guess missing details.

Toggling Cyclic to close your curve

Once you are satisfied, you will want to close your curve so it is a solid outline of our profile. An easy way to do that is to use the **Toggle Cyclic** feature. The steps are:

1. If necessary, switch to **Edit Mode**.
2. Click the **Tools** tab in the **Tool Shelf** on the left side of your screen.
3. Under the **Curves Tools** section, look for **Curves** and click the **Toggle Cyclic** button. Alternatively, you can hold down *Alt + C* as a shortcut.
4. This will connect the two open control points of your curve. Like any other curve section, you can adjust the handles to get the shape you desire:

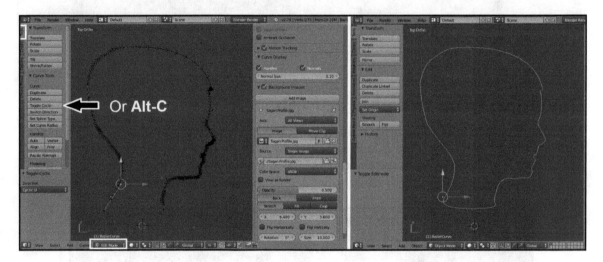

Hitting Toggle Cyclic or Alt + C will close up your curve.

Summary

In this chapter, you learned how to import a photograph in Blender to use as a background image. You learned about adding new Bezier curves and how to use the control points and handles to alter the shape of that curve. Finally, you learned how differences in perspective, view modes, and object interaction modes can help you evaluate the quality and aesthetics of your design.

In the next chapter, we will work on getting this 2D curve one step closer to 3D printing by turning it into a 3D mesh.

3
Converting a Bezier Curve to a Properly Sized 3D Mesh

In this chapter, we will convert the 2D curve of our profile into a 3D mesh that is properly sized for our pendant. The skills that will be covered are as follows:

- Converting a Bezier curve into a mesh
- Using different selection modes to select vertices, edges, and faces
- Creating new faces
- Using the Extrude tool to make a 2D face into a 3D object
- Understanding Blender units and sizing your object to specific dimensions

Converting a Bezier curve into a mesh

Now that we have finalized the shape of our curve, we want to translate that layout to a format that will be easy to combine with other 3D objects. We want to make our curve into what's called a **mesh**. As a curve, each segment is defined by two control points and two handles, which makes it easy to define and edit.

That same shape as a mesh is comprised of numerous points (**vertices**) and line segments (**edges**):

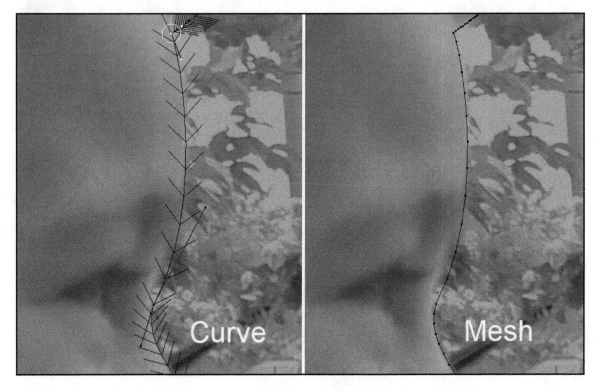

As a curve, the forehead is defined by two control points and two handles. As a mesh, that is translated to specific vertices.

Viewing the curve in **Edit Mode** gives you a preview of where the final vertices will be. The arrows that show the direction of the curve also illustrate where the points will be.

You can select how many vertices will ultimately define each curve segment. On the bottom right of your screen is an area known as the **Properties Window**. When you have an object selected, that section will allow you to view and change its characteristics. Properties are grouped by category and you can use a series of icons to navigate between them. When you select a Bezier curve, there is a little arc icon with two endpoints that displays properties specific to curves:

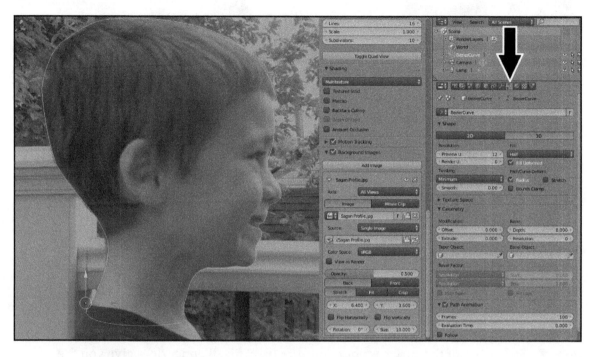

The Properties Window is on the right side of your screen. There is a special curve subsection to edit curve information.

Under the **Active Spline** section, there is a **Resolution Setting**. This is the number of vertices that will comprise each section of the curve. If you'd like a smoother resolution along your curve edge, you can increase that number to more vertices. Increasing the **Resolution** from **12** to **24** will double the vertices being created between control points:

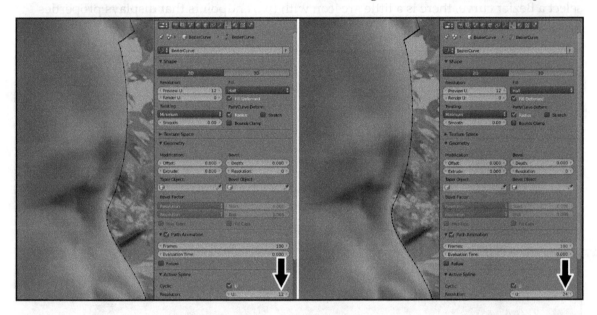

The Resolution setting determines how many vertices will be created in your mesh

Consider making a backup before converting to a mesh

Before converting your curve to a mesh, you may want to make a backup copy of the curve or your entire `.blend` file. Blender does give you the ability to convert meshes back to curves, but you'll find it does not keep your original control points and handles. If you do decide you would like to make edits to your original curve, working with a backup copy may prove to be easier.

The steps to convert your curve to a 3D mesh are as follows:

1. If necessary, switch to **Object Mode** as we want to perform an action on the whole object. Right-click on the curve to select it.
2. In the **Properties Window**, click on the Curve icon and make any desired adjustments to the **Active Spline Resolution** setting.

3. At the bottom of your screen, go to the **Object** | **Convert to** | **Mesh from Curve/Meta/Surf/Text** menu option. Alternatively, you can hit *Alt + C* as a keyboard shortcut and then select **Mesh from Curve/Meta/Surf/Text**:

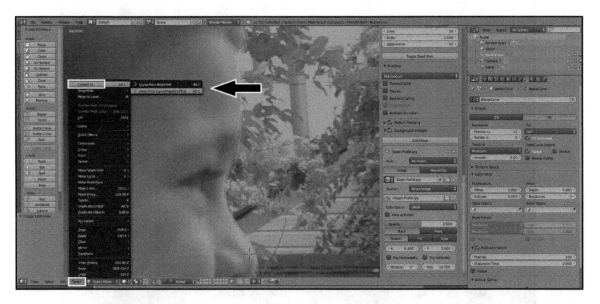

Converting a curve to a mesh by going to Object | Convert to | Mesh from Curve/Meta/Surf/Text

Selecting vertices and making a new face

Now that our profile is a mesh, you will be working in terms of vertices, edges, and faces. Vertices are the points that make up the edges. Edges, in turn, are the borders that make up **faces**. In 3D printing, the slicing software is ultimately concerned with the faces of your object. An object with just vertices and edges would not print.

When you are in **Edit Mode**, you have the ability to view and edit all three elements of a mesh. There are now icons at the bottom of the screen that will let you switch your **Selection Mode.** If you select the leftmost icon, which is a yellow point on a cube, you will be in **Vertex Select** mode, where right-clicking will select specific vertices in your model. Selecting the middle icon, a yellow line on a cube, will put you in **Edge Select** mode and allow you to pick the edges or the outline of our profile. There is a final icon for **Face Select** mode which won't let us select anything at the moment.

Right now, our profile is just a collection of vertices and edges. In other words, our profile is not printable:

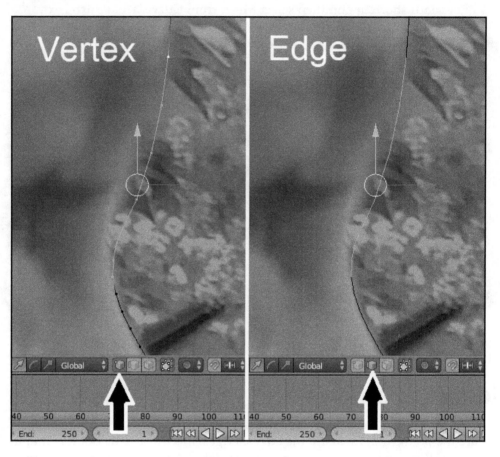

Vertex Selection Mode and Edge Selection Mode

We'll start to rectify that by using the vertices and edges we already have to create a new face. The steps are as follows:

1. Switch to **Edit Mode** as we'll be changing just a specific part of our object.
2. At the bottom of the screen, select the Vertex Select icon.
3. Under the **Select** menu, pick **(De)select All** to select all the vertices in your model. You can also type A as a shortcut:

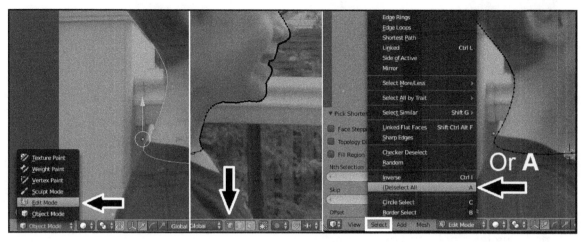

Selecting all the vertices

4. Every vertex in your model will be highlighted in yellow to show it is selected. You can now tell Blender to make a new face out by going to **Mesh | Faces | Make Edge/Face**. Alternatively, you can hit the *F* key on your keyboard:

Creating a new face.

At this point, your background image is suddenly obscured. There is a newly created face blocking the view.

Extruding to make 3D objects

You have your first face, but your model is not yet a full 3D object. You are going to need to give your object some height to give your printer something to do. Before we do that, let's learn a little more about our face and how it will behave.

Understanding and viewing face normals

Although it is completely flat and 2D, your first face already has an inside and an outside, a front and a back. A quilt square is also flat, but there is a definite outside, the part with the pattern that will be seen, and a definite inside. Your face doesn't have the fancy colors of a quilt square, but you can still tell which part is the "front" and which part is the "back." The 3D modeling terminology is **face normal**:

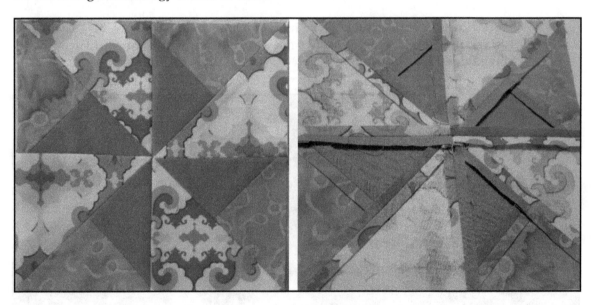

Like a quilt square, your faces have a front (outside) and a back (inside)

The steps for viewing your face normals are as follows:

1. If necessary, switch to **Edit Mode**.
2. In the **Properties Shelf**, go to the **Mesh Display** section. Under **Normals**, select the icon that has a cube with a yellow side.
3. This will put a blue line on your faces, pointing out from what will be the outside of your object. If the lines are hard to see, you can increase their **Size** and make them longer for better visibility:

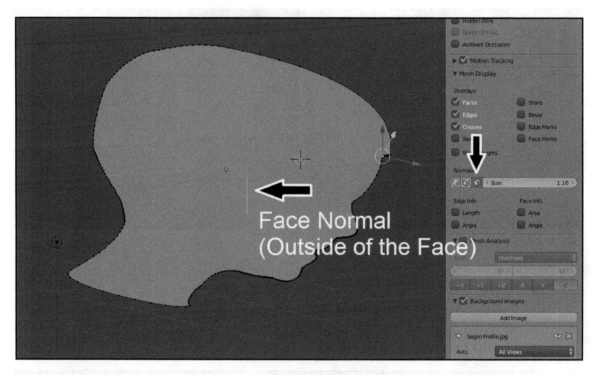

A light blue line helps you tell which side of your face is out

Not only will face normals show you the outside of your face, they'll also give you an idea of the direction in which the face is pointing and how it will behave if you grow, or Extrude, that section.

Using Extrude Region

The **Extrude** tool in Blender can take a 2D face like our profile and make it 3D by copying that face, and then adding all the supporting faces to connect the two. In the example of our profile pendant, after we extrude we will have two identical faces in the shape of the subject's profile—one for the top of pendant and one for the bottom. In addition, numerous faces will be automatically added to make up the sides of the pendant:

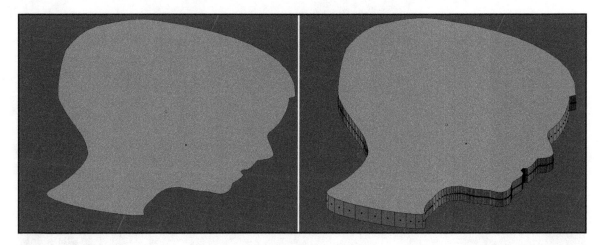

Before and after of extruding a face

The steps for extruding a face are as follows:

1. If necessary, switch to **Edit Mode** using the drop-down menu at the bottom of the screen.
2. Use the icon to switching to **Face Select** mode:

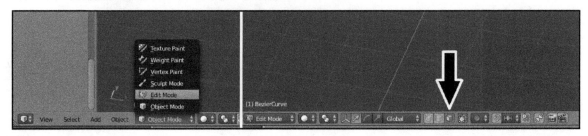

Switching to face selection mode.

3. Right-click to select the face you wish to Extrude.
4. If necessary, click on the **Tools** tab on the **Tool Shelf** on the left side of the screen.
5. Under **Mesh Tools**, look for the **Add** section and click on the **Extrude Region** button. You can also hit *E* on the keyboard as a shortcut.
6. Move your mouse to increase or decrease the extrusion amount. By default, the system is extruding in the same direction as the face normal. When satisfied, left-click to commit the change. Alternatively, you can hit the *Enter* key:

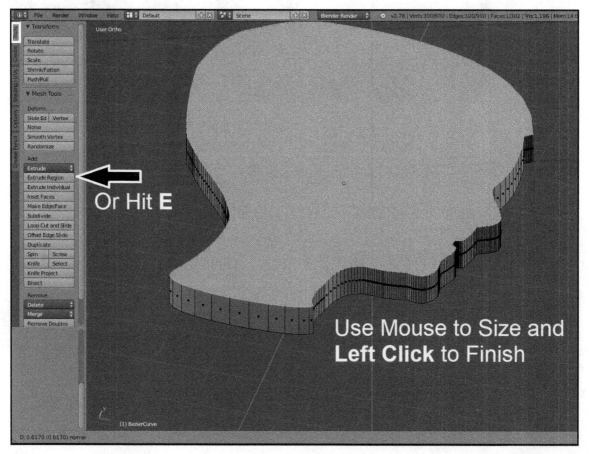

Extruding to a 3D mesh.

Extruding to exact dimensions

When extruding, instead of using your mouse to size, you can also type in specific dimensions. Positive numbers will move in the direction of the face normal. A negative number will move backward:

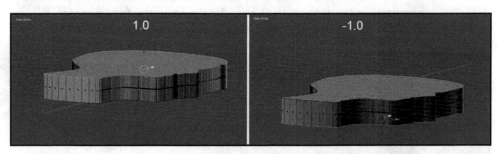

Extruding by typing E 1.0 and by typing E -1.0

Scaling and sizing the mesh

Before we go any further, this is a good point to reflect on the thoughts from Chapter 1, *Thinking About Design Requirements*, and to size our piece appropriately for the function and the printing process you have in mind. Looking at pendants I already own, I'm thinking a suitable size for this pendant would be 1 1/2" tall. This is an item that may look fantastic in cast metals from a 3D Printing Service Bureau. If I did decide to go that route, I would make the piece thinner to save on cost.

My starting dimensions would likely be as follows:

Dimension	Service Bureau (Shapeways Plated Metals)	At home (FFF/FDM)
Length	1 1/2" (38.1 mm)	1 1/2" (38.1 mm)
Width	Proportional to length	Proportional to length
Height (thickness)	0.8 mm	2 mm

Converting to the metric system

For those of us used to the **United States Customary System** and inches, I highly recommend thinking and modeling in the **International System of Units** and millimeters instead. 3D printers and slicing software work in microns and millimeters. In addition, the default coordinate system Blender uses is identical to millimeters when you export a file for 3D printing. When you model with millimeters in mind, you can use the Blender measurement system as is without changes.

Unit settings in Blender

Although you do have the ability to change the units in Blender, I recommend sticking to the default *Blender units* and treating them as millimeters:

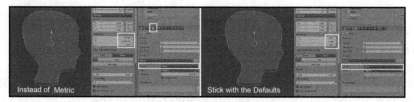

Default Blender units are recommended

If you do have a measurement in inches, you don't have to worry about remembering there are 25.4 mm in an inch. Like most things in life, you can Google it. The large search engines such as Google or Bing, and even tools such as Amazon Echo, will readily answer conversion questions:

Using a search engine to convert units of measurement

Reading the current dimensions and scale

When you are in **Object Mode**, the **Properties Shelf** shows you information about the selected object. This includes the current Scale and Dimensions, which you can find under the **Transform** section. Each dimension corresponds to a specific axis. These will become second nature, but at first you can rely on the color coding of the arrows and axis grid lines:

Axis	Color of arrows and grid lines
X	Red
Y	Green
Z	Blue

Treating the Blender units as millimeters, the dimensions of my pendant are currently 6.44 mm x 8.195 mm x 1.0 mm:

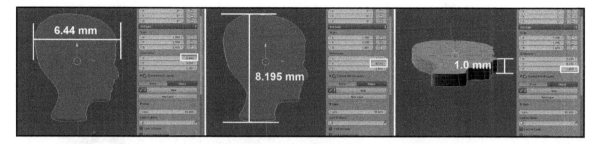

Originally dimensions of the pendant.

Preceding the **Dimensions** is another section you can use to change the size of your model. It lets you update the **Scale**. Currently, everything is set to **1**. If I wanted to double the size of every dimension, instead of entering specific measurements, I could simply update the scale to **2**:

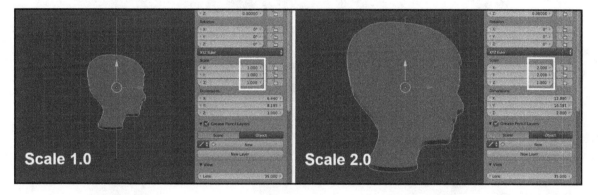

The impact of scaling.

Scaling a model by typing dimensions

With the pendant, I have decided I would like the head to be 1 1/2" high, which is 38.1 mm. Referring to the color coding of the grid lines and the axis arrows, I want to update the **Y** (green) dimension. The steps are as follows:

1. If necessary, switch into **Object Mode** and right-click on your object to select it.

2. In the **Properties Shelf**, under the **Transform** section, look for **Dimensions** and click in the **Y** box. Type in the new dimension and hit *Enter* or click out of the **Y** box to commit the change, In this example, I type in 31.8:

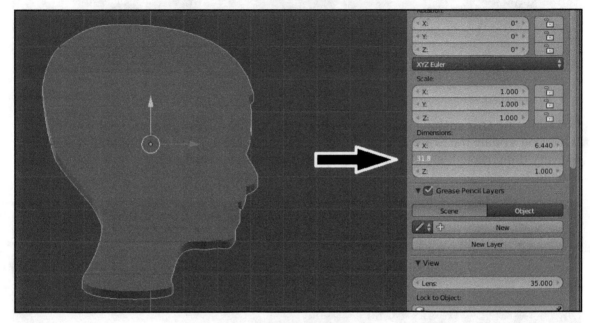

Updating the Y dimension.

Repeat these steps to update the **Z** dimension to the desired thickness of the pendant. In my example, I decided I would use 0.8 mm for a 3D Printing Service Bureau or 2.0 mm for at-home printing:

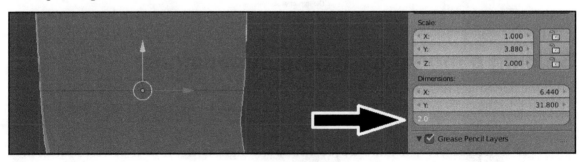

Updating the Z dimension.

Fixing proportions by updating scale

At this point, when I look at the pendant, it no longer looks like my background image. This is because our final dimension, the X (red) axis, is out of proportion with the Y (green) axis:

The pendant is out of proportion.

We can correct this by updating the scale of the X axis to match the Y axis. The steps are as follows:

1. If necessary, switch to **Object Mode** and right-click on your object to select it.
2. In the **Properties Shelf**, under the **Transform** section, look for **Scale** and click in the **Y** box. Hit *Ctrl + C* to copy that exact scale measurement to your computer clipboard.

3. Click in the **X** box under **Scale**. Hit *Ctrl* + *V* to paste the copied measurement into that box. You can also type in the number if you prefer:

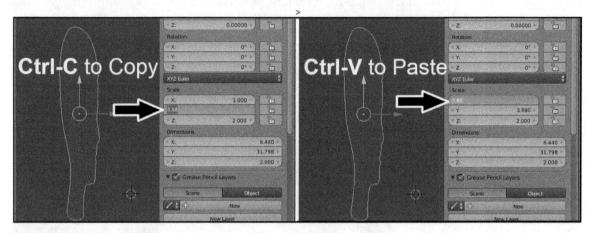

Copying the X Scale to Y.

4. Hit *Enter* or click out of the **X** box for the change to take effect.

Now that the X dimension and the Y dimension have matching scales, our pendant is recognizable again:

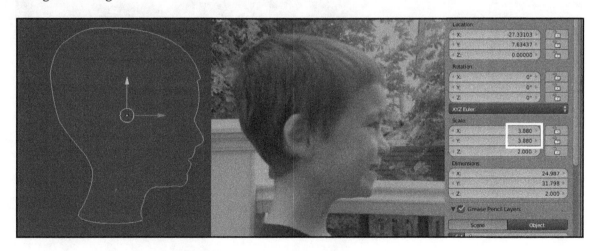

The pendant is back in proportion.

Summary

In this chapter, you converted a Bezier curve into a mesh. You learned how to select vertices and edges and how to create a brand new face. Next, you learned about the Extrude tool and how to make that 2D face into a 3D object. Finally, you learned how to update the dimensions and scale of your object to make sure it is properly sized for your needs.

In Chapter 4, *Flattening a Torus and Boolean Union*, you will finalize your pendant by adding a hook at the top.

4
Flattening a Torus and Boolean Union

In this chapter, you'll be adding a little hook at the top of the pendant so it can be worn on a necklace. The skills that will be covered include:

- Adding a new torus object to your project
- Rotating and laying out objects with the Transform tools
- Using Border Select to select multiple vertices at once
- Using Scale to standardize a group of vertices to a specific height to make a flat base
- Using the Boolean Union Modifier to make multiple objects into a single mesh
- Exporting your work into the STL file format for 3D printing

Creating and laying out a torus

With this project, you have made a custom-shaped mesh from a Bezier curve. Blender also has a library of standard meshes you can use to build your model. One such standard mesh is the **torus** which adds a donut-shaped object to your project. The torus is the perfect shape to add a little hook to our pendant.

When you create a torus, Blender gives you additional properties to determine the size. Two properties of note are:

- **Interior Radius**: This is the measurement from the center of the torus hole, to the inside of the ring around the hole
- **Exterior Radius**: This is the measurement from the center of the torus hole to the outside of the ring:

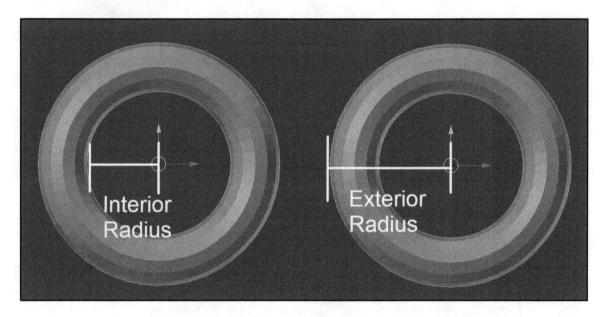

Interior Radius and Exterior Radius of a torus

Thinking about the concepts in Chapter 1, *Thinking About Design Requirements*, you may have specific dimensions in mind. For example, my chain would require a hole that is 3 mm wide, so I would want to make sure the Interior Radius is at least 1.5 mm (half of 3 mm) to accommodate that. The printing process would be the driving force for determining the thickness of the ring that would decide my Exterior Radius. For Plated Metals from a 3D Printing Service Bureau, the minimum wall thickness is listed as 0.8 mm, so I would want my ring to be that thick. At home, printing in plastic, I'd like the ring to be 2 mm thick as the material is not as strong.

My starting dimensions might be:

Dimensions	Service Bureau (Shapeways Plated Metals)	At home (FFF/FDM)
Interior Radius	1.5mm (for a 3mm diameter hole)	1.5mm (for a 3mm diameter hole)
Exterior Radius	2.3mm (1.5mm plus the 0.8 minimum wall thickness)	3.5mm (1.5mm plus 2mm for wall thickness)

Adding a new torus object

To add the torus object to the project, take the following steps:

1. Since you are adding a brand new object, make sure you are in **Object Mode**.
2. Left-click your screen to move the 3D Cursor to where you would like to add the torus:

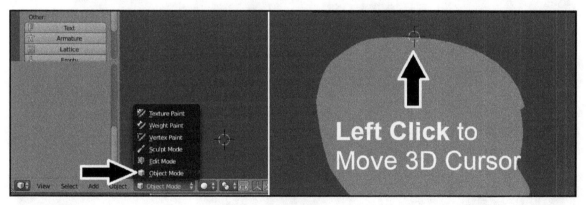

Moving the 3D Cursor.

3. In the **Tool Shelf** on the left side of the screen, click the **Create** tab. Left-click the **Torus** button. A new torus appears on your screen. In addition, a new **Add Torus** section appears at the bottom of the **Tool Shelf** to allow for further customization:

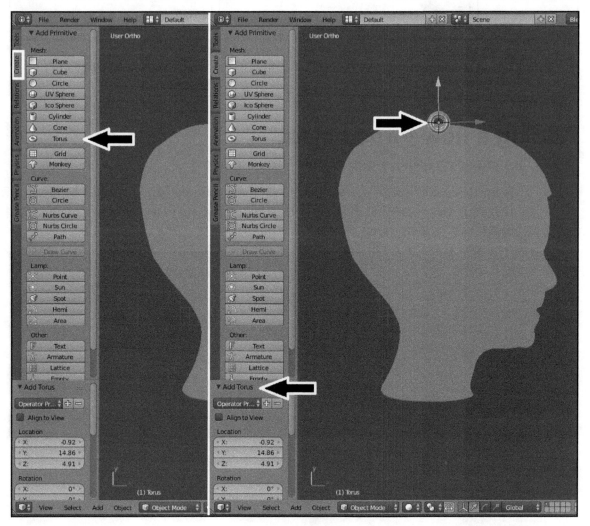

Adding a new torus to the project.

4. Immediately scroll down to the new **Add Torus** section of the **Tool Shelf**. Under **Torus Dimensions**, click **Exterior/Interior**. Update the **Exterior Radius** and **Interior Radius** properties accordingly:

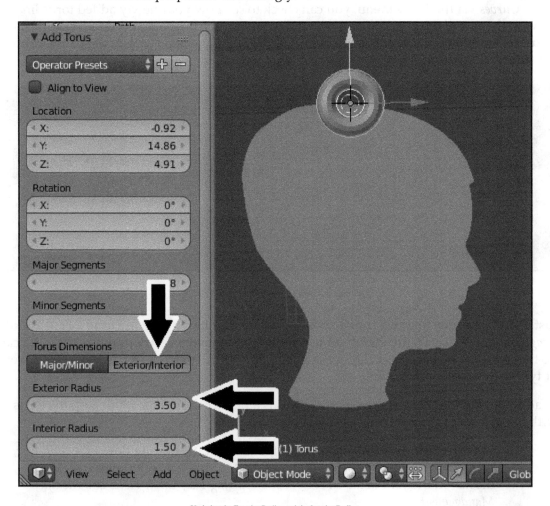

Updating the Exterior Radius and the Interior Radius.

Your new torus has been added with the proper dimensions.

Positioning the torus

Using the techniques of switching viewpoints from Chapter 2, *Using a Background Image and Bezier Curves* via the **View** menu, you can check to see how your newly added torus lines up with the rest of the pendant and what adjustments need to be made. As an example, the torus in the following image is not lined up appropriately when I look at the pendant from the side:

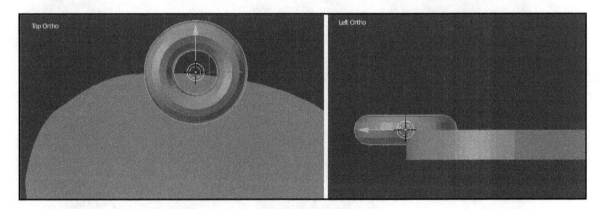

Checking the placement by going to View | Top and View | Left

Just as we were able to move control points and handles in Chapter 2, *Using a Background Image and Bezier Curves*, Blender gives us the ability to move objects around as well. We can do that with the exact same techniques of using the white circle, the axis arrows, the G key, or typing in specific positioning.

In addition, Blender has an align feature. This is a perfect shortcut for lining up the torus with the bottom of the pendant. The steps are:

1. In **Object Mode**, right-click the profile to select it. Holding down the *Shift* key, right-click the **torus** to select that as well. Multi-select techniques will be discussed in more detail in Chapter 6, *Cutting Half Circle Holes and Modifier Management*.
2. In the menu at the bottom of the screen, click **Object**. Next, pick **Transform** and select **Align Objects**:

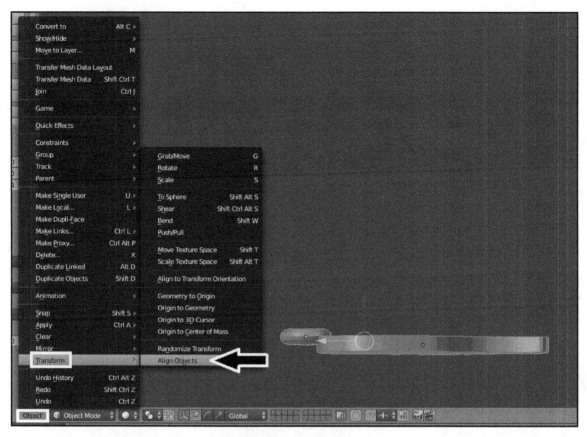

Preparing to align the pendant and the torus.

3. In the **Tool Shelf** on the left side of the screen, there is a new **Align Objects** section. Under the **Align** header, pick the axis you wish to sync up. In this case, I pick **Z**:

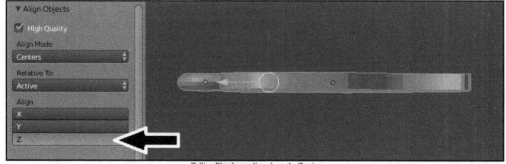

Telling Blender to align along the Z axis.

Change your perspective, check your work from different views, and make any necessary adjustments. They may be manual adjustments such as moving the torus along the Y axis to control how deep it goes into the pendant. You may also use the same Align technique on the X axis to center the torus with the pendant:

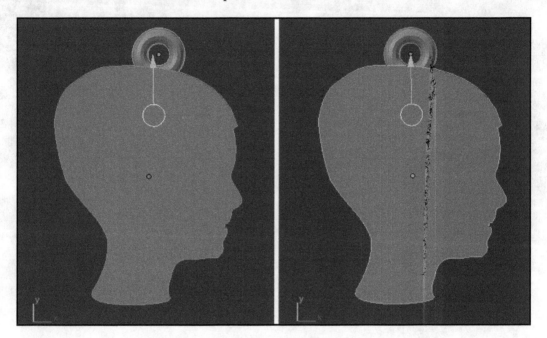

Aligning on the X axis can center the torus with the profile.

Rotating the torus (for Service Bureau)

If you are planning on printing at a 3D Printing Service Bureau, their industrial printers can handle designs that don't have flat bases and designs that do have large overhangs. As a result, you can consider rotating the torus. This could better suit the aesthetic you are looking for.

Often, the hardest part of rotating an object is figuring out which axis you want to rotate around. Here, switching to different views (discussed in Chapter 2, *Using a Background Image and Bezier Curves*) and referring to the color coding of the axis arrows (discussed in Chapter 3, *Converting a Bezier Curve to a Properly Sized 3D Mesh*) can help guide the way.

Think about each axis line and what the object would look if it was spun around that line. If you aren't quite sure which axis to rotate on, there is no shame in trial and error:

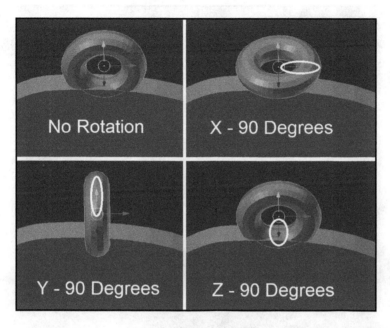

Impact of rotating around various axes.

Object Origin and Rotation

The rotation will occur around the object's point of origin which displays as a yellow dot when your object is selected. In this case, it is the very center of the torus, which is perfect for our needs. If you ever need to rotate around a different point, Chapter 5, *Building a Base with Standard Meshes and a Mirror* will discuss how to change an object's origin.

If you do want to rotate the torus, the steps are:

1. If necessary, make sure you are in **Object Mode** and right-click the object to select it.

2. Go to the **Object** | **Transform** | **Rotate** menu option. Alternatively, you can type *R* on your keyboard:

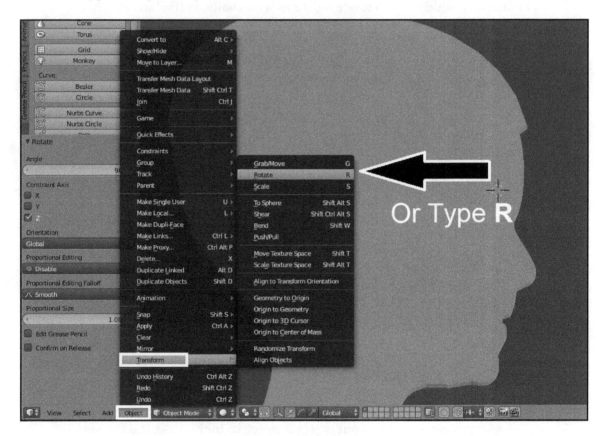

Using the Object | Transform | Rotate menu.

3. Type the axis you would like to rotate around: **X** for X (red), **Y** for Y (green), or **Z** for Z (blue). A line of the appropriate color will display to show you what you will be rotating around:

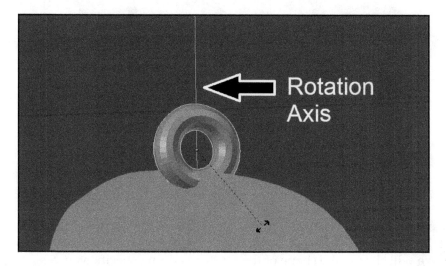

A colored line shows you are rotating along a specific axis.

4. You can move your mouse to rotate. I recommend typing in the exact degrees. In this case, type 90.
5. Hit the *Enter* key or left-click to apply the change.

The hook for your chain is now rotated. Since you are working toward printing at a 3D Printing Service Bureau, you may skip the next section and proceed to *Combining objects together with Boolean Union.*

Giving the torus a flat bottom (for home)

Naturally, the torus object is rounded, which does give a nice look and feel to the pendant's hook. However, the rounded nature of the bottom may be tricky for the FFF/FDM printers. Looking at the slicing preview from the bottom up, I can see that perhaps there are some tricky overhangs for the printer.

In the following preview, I can see some places where lines of plastic would have nothing underneath it:

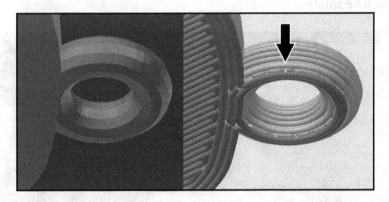

How our torus looks in Blender and how it looks in the slicing preview (looking from the bottom up).

Since no one sees the back of the pendant, we can flatten the bottom of that torus to help the printer out. To do that, we'll be getting more familiar with a technique called **mesh modeling**. We will change the shape of the torus by editing specific vertices.

Toggling vertex visibility and using border select

To flatten our vertices, we first want to select them. When you are in **Edit Mode** by default you see just the vertices that are visible from your perspective. If I'm looking at the left side of the torus, for example, I only see the faces, edges, and vertices of that side. Just like in reality, everything on the other side is obscured by my perspective. Blender calls it **Limit selection to visible**.

You do have the ability to turn that off, which gives you something akin to X-ray vision where you can see everything even if it is behind a solid surface. The icon to turn Limit selection to visible on and off is directly to the right of the three selection mode icons. It will work for any of the three selection modes, allowing you to see hidden vertices, edges, and faces:

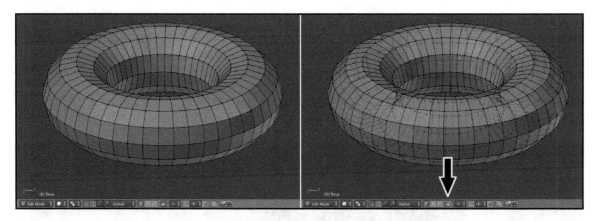

Turning off the "Limit selection to visible" mode allows you to see everything even if it would normally be hidden from your point of view.

As you may recall, you can right-click items to select them. Blender also gives you the ability to select multiple items at once. We'll talk a little more about using the *Shift* and *Control* keys to multiselect in Chapter 6, *Cutting Half Circle Holes and Modifier Management*. For this chapter, we are going to explore a tool called **Border Select**, which allows you to draw a square and select all the items within.

Find a good view

With Border Select, how you are looking at your model will impact how easy it is to make your selections. Border Select draws a rectangle with perfect straight lines. Try to find a good view so everything is lined up in a manner that is easy to select. If I'm looking at my torus from an angle, I will have to make multiple selections to get everything and I'm more likely to select vertices I don't want. If I change my view so I'm looking directly at it from the side, it is much easier to make my selection with a single rectangle:

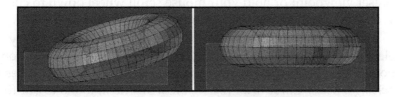

Looking at the torus at an angle makes it harder to select the vertices I want with a Border Select rectangle.

It is not always possible to get everything in one try. Luckily, Border Select will add the new selections to anything you already have selected. This means you can do multiple Border Selects in succession to get everything you want. However, this also means you want to make sure to deselect anything you don't want before you begin.

For example, if I had two vertices already selected at the top of my torus, after my Border Select, those two vertices will still be selected even though they weren't in the selection box:

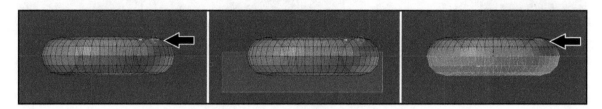

Two vertices at the top of the torus are already selected. The Border Select adds to that selection, so they are still selected afterward.

With our pendant hook, we are going to want to select all the vertices on the bottom half of our torus so we can flatten them out. The steps to do that are:

1. If necessary, right-click the torus to select it and switch to **Edit Mode**.
2. Click the Vertex select icon.
3. Click the Limit selection to visible icon to show all the vertices:

4. Now that all the vertices are displayed, change your viewpoint for easier selection. You can use the **View** menu at the bottom of your screen to pick from the preset viewpoint or hold your mouse scroll wheel down to customize your view. In this case, I recommend going to **View | Left**.
5. Make sure no other vertices are selected. If there are some, an easy way to unselect them is to click on **Select | (De)select All** menu or hit *A* on the keyboard. That is the same feature we used to select all the vertices in Chapter 3, *Converting a Bezier Curve to a Properly Sized 3D Mesh*, to make our first face. If something is already selected, that same menu option will unselect them.
6. In the **Select** menu at the bottom of your screen, click **Border Select**. Alternatively, you can hit the *B* key on your keyboard.

7. A dotted cross shows up on your screen. Much like cropping a photo, use your mouse to position the cross at one of the corners of your eventual rectangle. Left-click to set that corner, drag your mouse until you are satisfied with the rectangle, and left-click again:

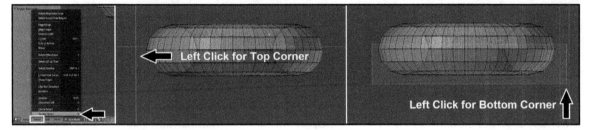

Drawing the selection box.

When you are done, all the vertices in the bottom half of your torus should be yellow and selected. Often it is handy to take a moment and switch views, to make sure nothing was missed and there are no extra vertices along for the ride:

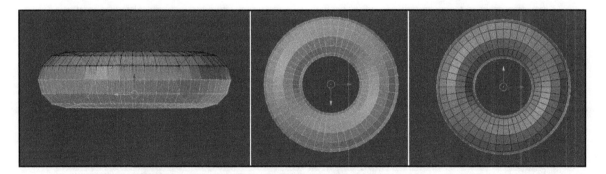

The bottom vertices of the torus are selected. Switching views lets you double-check your work.

Using Scale to align vertices

Now that we have all the vertices selected, we want to set them all to the same height on the Z (blue) axis to make a flat base. Your first instinct may be to look over to your **Properties Shelf** and type in a new **Z** coordinate under the **Transform** section. If you look closely, however, you'll notice the caption reads **Median**.

When you change a coordinate there, it is going to move every vertex in equal amounts, keeping the rounded shape of our bottom:

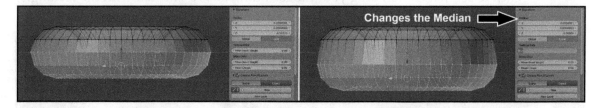

Changing the Z value under Transform | Median doesn't set everything to the same level. It keeps the curved shape.

Luckily, Blender's Scale feature can sync up all the vertices on the same level. You can think of it as an align tool. If you scale everything to 0, it will move all the vertices to the exact same spot, making the bottom of the torus come together to a single point like a gemstone (note: all the individual vertices are still there). You can also scale along a particular axis. For example, you can set just the X coordinates for vertices to be the same:

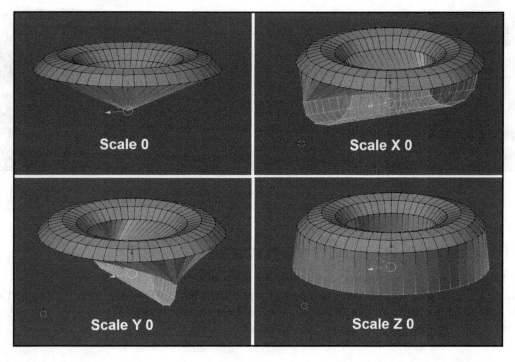

The differences in using the Scale feature on vertices. Scale 0 will set all vertices to the same position. Scale X 0 lines all up the X coordinates. Scale Y 0 lines up the Y coordinates. Finally, Scale Z 0 lines up the Z coordinates.

As you can see from the preceding image, we want to scale our torus on the Z axis. Our steps would be:

1. Go to the **Mesh | Transform | Scale** menu option or hit *S* on the keyboard:

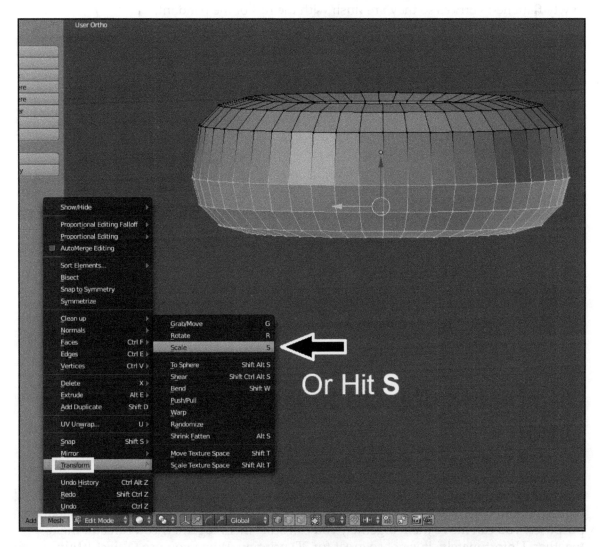

Using the Mesh | Transform | Scale menu option.

2. Type z to tell Blender you want to adjust the position along the Z-axis. A color-coded line, in this case blue, shows on your screen to show you which axis you are scaling to.

3. Type the number 0.

With the Z coordinates all lined up, our torus has a nice flat base for 3D printing. Evaluate your work from different angles and if necessary, right-click the Z arrow and adjust those newly flattened vertices so they are flush with the rest of the pendant:

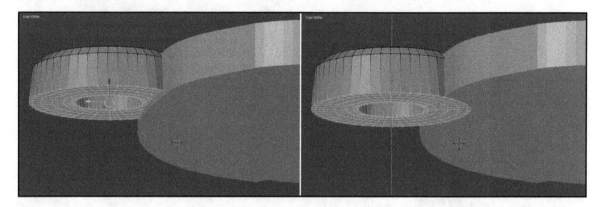

After flattening, the bottom of our hook is higher than the rest of the pendant. You would like that to be flush with the bottom of the profile.

Exact Z Coordinates

Once the vertices are all lined up, because they are all at equal heights, you can now type in a specific Z coordinate under the **Transform Median** section and confidently know they will all move together to that same height.

Combining objects together with Boolean Union

At this point, we have two separate objects making up our pendant—the profile that we made from a Bezier curve and then a torus to serve as a hook. We want to print them together as one, so we want to combine them both into a single object. It is tempting to highlight both objects and use the **Object | Join** menu option. It is convenient for Blender purposes: you can move them together, you can scale them together, you can edit them together. Unfortunately, it is not so great for 3D printing. When you use **Object | Join**, Blender keeps all the geometry for both the selected objects. If I join the profile and the hook, I can still see all the vertices of the torus inside of the pendant.

In `Chapter 3`, *Converting a Bezier Curve to a Properly Sized 3D Mesh*, we talked a little about face normals and how faces have insides and outsides. With **Object | Join**, all that internal geometry is going to send your slicer mixed signals as to what's inside and what's outside:

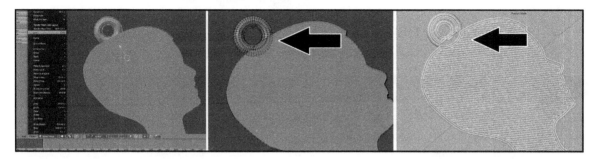

Using Object | Join leaves remnants of the original objects inside, which can confuse the slicing software.

There are tools to repair such issues, one of which will be highlighted in `Chapter 15`, *Troubleshooting and Repairing Models*. Nonetheless, I find it easier to keep your meshes clean and concise as you go. Instead of **Object | Join**, I recommend using what's called a **Boolean Modifier**.

The Boolean Modifier tool has a Union option that will combine two objects into one. The difference is the Boolean Modifier will consolidate the geometry to make the new object. It'll recognize the unnecessary vertices and faces of the torus and remove them, producing a much cleaner object for 3D printing:

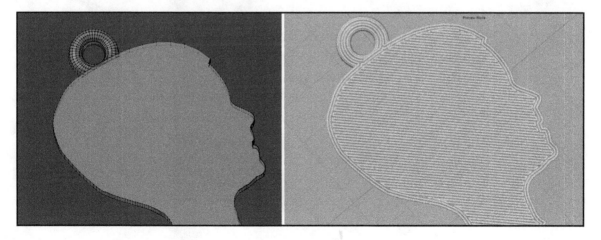

Applying a Boolean Union Modifier cleans up internal vertices and unnecessary geometry, producing a much cleaner slice.

The steps to add the Boolean Union Modifier to an object are:

1. If necessary, switch to **Object Mode** and right-click one of your objects to select it. In this case, I recommend selecting the person's profile.

2. In the **Properties Window** on the right bottom of the screen, click the wrench icon to access your **Modifiers**.

3. Click the **Add Modifier** drop-down and select **Boolean**:

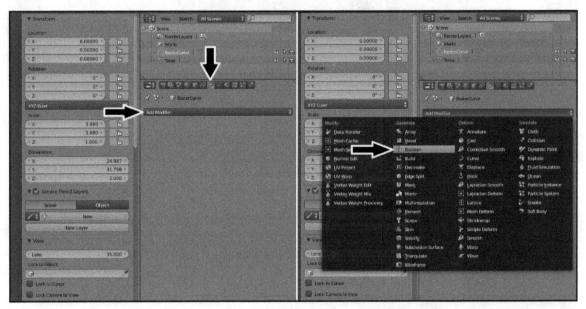

Adding a new Boolean Modifier.

4. For **Operation**, pick **Union**. This tells Blender you will be combining two objects into one, making a union of them both.

5. Under **Object**, pick the object you want to combine with this one. In this case, pick the **torus**.

6. Set the **Overlap Threshold** to 0:

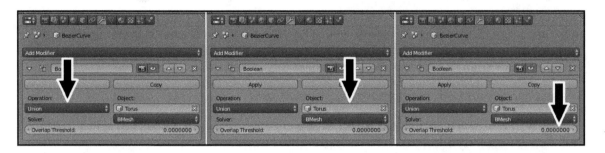

Setting the properties for the new Boolean Modifier.

7. When you hit **Apply**, the second object (the one we selected for Object, in this case, the torus) will remain intact, but the first object (the one we are adding the modifier to, in this case, the profile) will have its vertices, edges, and faces permanently changed.

Delay Applying Modifiers

The **Apply** button will make permanent changes to your object. When you export a file for 3D printing, Blender will automatically apply any pending modifiers. As a result, you can delay applying modifiers unless you absolutely need them for additional modeling. This makes adjustments and edits easier.

Troubleshooting Tips in Chapter 15, *Troubleshooting and Repairing Models.*

If you ever have unexpected behavior with a Boolean Modifier, there may be something wrong with your meshes. For example, perhaps the face normals are backwards so the inside of an object is marked as the outside. Tips on troubleshooting and fixing models are available in Chapter 15, *Troubleshooting and Repairing Models.*

At this point all our work is combined into a single, print-friendly object.

Exporting your work for 3D printing

Our final step is to export the model into a format for the slicer and 3D printer. Currently, there are a few file formats that work well. The most common format is Stereolithography. You can think of it as a **Standard Triangle Language** (**STL**) as it will convert all your faces into a series of triangles for the slicer to read.

The steps to export your pendant for 3D printing are:

1. If necessary, switch to **Object Mode** and right-click your object to select it. Make sure everything you want is highlighted in yellow.
2. In the menu at the top of your screen, select **File** | **Export** | **Stl (.stl)**:

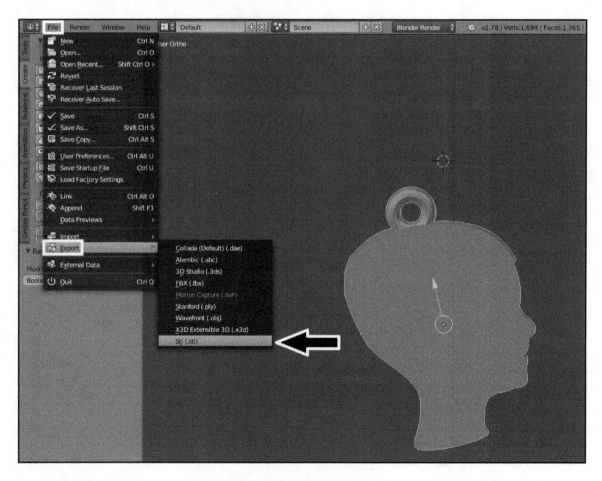

Exporting the model to an STL file.

3. You can click on the folder icon and the white up arrow to browse your computer's folder structure to pick where you want to save the file.

4. By default, the STL will be named the same as your `.blend` project. You can customize that file name if necessary. Check the **Selection Only** box. Otherwise, Blender will include everything in the STL, even objects that are hidden or redundant. Click the **Export STL** button:

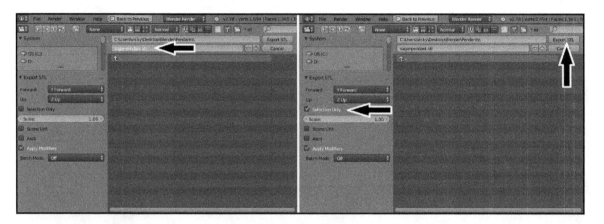

Picking the file name and finalizing the export.

With that, your custom profile pendant is ready to upload to a 3D Printing Service Bureau or for slicing for your own printer at home.

Summary

In this chapter, you learned how to add a standard torus mesh to your project. You learned how to adjust its size and how to position it. For Service Bureau printing, you learned how to rotate the torus. For home printing, you learned how to use the Border Select and Scale features to flatten the back of the torus. You learned how to combine your profile and your torus into a single object using the Boolean Union Modifier. Finally, you learned to export your work into an STL file for 3D printing.

In the Chapter 5, *Building a Base with Standard Meshes and a Mirror*, you'll use standard meshes and a mirror to start another jewelry piece, a customized coordinate bracelet.

5
Building a Base with Standard Meshes and a Mirror

In this chapter, you are going to start a second jewelry project, a bracelet plate you can customize with the coordinates of a special location. You'll start by learning more about making objects with a combination of standard meshes and the Boolean Modifier. You'll also learn about using the Mirror Modifier to save time and make your work symmetrical. Finally, you'll learn how to add text to your project, which is handy for custom engraving or embossing. In this chapter, we'll start by building the base plate for our bracelet. The skills you'll learn include:

- Adding a cube and a cylinder to a project
- Placing objects with the Transform section of the Properties Shelf
- Changing an object's Origin
- Using the Mirror Modifier to make symmetrical objects

Working with a cube and cylinder

Before we begin, let's reflect on the concepts from Chapter 1, *Thinking about Design Requirements,* and think about the sizing of our plate. Using my own wrist as a guide, I determine how long and wide I want it:

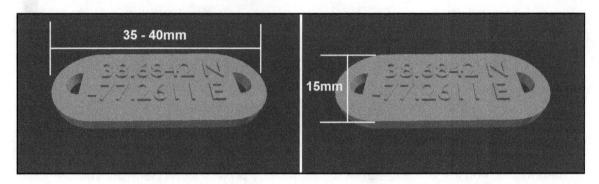

Brainstorming dimensions of the final piece

For the height (thickness) of the piece, the printing process is going to be the determining factor. The sizing I end up with is as follows:

Dimension	Service Bureau (Shapeways Strong & Flexible Plastic)	At Home (FFF/FDM)
Length	35-40mm	35-40mm
Width	15mm	15mm
Height	1mm (Slightly bigger than the minimum wall thickness of 0.7 mm)	2.5mm

Resizing the default cube

For this project, the default cube can contribute to our final model. Instead of deleting it, like we did in Chapter 2, *Using a Background Image and Bezier Curves,* we can resize it to our needs. We are going to use the Mirror Modifier later in this chapter, so we will only be modeling half of the base. Since the eventual curved edges will add to the total length, I'm going to make this cube 10 mm long (X), 15 mm wide (Y), and 2 mm high (Z).

As we saw in `Chapter 3`, *Converting a Bezier Curve to a Properly Sized 3D Mesh*, the **Transform** section of the **Properties Shelf** is a great way to size objects when you have specific dimensions in mind. The steps for resizing the default cube are as follows:

1. The default cube should automatically be selected when you start a new project. If not, right-click on it to select it.
2. Click on the **+** icon or hit *N* to display the **Properties Shelf**.
3. Under **Transform**, find **Dimensions** and set the **X**, **Y**, and **Z** dimensions accordingly. The example I'm going with is `10`, `15`, and `2`:

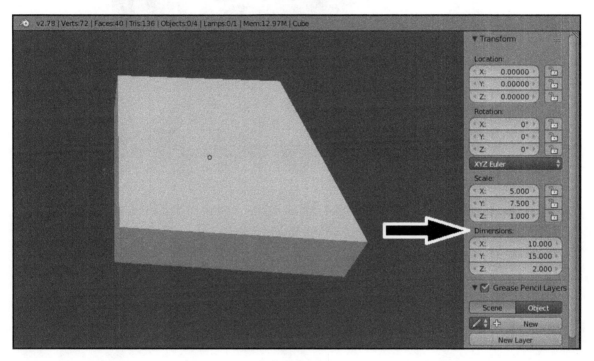

Setting the dimensions.

Adding and sizing a cylinder

To give our bracelet plate a more polished look, we are going to add a new cylinder to round out the edges. To ensure our cylinder and cube match, we'll want to set the diameter of the cylinder to be the same as the width (Y) of the cube. In other words, we want the diameter of the cylinder to be 15 mm, which would make a radius of 7.5mm:

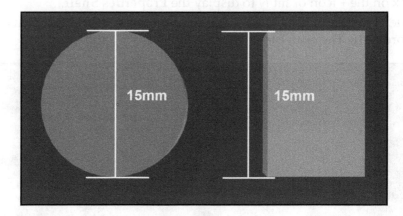

The cylinder diameter should match the width of the cube

We'll also want it to have the same thickness, or depth, as the rest of the base. In this case, 2mm for at-home printing and 1mm for Service Bureaus.

The steps to add and size the new cylinder are as follows:

1. In **Object Mode**, left-click to place the 3D Cursor where you'd like the new cylinder to be. Don't worry if it is not exact.
2. In your **Tool Shelf** on the left side of the screen, look under the **Create** tab and click on **Cylinder**:

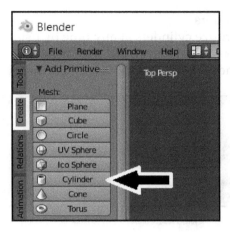

Adding a new cylinder

3. At the bottom of the **Tool Shelf**, an **Add Cylinder** window appears with additional options. Update the **Radius** and **Depth** accordingly. Here, I am going with 7.500 and 2.000:

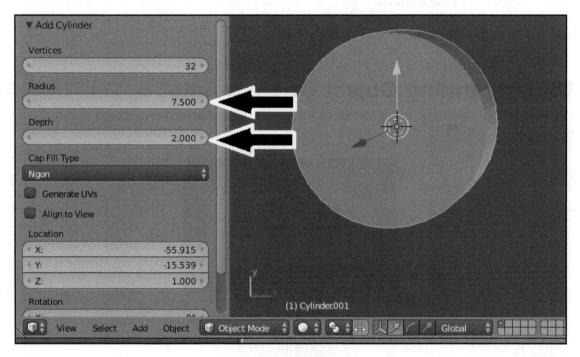

Setting the Radius and Depth of the cylinder

Resizing cylinders
You can also resize cylinders at any time by using the **Dimensions** section in the **Properties Shelf**, like you did with the cube. In addition, you can produce elliptical cylinders by giving the **X** and **Y** dimensions different values:

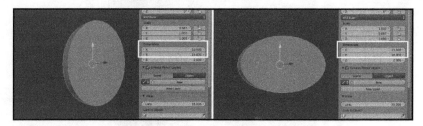

Cylinders can be resized in the Properties Shelf as well.

Using Object Origins to line up objects

Now that we have both a cube and a cylinder in our project, we want to move the cylinder so it rounds out our cube perfectly. To do that, it is helpful to understand the Object Origin and how Blender uses it to interact with your shapes.

Understanding Object Origin points

Whenever you select something in Object Mode, a yellow dot indicates what is known as the **Object Origin**:

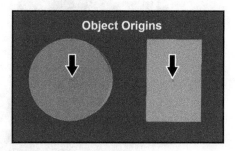

Examples of Object Origins.

By default, the Object Origin is the key point when Blender is manipulating and interacting with your selection:

- **Scaling**: When you scale an object, it scales outward from that Object Origin. If your origin is in the center, the object will grow equally on both sides. If your origin is in a corner, however, that side will stay stationary and the object will grow on the other side:

Scaling works outward from Object Origin

- **Rotating**: The Object Origin serves as the default pivot point when you are rotating. That pivot point could alter the final placement of your object after rotation:

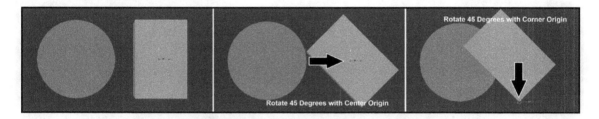

By default, rotating works around Object Origin

- **Mirroring**: Mirroring, which you will do later in this chapter, also uses the Object Origin. Symmetrical objects, such as a cylinder, may not look any different when being mirrored over the center of the object. Once that Object Origin is off-center or on an outside edge, mirroring will have a much greater impact:

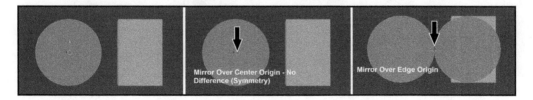

Mirroring with different Object Origins

- **Positioning**: Finally, when you are looking at the **Location** coordinates of an object, you are looking at the coordinates of that Object Origin point. When your object is moved, it is the coordinates of the Object Origin that are getting updated:

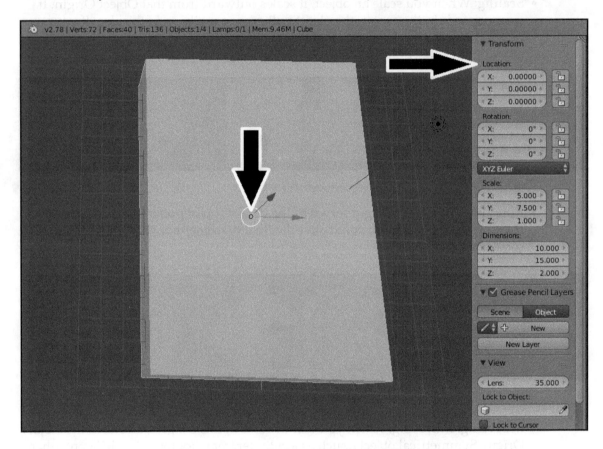

The Location of an object is the coordinates of the Object Origin

Moving the cylinder into place

By default, the Object Origin for both cubes and cylinders is the very center of the object. When Blender starts a new project, the default cube is placed at **0,0,0** for X, Y, and Z. We'll want our cylinder to line up perfectly on the Y and Z axis, so we'll want to make sure they are set to **0** as well. For the X coordinate, we have to do some light math. We want the very center of our cylinder, where it is the widest, to line up to the left edge of our cube.

Our cube is 10mm in the X dimension. The Object Origin is right smack in the middle at 0. The axis arrows point in the positive number direction. That'll put our right side at 5 mm and our left side at -5mm:

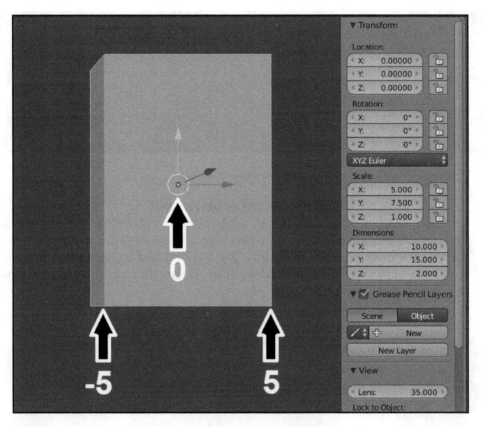

The coordinates of the center and sides of the cube.

Since we want to place the center of our cylinder (conveniently where the Object Origin is) flush with that left side, we'll want to set the X coordinate to -5. Our steps for adjusting the position of the cylinder are as follows:

1. In **Object Mode** and right-click on the **cylinder** to select it
2. On the **Properties Shelf**, change the **Location** coordinates:
   1. Set **X** to -5 (the X coordinate of the cube minus half of the X dimension)
   2. Set **Y** to 0 (the Y coordinate of the cube)
   3. Set **Z** to 0 (the Z coordinate of the cube):

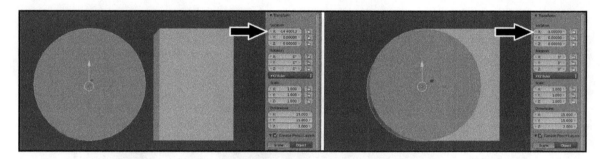

Setting the coordinates of the cylinder

Working with odd dimensions or placement?

This kind of placement is easy when an object is centered on our grid and we are working with clean, whole number dimensions. If you are working with a more complex situation, you can find and copy exact coordinates for a vertex in **Edit Mode**. Make sure you are viewing **Global** coordinates instead of **Local**:

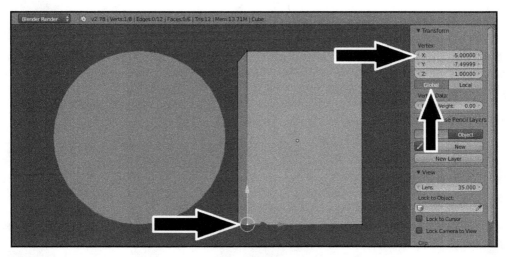

Exact coordinates can be copied in Edit Mode

Our cylinder should now be lined up with the cube. Take a moment to switch viewpoints and check your work from different angles:

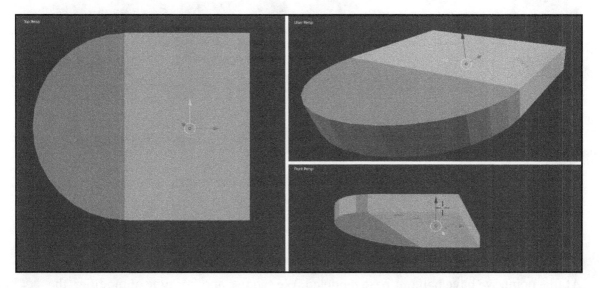

Checking the cylinder position from different viewing angles

Making the base whole

Now that our cylinder is in place, let's go ahead and use the Boolean Modifier we learned about in Chapter 4, *Flattening a Torus and Boolean Union*, to make a union with the cube and the cylinder. The steps are as follows:

1. In **Object Mode**, right-click on the **cube** to select it.
2. In the **Properties Window**, click on the wrench icon to get to **Modifiers**.
3. Click on the **Add Modifier** dropdown and select **Boolean**.
4. For **Operation**, pick **Union**. Under **Object**, pick the **cylinder**. Set the **Solver** to **Carve**:

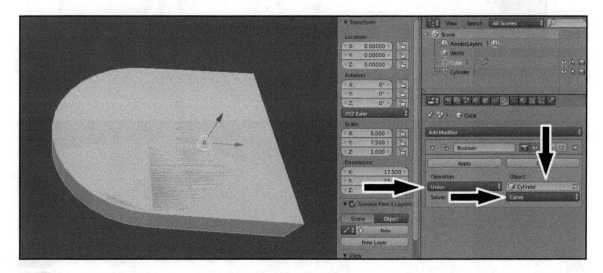

Adding the Boolean Union to combine the cube and cylinder

Do not hit **Apply** at this time.

Understanding the mirror axis

At this point, we have half our base modeled. We can use another type of modifier, the Mirror Modifier, to make our base whole. When mirroring, you are given the option of which axis you wish to mirror. Extra vertices, edges, and faces are added by adjusting just the coordinates of the selected axis. In other words, if you are mirroring the X axis, then only the X axis coordinates will be adjusted.

Whichever axis you choose, you can envision the other two axes as forming the mirror itself. The following image is the profile from our earlier jewelry project. If I select to mirror the X axis, you can pretend the Y-Z arrows make up the corner of an invisible mirror:

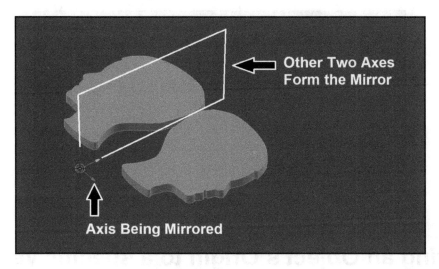

When mirroring the X axis, you can think of the Y and Z axes as making the mirror

Similar to the rotation we did in `Chapter 4`, *Flattening a Torus and Boolean Union*, it may take some time to get your bearings and know immediately which axis you wish to mirror. It will become more intuitive with practice. In the meantime, there is no harm in trial and error:

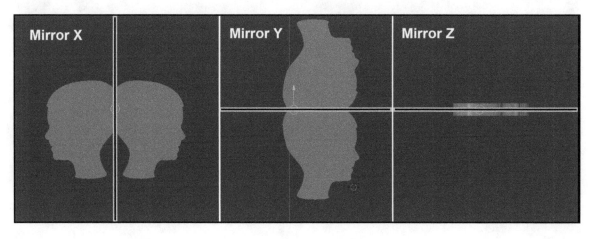

Examples of mirroring different axes of the profile pendant

Advanced mirror options

For specialized needs, you can mirror multiple axes at a time. In addition, you can tell Blender to use a specific object such as a plane to mirror over, allowing you to mirror at any angle and any direction:

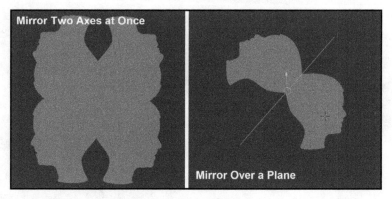

Examples of advanced mirroring

Updating an Object's Origin to a specific vertex

Mirroring is another Blender process that relies heavily on the Object Origin. That point is going to determine where the invisible mirror is going to be placed. Our newly modeled base is a great illustration. By default, the Object Origin is still right in the middle of our default cube. We put thought into the sizing of our plate. With a mirror placed there, we would be losing some of the length of our base.

Our final dimensions would fall short of the plan:

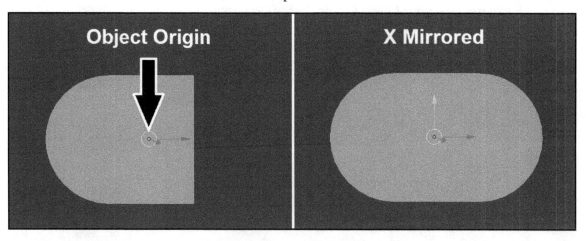

Blender mirrors according to the Object Origin

However, if the Object Origin was moved to the right edge of our base, then mirroring would truly duplicate our work:

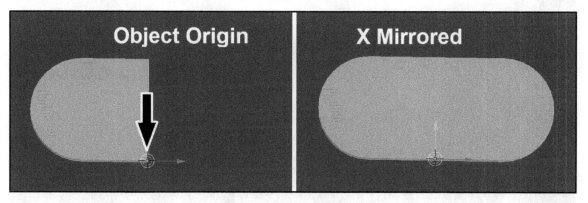

When the Object Origin is moved to the right edge, the final object is longer

Blender allows the Object Origin to be changed on demand. For our bracelet plate, we are going to set the Object Origin to a specific vertex on the far right side of our model. The steps are as follows:

1. In **Object Mode** and right-click on our object (in this case, the cube) to select it.
2. Switch to **Edit Mode**.

3. If necessary, click on the **Vertex Select** icon. Right-click to select the vertex you'd like to make your Object Origin. In the case of our bracelet plate, select one of the vertices in what will be the middle, the straight side of the plate:

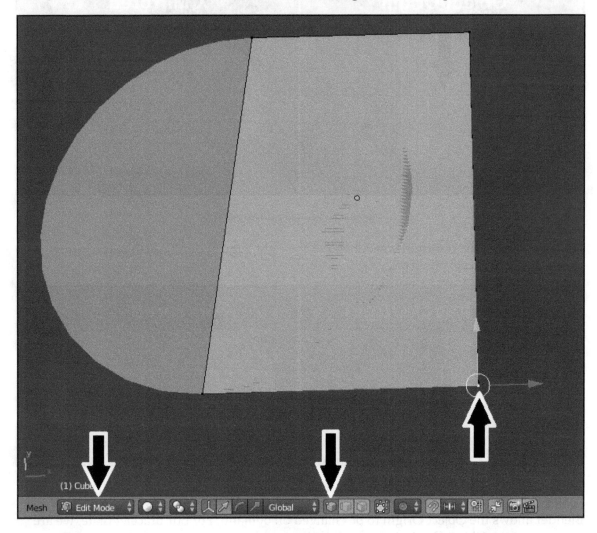

Selecting a vertex at the far right.

4. In the menu at the bottom of your screen, select **Mesh** | **Snap** | **Cursor to Selected**. This moves the 3D Cursor to the exact position of the selected vertex:

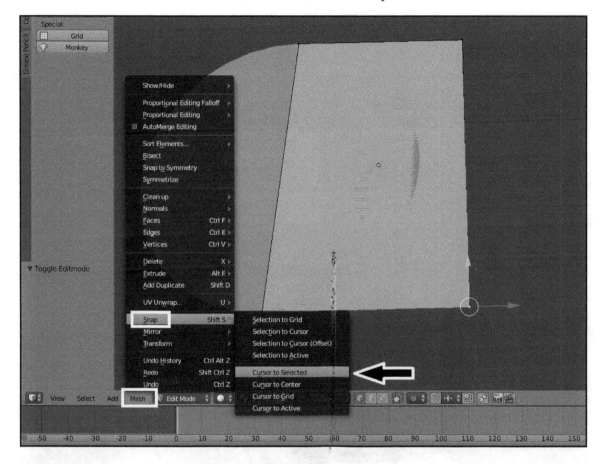

Moving the 3D Cursor to the selected vertex

5. Switch back to **Object Mode.**

6. In the menu at the bottom of the screen, select **Mesh | Transform | Origin to 3D Cursor**. This tells Blender to change the Object Origin to where the 3D Cursor is:

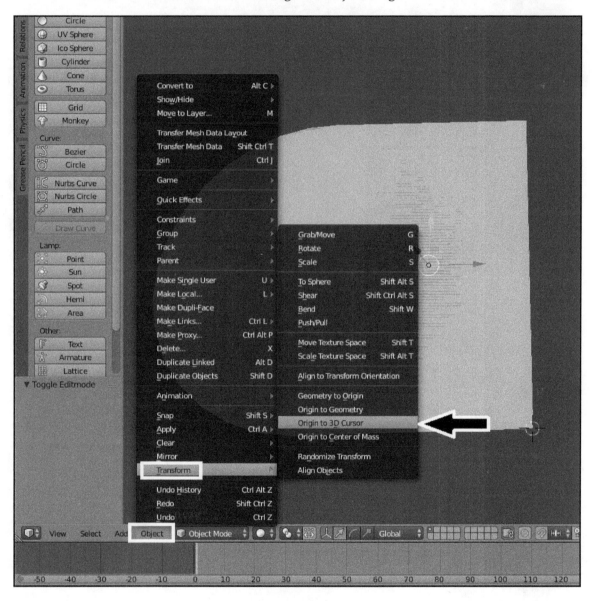

Moving the Object Origin to the location of the 3D Cursor

After these steps are performed, the yellow dot and axis arrows are moved and reflect our newly-defined Object Origin:

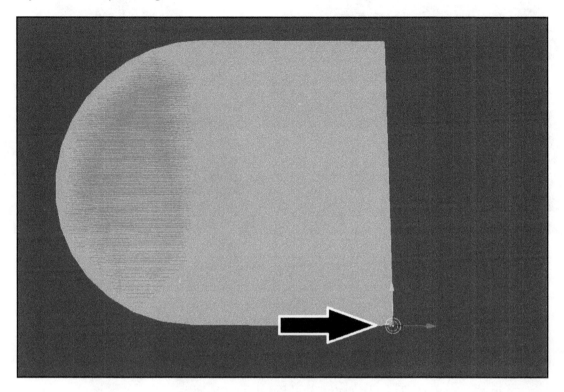

The newly-placed Object Origin

Adding a Mirror Modifier

Now, we are ready to add the Mirror Modifier to our model to copy and flip our base along the X axis. The steps are:

1. In **Object Mode** and right-click on the object (in this case, the cube) to select it.
2. In the **Properties Window**, click on the wrench icon to access the **Modifiers**.

3. Click on the **Add Modifier** dropdown and select **Mirror**:

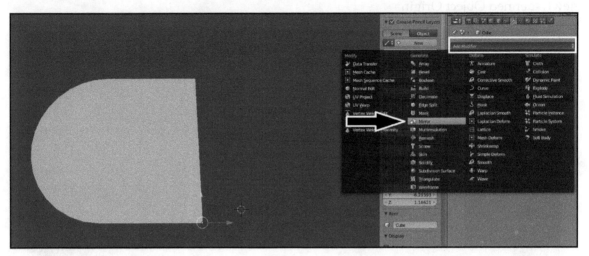

Adding a new Mirror

4. Mirror options will appear at the bottom of your Modifiers list. In this case, it'll be listed under the **Boolean Union Modifier** we added earlier. For **Axis**, make sure **X** is selected as we want to copy and mirror our X coordinates.

5. Under **Options**, uncheck **Merge**. The **Merge** option will automatically consolidate vertices that are in the same spot. I have found this automatic merge sometimes leads to issues that need to be repaired with the techniques described in Chapter 15, *Troubleshooting and Repairing Models*:

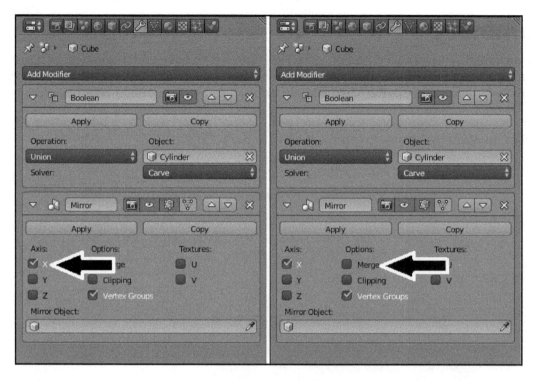

Picking the Mirror Axis and whether to Merge vertices

Do not click **Apply** at this time. At this point, the half base you have modeled is now whole:

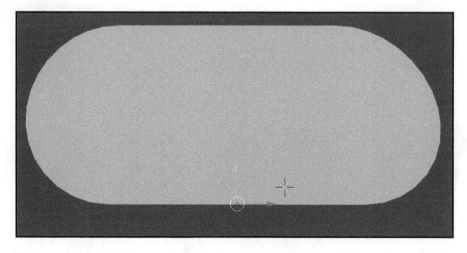

The mirrored cube and cylinder makes a whole base

Summary

In this chapter, you modeled half of a bracelet plate with a cube and a cylinder. You learned about the Object Origin, its impact on placement, and how to alter it to better fit your needs. Finally, you learned about the Mirror Modifier and used it to complete your bracelet plate.

In the `Chapter 6`, *Cutting Half Circle Holes and Modifier Management*, you'll be adding another modifier to the mix to carve out holes in the plate.

6
Cutting Half Circle Holes and Modifier Management

In this chapter, we are going to poke two holes in our plate to allow it to be added to a bracelet. The techniques and skills covered will include the following:

- Duplicating objects to save time
- Positioning based on the minimum wall thickness
- Using the *Ctrl* and *Shift* keys to multiselect items
- Mesh modeling to remove vertices and create new faces
- Using the Boolean Difference Modifier to cut holes
- Managing the order of the Modifier Stack

Duplicating and sizing a cylinder

Now that we are satisfied with the shape and size of our base plate for the bracelet, we should add holes so that it can be incorporated into a jewelry piece. The Boolean Modifier that we used in Chapters 4, *Flattening a Torus and Boolean Union*, and Chapter 5, *Building a Base with Standard Meshes and a Mirror*, can also subtract objects from each other:

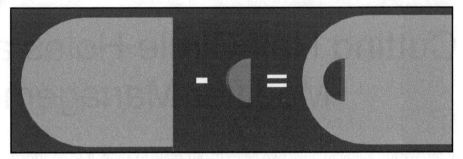

The Boolean Modifier can also subtract objects from each other

We can use that to poke holes in either side of our plate. That hole object could potentially be any shape. We could subtract a cylinder, a cube, or even the profile pendant we made in previous chapters:

Examples of the plate with different types of objects subtracted from it

For this project, I want to stay consistent with the curvature of the piece and use a semicircle for my hole. Thinking about the design requirements and the cording I want to use for the bracelet, I decided that the diameter of that semicircular hole should be 5mm:

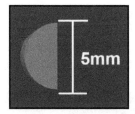

Deciding the sizing of the hole

In `Chapter 5`, *Building a Base with Standard Meshes and a Mirror*, we used a Boolean Union Modifier to combine a cylinder with our default cube. Since we added the modifier to the cube, that is the object that will be modified. The cylinder is still in our project and remains unchanged. Rather than starting from scratch, we can use that cylinder as a template. The steps to duplicate it and resize it are as follows:

1. If necessary, switch to **Object Mode** and right-click on the cylinder to select it.
2. In the **Tool Shelf** on the left-hand side of the screen, click on the **Tools** tab. Under the **Edit** section, click on the **Duplicate** button:

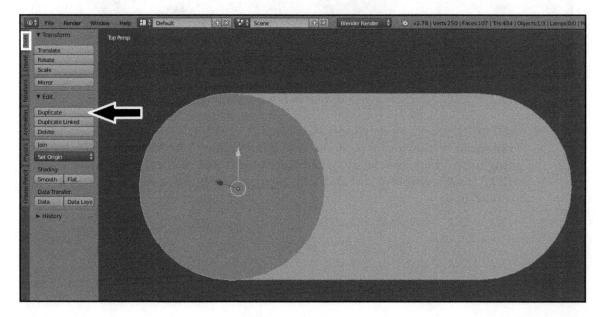

Duplicating the cylinder

3. Immediately, a new cylinder is added to your project in the exact same spot as the previous cylinder. If you look at the upper right-hand side of your screen, there is an area called the **Outliner** which will list all the objects in your project. There, you can see the brand new cylinder in the object listing:

The new cylinder is listed in the Outliner

4. Your newly duplicated cylinder is selected by default. You can go straight to the **Transform** section and type in the new **Dimensions**. Since this new cylinder is going to be a hole, we can give it a bigger height than the rest of the base. This will help with visibility and also with cleaner cuts. In this case, I'll set **X** to **5**, **Y** to **5**, and **Z** to **3**:

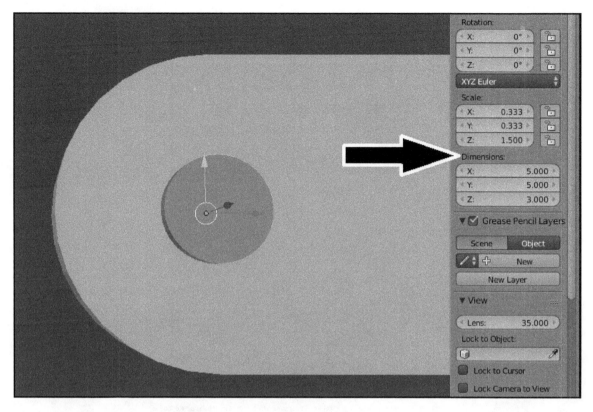

Setting the Dimensions of the new cylinder

Placing the hole and preserving wall thicknesses

The new small cylinder is centered within its larger predecessor. For aesthetics, and to make sure we have more space for our custom text, we'll want to move that new cylinder along the X axis and place it closer to the edge of our piece. For the most part, you can go with what looks good to the eye. The only stipulation is you will want to make sure you meet the minimum wall thickness of your printing process.

For Service Bureau Printing, I would consider leaving at least 1mm. For at-home printing, I would be more comfortable with 2mm:

You will want to keep minimum wall thickness in mind when positioning the new cylinder

Positioning with subtraction

We can determine the new position of our hole with some subtraction. Taking the leftmost point of our base and the peak of the rounded edge, subtract the desired wall thickness. That gives us the coordinate of where we want the outermost point of our hole to be. Anything closer will produce a thinner wall than desired. Since the Object Origin is the center of the cylinder, we'll want to subtract the radius (half of the 5 mm diameter). That will give us the new **X** coordinate of our hole:

X Coordinate of Far Edge - Wall Thickness - Radius of Hole = X Coordinate of Hole

In the case of our current base and hole, that puts our new coordinate at -8 mm for home printing and -9 mm for Service Bureau Printing:

Printing process	X coordinate of the far edge	Wall thickness	X coordinate of the outer edge of the hole	Radius of hole	X coordinate of the center of the hole
Service Bureau	-12.5 mm	2 mm	-10.5	2.5 mm (5 mm diameter)	-8 mm
Home printing (FFF/FDM)	-12.5 mm	1 mm	-11.5	2.5 mm (5 mm diameter)	-9 mm

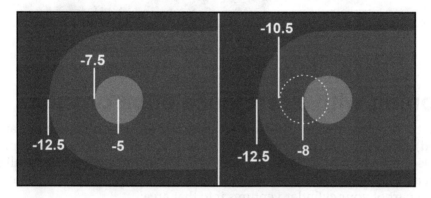

Current positions and desired positions for a 2 mm wall thickness (assuming at-home printing)

In Chapter 5, *Building a Base with Standard Meshes and a Mirror*, you learned about changing the Object Origin. If you would like to simplify the math, you could change the Object Origin to the outer edge of your hole using the same **Mesh | Snap to | Cursor to Selected** and **Object | Transform | Origin to 3D Cursor** menu options we used before. When you change your Object Origin to the edge of the circle, you no longer have to consider the radius when repositioning your hole. You would just have to subtract the desired wall thickness. The math becomes the following:

X Coordinate of Far Edge - Wall Thickness = X Coordinate of Hole

For a 2mm wall thickness and home printing, now I'm moving my hole to −10.5 (−12.5 + 2) instead of −8 (−12.5 + 2 + 2.5). Once you have determined your new coordinate, you can simply type in the new X Location in the Properties Shelf:

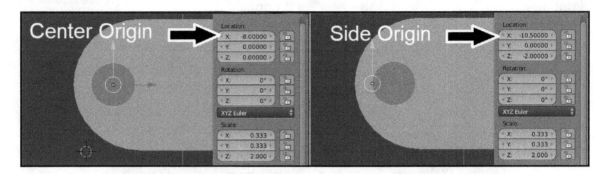

By changing the Object Origin, my math and thought process becomes simplified

Positioning with a reference cube or ruler

If you are not a fan of subtraction, instead of typing in exact coordinates, you can left-click on the X (red) axis arrow and move the hole to a spot you see fit. To help with placement, you could also add a temporary cube to your project, size it to your desired wall thickness, and use that as a math-free guide. Consider that little reference cube as "no man's land" and make sure no part of your cylinder ventures into that area:

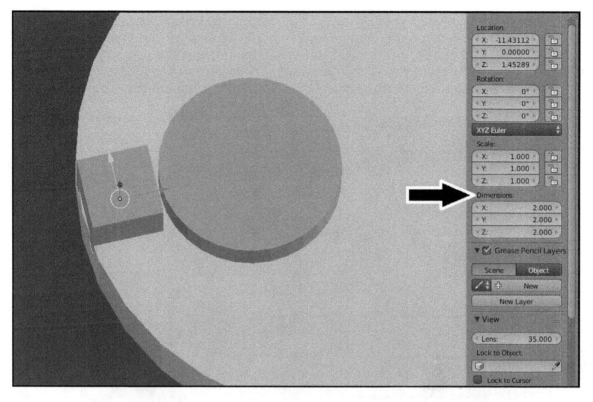

Using a 2 x 2 x 2 cube as a reference when moving our cylinder hole.

In addition, Blender has a Ruler/Protractor tool you can use to check your work. This tool works in both **Object Mode** and **Edit Mode**. We could use it to measure the difference between the outer edge of our base plate and the outer edge of our hole and make sure it is greater than the minimum wall thickness. The steps to measure that distance with the Ruler are as follows:

1. In the **Tool Shelf** on the left-hand side of your screen, click on the **Grease Pencil** tab.
2. Under **Tools**, click on the **Ruler/Protractor** button.

3. In our 3D View, left-click and hold on one spot you wish to measure. In this case, click and hold on the leftmost point of our base plate. As you move your mouse to the other side, Blender will give you a running measurement. Once you are at the second point you wish to measure, such as the outer edge of our hole, you can let go of the left mouse button and see your final measurement:

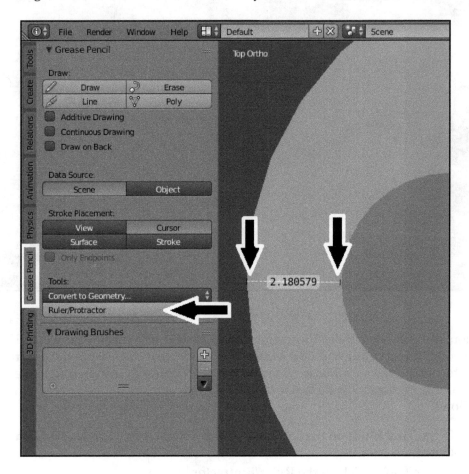

4. Hit the *Esc* button on your keyboard when you are done.

Mesh modeling to make a half cylinder

Satisfied with the placement of our hole, we are going to use mesh modeling techniques to change our full cylinder into a half cylinder. In Chapter 4, *Flattening a Torus and Boolean Union*, you used the **Border Select** tool to pick a number of vertices at once. In this chapter, you'll practice another way to multiselect: using the *Ctrl* key and *Shift* key in conjunction with right-click.

Using Shift to multiselect

Anytime you are using the right mouse button to select, you can use the *Shift* key to add additional items to the selection. This includes entire objects in **Object Mode** as well as vertices, edges, or faces when you are in **Edit Mode**. Let's look at vertices in a cylinder as an example. If I right-click on a vertex, it becomes the only active selection. It's highlighted in yellow and I have the usual axis arrows to reposition it. Next, if I hold down the *Shift* key and right-click on another vertex, instead of resetting the selection, that vertex is also highlighted with the first one:

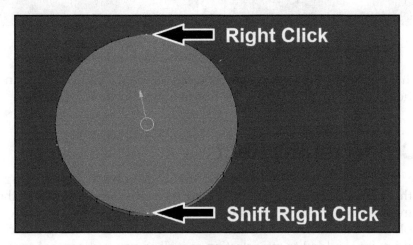

Right-clicking on a vertex and then Shift + right-clicking on another will select both vertices

You don't have to stop at two selections; you can hold down the *Shift* key and right-click on as many vertices as needed. Because you are clicking on each selection, you have the power to pick exactly what you want. If I wanted to give my cylinder a star-like taper, I could select every other vertex:

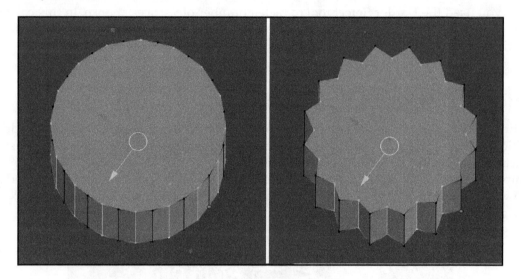

An example of using Shift to select every other vertex. Shift + right-click can also deselect

In the event that you select the wrong item, you can use *Shift* + right-click to unselect just that item without hindering or resetting the rest of your selection.

Using Ctrl to multiselect

In **Edit Mode**, you can also hold down the *Ctrl* key while you are right-clicking. The difference is this will add the newly selected item, as well as anything else in the shortest path connecting the two. With the cylinder example, if I right-click on a vertex, that will become the sole active selection. If I then hold down the *Ctrl* key and right-click on another vertex, that end point is added to my selection as well as any vertices that are in between:

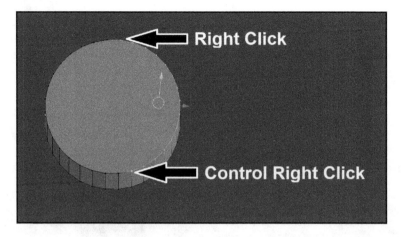

Ctrl + right-click will add all the vertices leading up to the new selection

There is a catch with *Ctrl* + right-click. Blender will use the defined edges of your model to select the shortest path between the two selections. That may not necessarily be what you have in mind. If you pick the topmost vertex of the cylinder and the bottommost vertex of the cylinder, you may be hoping to pick all the vertices traveling along the right side, but Blender picks the left side.

You can also be thwarted by internal edges. In Chapter 7, *Customizing with Text*, we'll be working with text. When Blender creates meshes from text, it automatically triangulates them. Every surface is composed of a number of little triangles. Those extra edges give Blender tempting shortcuts between vertices, particularly along curves. If I click on either side of a zero, instead of selecting the outside curve, Blender selects the shortest route between the two:

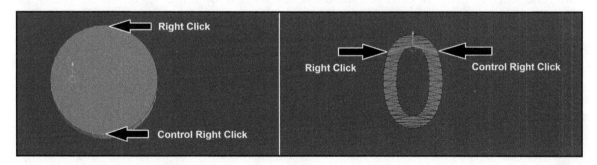

Ctrl + right-click takes the shortest path between vertices, which may not be what you intended to select

In both cases, you can still achieve your intentions with *Ctrl* + right-click. The trick is to *Ctrl* + right-click on an interim vertex in between to make sure Blender follows your intended path. In the example of the cylinder, if I *Ctrl* + right-click on a vertex along the right side before I *Ctrl* + right-click my bottom vertex, I force Blender to travel along the right-hand side instead of the left-hand side:

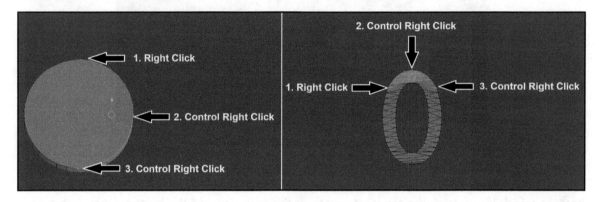

By Ctrl + right-clicking a vertex in the middle, you can better define Blender's selection path. Ctrl + Z to undo selections

When you are working with tedious, in-depth selections, you might find yourself frustrated when you accidentally mess up your selection. Perhaps Blender took an unanticipated shortcut or perhaps you forgot to hold down *Shift* or *Ctrl* and you wiped out your previous work. You do not have to start from scratch. If you hold down the *Ctrl* key and the Z key, you can undo your erroneous selection.

As you are working with selections, if you need a mnemonic device to remember the difference between *Shift* or *Ctrl*, you can think of it as "*S* is for single selections" and "*C* is for connected selections":

KeyColumn	Selection Type
Shift	Single, separate selections
Ctrl	Connected, combined selections

Deleting vertices in the cylinder

We can put these concepts to use by deleting unnecessary vertices and creating new faces to make our half cylinder. We'll want to keep the topmost and bottommost points of our cylinder, but delete everything on the right-hand side. The steps are as follows:

1. If necessary, switch to **Object Mode** and right-click on our hole to select it.
2. Switch to **Edit Mode** and, if necessary, click the icon to select **Vertex Select** mode. I also recommend turning off Limit selection to visible so that you can see all of the vertices:

Making all vertices visible

3. We want to keep the vertex at the highest point of our circle. Right-click on the vertex immediately to the right of that point. Holding down the *Ctrl* key, right-click on the vertex immediately to the right of the lowest point. This selects all the vertices on the top right-hand side of our cylinder:

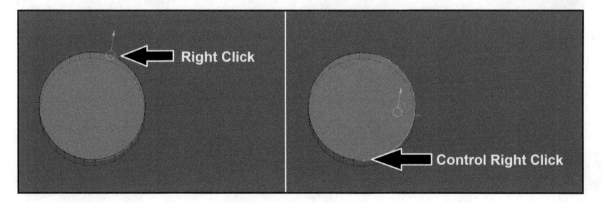

Selecting top vertices to remove

4. So far, I have only selected vertices on the top of my cylinder. I don't want to forget the same vertices on the bottom. Holding down the *Ctrl* key, right-click on the vertex immediately following the one you just selected. Finally, *Ctrl* + right-click on the vertex immediately below the very first one you selected. Every vertex on the right-hand side of the cylinder will be highlighted yellow:

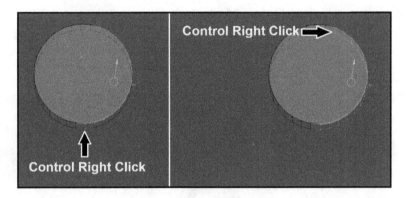

Selecting the bottom vertices to delete

5. Hit the *Delete* button on your keyboard. A menu lets you select exactly what you wish to delete. Select **Vertices**. This will delete all the selected points. Any edges and faces related to those deleted vertices will also be removed:

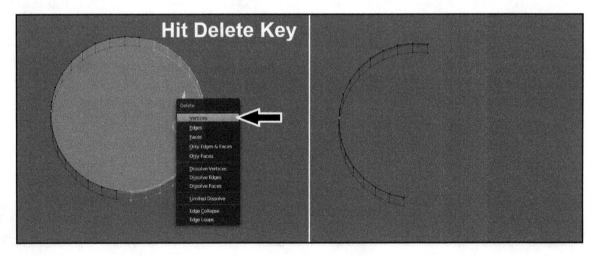

Telling Blender to delete the selected vertices

Creating new faces

Our cylinder is now just a shell, not a complete 3D object. To turn it back into a workable 3D mesh, we'll need to create three new faces: two half-circle shaped faces to make up the bottom and top, and then a rectangle-shaped face to close up the object and make it whole:

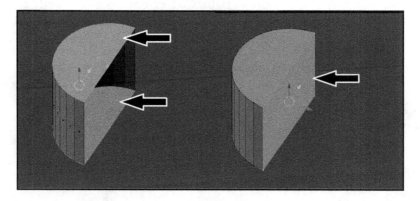

The three new faces we will need to create to complete our half cylinder

Making the new faces will give you more practice of using the *Shift* and *Ctrl* keys to select vertices. The steps are as follows:

1. Top half circle face:
   Right-click to select the vertex at the highest point of the top half circle.
   Ctrl + right-click on the lowest point of that top half circle. Take a moment to make sure all the vertices are selected and that you didn't accidentally pick a point on the bottom of the cylinder. Hit *F* on the keyboard to create a new face:

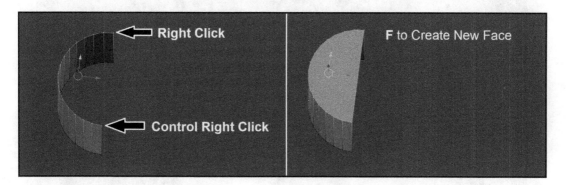

Selecting the top vertices and creating a half circle face

2. Bottom half circle face:

   If necessary, change your viewpoint to see the bottom vertices better. Right-click on one of the endpoints of the bottom half circle. This starts a new selection with just that point. Thanks to our new top half circle face, there is a new edge that gives Blender a shortcut to the other side of the bottom circle. To circumvent Blender using that new shortest path, *Ctrl* + right-click on a vertex midway and then *Ctrl* + right-click on the lowest point of our bottom half circle. Hit *F* on the keyboard to create a new face:

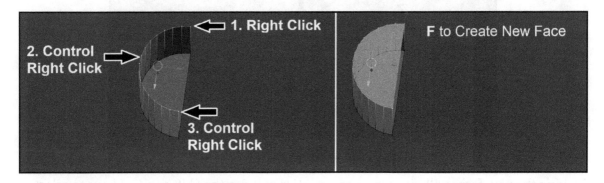

Selecting the bottom vertices and creating a second half circle face

3. Rectangular side face:

   Finally, to close up our mesh, right-click on one of the corners of our opening. Holding down the *Shift* key on the keyboard, right-click on the remaining corners. Hit *F* on the keyboard to create a new face:

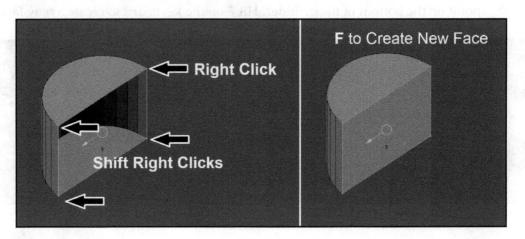

Creating the final face to close up the object

At the end of this process, we have a half cylinder mesh we are ready to carve out of our base plate:

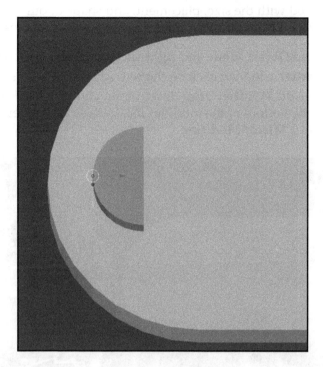

Half circle ready to be used

Many ways to make a half cylinder

This is just one approach to making a half cylinder. You could, of course, use **Border Select** to pick the unnecessary vertices and align their X values. You could start with a 2D circle or a Bezier curve and extrude it as we did with the profile pendant in Chapter 3, *Converting a Bezier Curve to a Properly Sized 3D Mesh*. Finally, you could use the Boolean Modifier to subtract a cube from the cylinder to "erase" the parts you don't want. You'll learn more about subtracting with the Boolean Difference Modifier in the next section.

Making a hole with Boolean difference

Now that we are satisfied with the size, placement, and shape of our half cylinder, it is time to tell Blender to subtract it from our base cube. The steps are as follows:

1. Switch back to **Object Mode** and right-click on our base cube to select it.
2. In the **Properties** window, click on the wrench icon to access the **Modifiers**.
3. Click on the **Add Modifier** drop-down menu and pick **Boolean**. A new modifier is added to the bottom of the modifier list. In this case, underneath our **Boolean Union** and our **Mirror Modifier**:

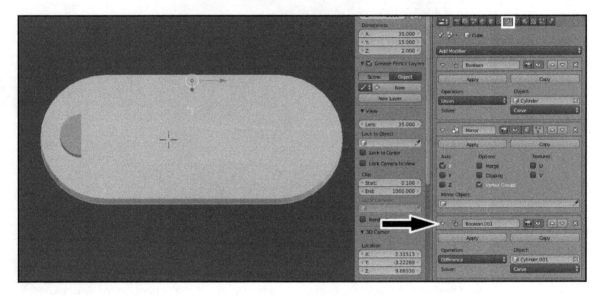

Adding another Boolean Modifier

4. For **Operation**, pick **Difference**. For **Object**, select what you want to subtract. In this case, I want to subtract our half cylinder, which is named **Cylinder.001**. Finally, for **Solver**, select **Carve**:

Setting up the properties for the Boolean Difference

Do not click **Apply** at this time. We've added our **Boolean Difference Modifier**, but at first glance, nothing looks different on our screen. That's because the Boolean Modifier only changes the parent object, the one we added the modifier to. The object we are subtracting, in this case, the half cylinder, remains unchanged and in place. We can't see our hole because the template for that hole, the half cylinder, is blocking it.

The Outliner window on the upper right-hand side of your screen lists all the objects that are a part of the project. To the right of each object, there is an eye icon. Clicking on that eye icon will toggle whether that object is visible or not. If we turn that icon off for our half cylinder, we are able to see what is underneath it:

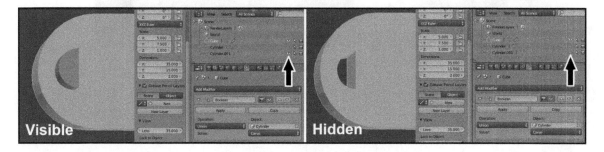

Turning off the viewport visibility allows us to see our new hole

Previewing Boolean modifiers in Wireframe Mode

Another good way to review your Boolean Modifiers is to switch the **Viewport Shading** from **Solid** to **Wireframe**. This gives you a glimpse of all the new and revised edges, including edges that are normally obscured by solid faces. **Wireframe Mode** will be illustrated and discussed in more detail in Chapter 11, *Applying Textures with Boolean Intersection*.

Changing your object with modifier order

Once our half cylinder is hidden, we can see the hole in the left-hand side of our bracelet plate. The right-hand side, however, is still completely solid:

The base with just a single hole.

This is due to the order of the modifiers, the Modifier Stack. Blender applies the modifiers from top to bottom, as they are listed in the **Properties** window. In the case of our bracelet base, Blender currently does the following:

1. Combines the cylinder and the cube to make a rounded half base
2. Mirrors the rounded half base to make a full base
3. Subtracts the half cylinder to make a hole

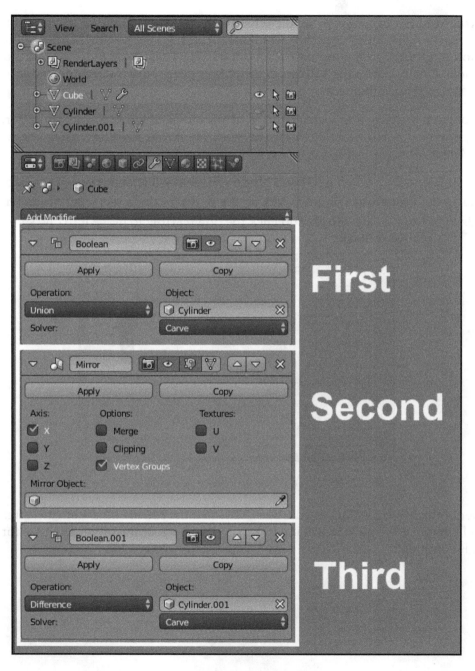

Modifiers are applied in order from top to bottom

The **Mirror** Modifier cannot copy a hole which is yet to exist. Changing the order of the Modifier Stack can produce very different objects. Suppose we put the **Mirror** Modifier last. The **Union** is applied, giving our base a rounded edge. The half-cylinder is subtracted to make a hole. Finally, when the **Mirror** Modifier is applied, both the rounded edge and the hole are copied to the other side.

We do not have to delete and recreate our modifiers to get them in the proper order. Blender gives us up-arrow and down-arrow icons to sort our Modifier Stack. The steps to put the **Mirror** Modifier last are as follows:

1. If necessary, switch to **Object Mode** and right-click on our object to select it
2. In the **Properties** window, click on the wrench icon to reach the **Modifiers**
3. Find the existing **Mirror** and click the down arrow to move it to one step later in the **Modifier Stack**:

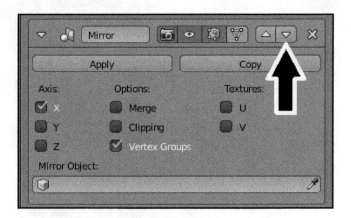

Clicking the down arrow to move the Mirror later in the process

The order of the Modifier Stack is adjusted. Now that the **Mirror** Modifier runs after our Boolean Difference, we have two equal holes on either side of the piece. The base for our bracelet is complete:

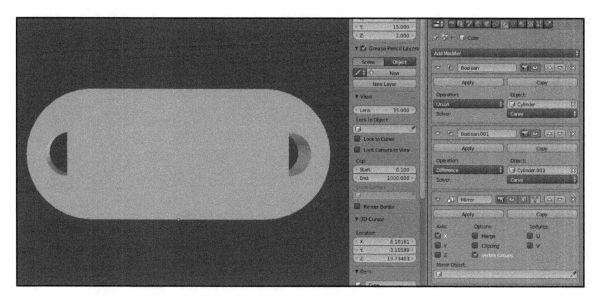

Mirroring last copies everything, including our half cylinder hole

Summary

In this chapter, you learned to duplicate an existing cylinder to make a template for a hole. You resized and repositioned the hole, keeping the minimum wall thickness in mind. You learned new techniques for selecting multiple items at once. You deleted unnecessary vertices and practiced mesh modeling to make new faces for your half cylinder hole. You learned how to use the Boolean Difference Modifier to subtract one object from another. Finally, you learned how the ordering of your modifiers can impact on your final object. Altogether, you finished the base of your bracelet plate.

In Chapter 7, *Customizing with Text*, you will learn how to add text to customize and finalize your bracelet.

7
Customizing with Text

One of 3D printing's great assets is its ability to customize. One way to do that is to add engraved or embossed text to a piece. In this chapter, you'll use the text object in Blender to add customized text to give the wearer an emotional connection to the bracelet. The skills you'll use include:

- Adding and editing new text objects
- Finding and using fonts already installed on your computer
- Converting text objects to 3D meshes

Adding a new text object

In Chapter 5, *Building a Base with Standard Meshes and a Mirror*, you used a cylinder and a cube as building block for your bracelet plate. Blender also has a specialized text object you can incorporate into your designs. You can add these the same way you would any other object:

1. In **Object Mode**, left-click to move your 3D Cursor where you would like to add the new text

2. In the **Tool Shelf** on the left-hand side of your screen, click the **Create** tab and under **Other**, click **Text**:

Adding a new text object.

This adds a new text object to your 3D View. By default, it simply reads, **Text**.

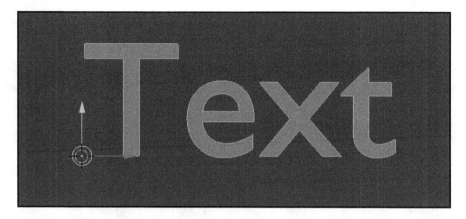

A newly created text object.

Like other Blender objects, you can use the **Properties Shelf** to transform the entire object, such as by changing its **Location** or **Rotation**:

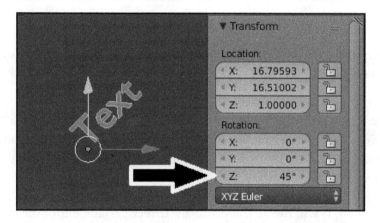

Normal transform functions, such as rotate, work on text objects.

Changing the text

To change the verbiage itself to something other than **Text**, you have to switch to **Edit Mode**. Once you do so, a cursor appears at the far right of the last **t** in **Text**:

In Edit Mode, a cursor allows you to edit the message.

You can use your keyboard to move that cursor and manipulate the text. Consistent with word processing applications such as Microsoft Word, there are a few shortcuts:

- **Arrow Keys**: You can use the left arrow and right arrow to move the cursor.
- **Home Key**: The *Home* key moves the cursor to the very front of the text.
- **End Key**: The *End* key moves the cursor to the very end of the text.
- **Shift Key**: Holding down the *Shift* key while you use the arrow, *Home*, or *End* keys highlights and selects multiple characters.
- **Backspace Key**: The *Backspace* key will delete any selected text. If nothing is highlighted, it will delete the character directly to the left of the cursor.
- **Delete Key**: The *Delete* key will remove any selected text. If nothing is highlighted, it will delete the character directly to the right of the cursor:

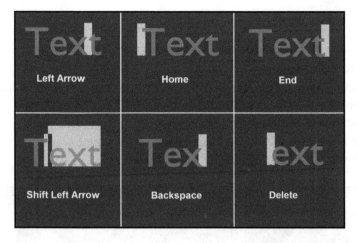

Using different keyboard shortcuts to highlight and remove text.

Once you remove the existing text, you can type in the coordinates you want to add to the bracelet. You can also paste in any text you have saved onto your computer's clipboard by holding down *Ctrl+ V*. The *Tab* key does not work when editing text. That is a keyboard shortcut to switch to **Object Mode**. However, you can use the *Enter* key to do a carriage return to put Longitude and Latitude on separate lines.

Finding out coordinates

If you don't know the coordinates of a place, give one of the major search engines a try. Both Google and Bing can field questions on coordinates:

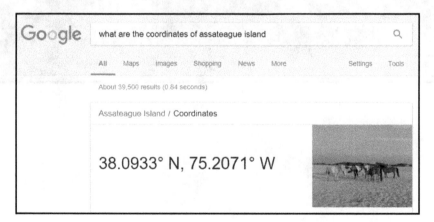

Search engines can help you find the coordinates of a special spot

The steps to edit the text object and fill in your custom coordinates are as follows:

1. If necessary, in **Object Mode**, right-click your text object to select it.
2. Switch to **Edit Mode**.
3. Delete the existing **Text**. One way is to hit the *Backspace* button four times. Another way would be to hold down the *Shift* key, hit the *Home* key to highlight all the text, and hit the *Delete* key.
4. Type or use *Ctrl + V* to fill in your **Latitude**. Hit the *Enter* key to start a new line. Type or use *Ctrl + V* to fill in the **Longitude**:

Pasting in the coordinates.

Your coordinates have been added to Blender, but they may not be the font you desire or the right size:

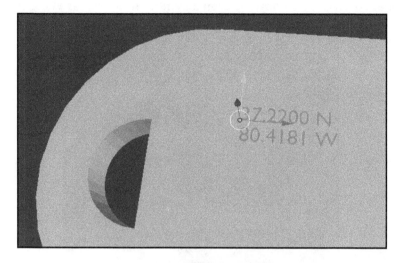

Newly added coordinates are in a default font type and a default size of one.

Changing font settings

When you create a new text object, it uses the Blender default font, Bfont, for your text object. I find it to be a solid font, though the capital J does strike me as out of proportion with the other letters:

The Blender Default Font.

The default font could very well meet your purposes. If it doesn't, Blender gives you the ability to fine-tune settings for your text objects, including the font type. You can use any font already installed on your computer, even a symbol font such as Wingdings:

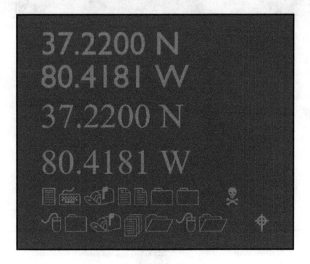

Same text, three different fonts.

Finding the font filename

When you do try to change a font in Blender, you are picking it by the filename of the **True Type Font** (`.ttf`) file that is installed on your computer. Sometimes, these are pretty easy to guess or recognize. The filename for Arial, for example, is `arial.ttf`. Arial Black, a thicker version, gets a little more obscure with a filename of `ariblk.ttf`. If you are unsure of the filename of a particular font, you can look it up on your computer.

The steps on Windows 10 are as follows:

1. Open up **File Explorer** to browse the folder structure of your computer.
2. Browse to the `C:\Windows\Fonts` directory. You will see a listing of all the installed fonts with a handy preview of what the text would look like:

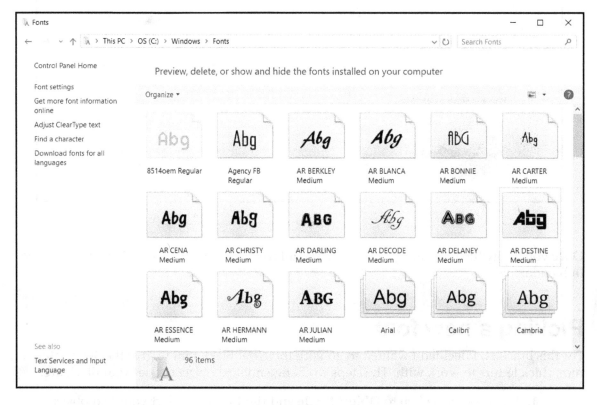

Browsing the Fonts directory in Windows

3. Right-click the desired font and choose **Properties**. The pop-up window will list the filename at the top of the screen:

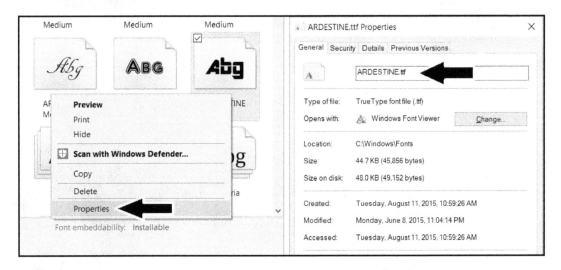

Finding the filename

Once you know the filename, you have all the information you need to switch the font type in Blender.

Picking a new font

For this bracelet, I decided I wanted to go with the Arial Black font to give the 3D printer nice, thick letters to work with. The steps to change my text object to use Arial Black are:

1. If necessary, switch to **Object Mode** and right-click to select your text object.
2. In the **Properties Window** on the right-hand side of the screen, click on the **F** icon directly to the right of the wrench we have been using for Modifiers:

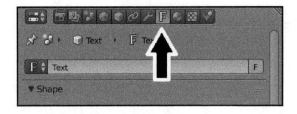

The F icon switches to Font properties

3. Under the **Font** section next to **Regular**, click on the folder icon to load a font from a new file.

4. A pop-up window lets your browse your file system for the new `.ttf` file. Use the white up arrow and folder icons to navigate to the directory your fonts are installed in. For Windows systems, this is typically `C:\Windows\Fonts`. Click the font filename you want to load and click the **Open Font** button. In this example, I select `ariblk.ttf`:

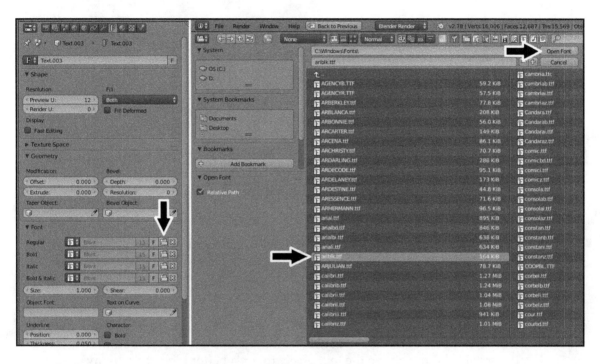

Selecting the font file

The font for your coordinates is now Arial Black, but the font size could use some adjusting to fit the bracelet:

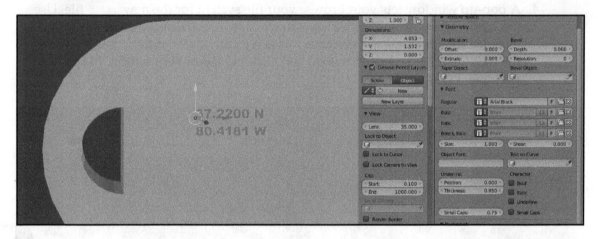

The new Arial Black text is too small for our bracelet.

Adjusting font size and line spacing

There is also a **Size** property we can adjust. By default that is set to 1. We can increase it to better fit our bracelet. The steps for increasing the font size are as follows:

1. If necessary, switch to **Object Mode** and right-click our text to select it. In the **Properties Window**, click the **F** icon.
2. Under the **Font** section, you can type in a new **Size**. You don't have to stick with whole numbers and can use decimals. It may take a few tries to find the best size. It may also help to move the text object to get a better idea of fit. In my case, I decided to use 5.500:

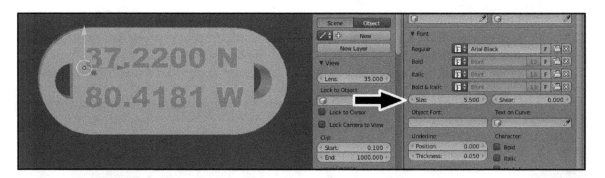

Increasing the text size

Once I updated the **Size**, I felt like I want to decrease the gap between the Latitude and the Longitude. The two lines seem a little too far apart for my taste. Under the **Paragraph** section of the properties, Blender gives you the ability to control the spacing between individual letters, entire words, and even lines:

Blender lets you control the spacing of the text, even between lines.

The steps to change the line spacing for our coordinates are as follows:

1. If necessary, switch to **Object Mode** and right-click our text to select it. In the **Properties Window**, click the **F** icon.

2. Under the **Paragraph** section, you can type in a new **Spacing** for the **Line**. Like sizing, you don't have to stick with whole numbers and can use decimals. Also like sizing, it may take a few tries to find the best value. In my case, 0.5 was too close and led to overlapping letters. 0.8 seemed to be what I was looking for:

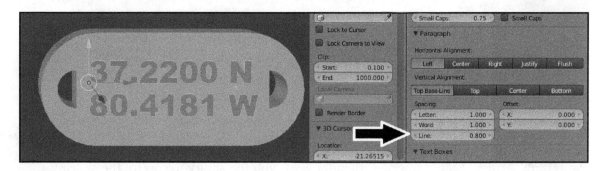

Updating the spacing between lines

When you are satisfied with your settings, there is one remaining problem. The text is only two dimensional. We need to find the best way to convert it to a 3D mesh.

Converting the text to a 3D mesh

Similar to the Bezier Curve in Chapter 3, *Converting a Bezier Curve to a Properly Sized 3D Mesh*, we want to convert our 2D text object into a mesh and make it 3D. Like most things in Blender, there are multiple ways to approach this.

Using the text object properties

You may have noticed in the **Geometry** section, there is a spot under **Modifications** where you can set up an **Extrude** height. This gives your text an exact thickness:

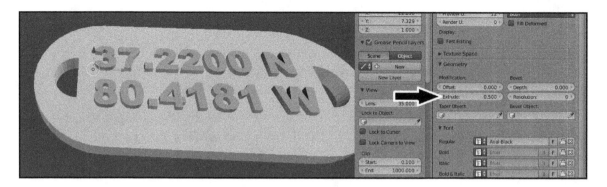

Setting the text thickness with font properties

You would still have to use the **Object | Convert to | Mesh from Curve/Meta/Serf/Text** menu option like we did in Chapter 3, *Converting a Bezier Curve to a Properly Sized 3D Mesh*, to convert your work to a 3D mesh. This approach does have a downside. The objects that are created this way tend to create a lot of **duplicate vertices** and an issue known as **non-manifold edges**, both of which are not optimal for 3D printing or interacting with other objects with the Boolean Modifier. Techniques for finding both issues, including using the optional 3D Print Toolbox seen here, are discussed in Chapter 15, *Troubleshooting and Repairing Models*. In my coordinates, I would find thousands of bad edges:

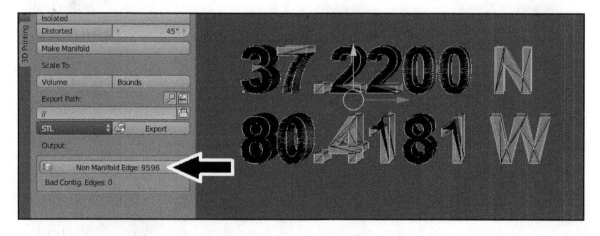

Using the Extrude property for the text object requires extra cleanup for the resulting mesh.

If this approach is what you are most comfortable with, Chapter 15, *Troubleshooting and Repairing Models*, also covers how these issues can be addressed and cleaned up.

Using the Extrude tool

My personal preference is to convert to mesh first and then use the Blender Extrude tool instead. This is an identical process to what we did in Chapter 3, *Converting a Bezier Curve to a Properly Sized 3D Mesh*, with the profile pendant. The steps are as follows:

1. If necessary, switch to **Object Mode** and right-click the text object to select it.
2. Go to the **Object** | **Convert to** | **Mesh from Curve/Meta/Serf/Text** menu at the bottom of the screen.
3. Switch to **Edit Mode** and hit the *A* key to select all the vertices.
4. In the **Tool Shelf** on the left side of the screen, click the **Tools** tab. Under the **Mesh Tools** section, click the **Extrude** button. Type in the desired height of the text. In my case, I type 0.5 to give it a height of 0.5mm:

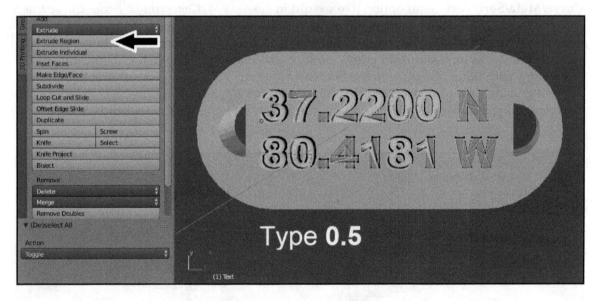

Extruding to give the coordinates a height of 0.5 mm.

When I use this approach, the resulting mesh looks the same. However, it has none of the issues of the previous approach. If I used the tools in Chapter 15, *Troubleshooting and Repairing Models,* to check for non-manifold edges, I would find none. No extra cleanup is required:

Extruding after converting to mesh produces a cleaner, error-free 3D object.

Finalizing the bracelet

When we use the Boolean Union Modifier, our main concern is getting rid of internal vertices and overlapping geometry that would potentially confuse the slicer and the 3D printer. In the case of our coordinates, if we align them perfectly flush with the rest of the base, there will be no such overlap. We would be able to safely export our work without having to do the formal Boolean Union.

Since the Object Origin of our coordinates is at the bottom of the letters, we will want to set that to match the Z position of the top surface of our bracelet plate to line them up. If the letters were higher than that, our text would not be connected to the base. If they are lower than that, the letters would extend inside the base and create the confusing overlap:

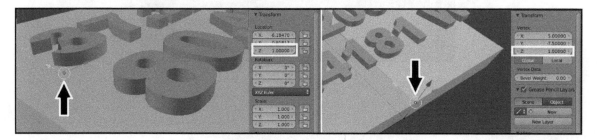

You want the bottom of the text to line up with the top of the base plate.

The steps to look up that perfect *Z* position and to adjust the **Location** of the text are:

1. In **Object Mode**, right-click to select the cube.
2. Switch to **Edit Mode**. If necessary, click the **Vertex Select** mode icon. Right-click an appropriate vertex to select it.
3. In the **Properties Shelf**, make sure the **Global** mode is selected and note the **Z** coordinate. In this case, I see a coordinate of 1.
4. Switch back to **Object Mode**. Right-click the text to select it. In the **Properties Shelf**, adjust the **Location** to match.

Finally, using the multi-select techniques we learned in Chapter 6, *Cutting Half Circle Holes and Modifier Management*, we can pick both the base plate and the coordinates and export them to STL format like we did in Chapter 4, *Flattening a Torus and Boolean Union*. The steps are:

1. If necessary, switch to **Object Mode** and right-click to select the cube.
2. Holding down the *Shift* key, right-click the text to select that as well.
3. At the top of the screen click the **File | Export | STL (.stl)** menu option. Make sure to check **Selection Only** and click the **Export STL** button.

Your custom coordinate bracelet plate is ready to print:

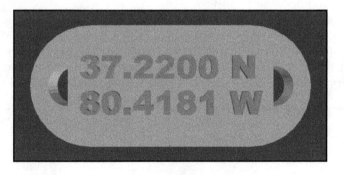

The final 3D model.

Summary

In this chapter, you finished your second jewelry piece. You learned how to add a text object in Blender and how to change the text, the size, the font type, as well as advanced settings such as line spacing. You learned two techniques to convert your text to a 3D mesh and how to align it flush with your bracelet plate. Finally, you reinforced earlier lessons by multi-selecting two objects and exporting them to STL format for 3D printing.

In the Chapter 8, *Using Empties to Model the Base of the House,* you'll begin another type of 3D printing project. You will start an architectural model by working on a house figurine.

8
Using Empties to Model the Base of the House

Another common 3D modeling project is an architectural model. In this section of the book, we'll model a small figurine based on photographs of a real-life house. In my case, I will be modeling the home my father grew up in, a home my grandfather designed and built.

In this chapter, we'll begin by using Blender objects called empties to add in multiple reference images. We'll then use mesh modeling techniques to make the shape of the house. The skills you will use are as follows:

- Adding and editing empty objects
- Scaling and using photos of different sizes
- Extruding faces of a 3D object
- Merging vertices to make a roof
- Adding new edges with the Loop Cut and Slide tool

Using Empties for reference images

To kick off our architectural model, we'll want to pull in reference images of multiple sides of our house. That will allow us to make sure our modeling efforts match the dimensions and the detailing of the original structure.

Missing an image? Try Google Street View or Google Earth!

Perhaps you are modeling a structure that is not nearby and you find you are missing details in your collection of photographs. You may be able to fill in the gaps by visiting Google Street View. Some details you can't photograph from the ground. If you are having trouble envisioning how the geometry of the house comes together, an aerial view from Google Earth may help pull the pieces together.

In Chapter 2, *Using a Background Image and Bezier Curves*, we set up a background image for the **Top** view to make our profile pendant. There were some limitations to that approach. You may remember that the image was only visible when we were viewing our project from a very specific spot, the **Top** viewpoint in **Ortho** mode. As soon as you moved to a different perspective, the image disappeared.

With this project, it would be beneficial to see multiple background images at once while we actively rotate around our house. Luckily, Blender gives us additional options for importing reference images. One such option is using an object called an **empty**.

Adding Empties

In some ways, empty objects behave just like normal Blender shapes such as cubes and cylinders. They can be added through the **Create** tab of the **Tool Shelf**. They can be moved and scaled and rotated. However, there is a distinct difference between an empty and other objects—empty objects will be "empty" as far as geometry goes. They will not have any vertices, edges, or faces. As a result, there is not an **Edit Mode** for an **empty**:

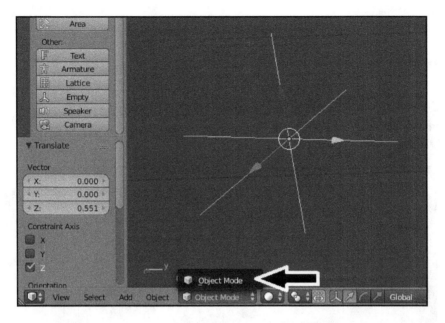

Empties do not have an Edit Mode as they not have any geometry to edit

You do have the ability to customize how your **empty** will display on your screen. For example, you can tell the **empty** to display as an image instead of the default plain axes lines:

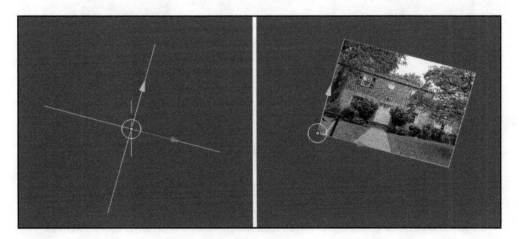

Default empty display of plain axes and an empty as an image

To start my modeling, I'm going to pull in images of two sides of my grandfather's house—the front and the left. The steps to add a new empty to your project and set it to an image are as follows:

1. If necessary, make sure you are in **Object Mode** and left-click to move your 3D Cursor to where you'd like to add the empty.
2. In the **Tool Shelf** on the left side of the screen, click on the **Create** tab. Under the **Other** section, click on **Empty**:

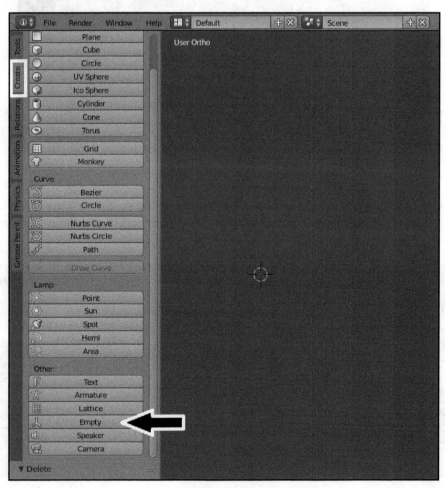

Adding a new empty

3. The new empty is added and displayed as plain axes lines. Directly underneath the **Tool Shelf**, a new **Add Empty** window displays. Change the **Type** to **Image**. Alternatively, you can change this at any time in the **Properties Window** by clicking on the axes icon and changing the **Display** to **Image**:

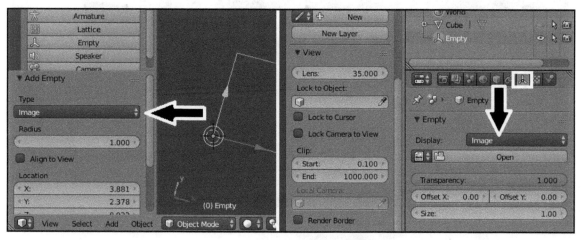

Two ways of changing the Type to Image

4. In the **Properties Window**, click on the axes icon. Underneath **Display**, click on the **Open** button. Use the white up arrow and the folder icons to browse the directory structure of your computer. Select the image you wish to use and click on the **Open Image** button:

Picking the image file

Repeat as necessary with additional reference photos. In my case, I also create an empty for the left side of the house. I end up with two empty objects in my project displaying photos:

Two empty objects displaying the front and side of my grandfather's house

Rotating the Empties

Both of my empty objects are side by side, which won't help me much when making a 3D model. We can rotate them as we learned in Chapter 4 , *Flattening a Torus and Boolean Union*. To keep everything intuitive as we model, I recommend rotating the empty objects so that they stay in conjunction with the common viewpoints. It'll be easier for me to visualize and navigate if I have the front image of the house synced with the **View | Front** menu option.

The steps for rotating the empty with the front of the house are as follows:

1. If necessary, switch to **Object Mode** and right-click on the **empty** you wish to rotate to select it.
2. In the **View** menu at the bottom of screen, select the **Front** view. Your empty may appear as just a line. Using the axis arrows as a reference, I determine I want to rotate around the **X** (red) axis:

The empty from the Front view.

3. In the **Properties Shelf** on the right-hand side of the screen, go to the **Transform** section and, under **Rotation**, give **X** a value of 90 degrees. Remember, trial and error with rotation is fine:

The empty after being rotated 90 degrees.

For the image of the left side of my grandfather's house, I want it synced with the **View** | **Left** menu option. I can repeat the preceding steps to make the picture upright in my 3D space and then add one extra step at the end:

4. In the **Properties Shelf** on the right-hand side of the screen, go to the **Transform** section and, under **Rotation**, also give **Z** a rotation of −90 (or 270) degrees:

Rotating the empty with the side of the house.

Now the two images are perpendicular to each other. You can use the drag and drop technique you used with the torus in Chapter 4, *Flattening a Torus and Boolean Union*, to better position the images for further review:

The two rotated empty objects are now perpendicular to each other

Scaling empties and adjusting for differences in pictures

If I compare our empty objects to a 2 mm x 2 mm x 2 mm cube, I can see that, by default, they are created substantially too small for my purposes:

Empty objects are tiny, much smaller than a 2 x 2 x 2 cube.

Reflecting on design requirements, I want my house figurine to be roughly 4 1/2" long across the front, which translates to 114.3 mm along the X (red) axis.

With empty objects, you can adjust the scale, but you can't type in specific Dimensions like you can for other objects. To cheat, let's first size a cube to the length we want and then use that to adjust the scale of the empty:

1. If necessary, switch to **Object Mode** and right-click on the cube to select it.

2. In the **Properties Window**, look for the **Transform** section. Under **Dimensions**, type in 114.3 for the **X** dimension:

Updating the X Dimension.

3. Your enlarged cube may now be hiding your empty. If necessary, move the cube and then right-click on your empty to select it.

4. Hit the *S* key for scale and move your mouse away from the Object Origin to make the empty larger. Left-click to apply the new sizing. Since this object is so small, you may run out of room in your 3D View window before the empty is as large as you like. If that is the case, you may repeat this step as necessary to enlarge it more:

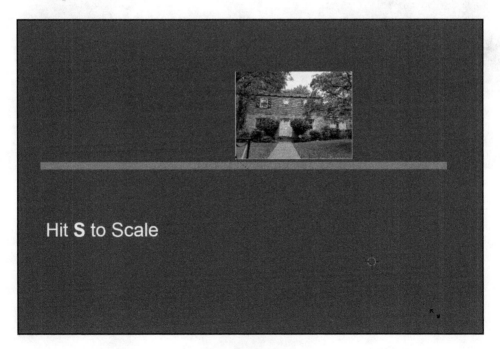

Scaling the empty to the right size.

5. You may have to adjust the positioning of the cube or the empty to get a better comparison of size. If you need to decrease the size, hit the *S* key and move the mouse toward the Object Origin.

After a few iterations, the front image of my grandfather's house is roughly the same size as my measurement cube:

The house image is now the desired size of our final model

The empty with the left side of my grandfather's house is still dreadfully small:

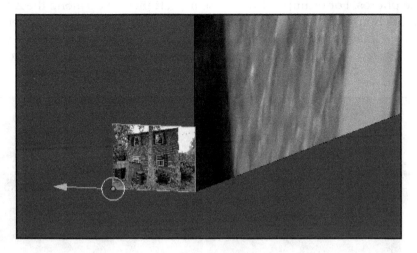

The Left empty needs to be resized as well

This is not necessarily going to be the exact same scale as the front. Variances in the position of the photographer means the pictures are not going to be taken from consistent distances. If you look at both of my pictures, you'll see that I was closer to the house when I took the picture of the side. The house is taller. What I'll want to do is note reference points that are in both images and sync them. In both pictures, the height of the house (without the roof) should be the same. So I'll scale my left image until the height of the house is equal with that of the front image:

These photos were taken from different distances. For our modeling, we'll want to scale the images so the height of the house matches in both.

I'll scale it, in the same manner, I did with the front. It helps to periodically adjust the position of the photos. For example, I will raise my left picture up along the Z (blue) axis so the bottom of the house lines up in both photos. I also pull it along the Y (green) axis to intersect the front image for better comparison. Finally, it is helpful to change your viewing perspective and use the mouse scroll wheel to zoom in closer to check your work and sizing:

Zooming in and changing positions can help you with your work.

Setting Transparency and X-Ray Mode

Now that the reference images are in place, there are two additional properties in Blender that can assist with your modeling:

- **Transparency**: You have the ability to set your image to be translucent, so items behind it are visible
- **X-Ray**: When you turn on X-Ray mode, then your image will display even if something is in front of it

In combination, these settings will make your reference images and your model visible no matter where you viewing your work and what is in the front:

Transparency in combination with X-Ray makes your reference images visible while you work.

The steps to add Transparency and X-Ray to your empty objects are follows:

1. If necessary, switch to **Object Mode** and right-click on the **empty** to select it.
2. In the **Properties Window**, click on the image icon to edit the empty properties. You can set the **Transparency** value by using the slide bar or typing in a value. 0 would be completely invisible and 1 would be completely opaque. In this case, I type in 0.40:

Setting the Transparency of the empty

3. In the **Properties Window**, click on the cube icon to access the **Object** properties. Under the **Display** section, check the **X-Ray** box:

Turning on X-Ray mode.

This image will now show through objects in front of it, but because of the transparency, you'll see both your reference image and your model. Repeat, as necessary, with your other reference image(s).

Modeling the base of the house

Before I start modeling my house, I'm going to take a moment and reflect on my plan. You are not limited to just the images you imported into Blender. You can refer to images outside Blender as well as your own memory and recollection. Looking at another image, I notice that the room to the right of the house is actually inset a bit from the main structure:

The side room is inset from the main structure

There are many ways to attack this shape. I'm going to start with the we used for scaling the empty earlier. I'm going scale it down to the length, height, and depth of the main structure. Then I'll raise that up to make the roof. Finally, I'll do an offshoot for that extra room.

There are two techniques I can use to size the cube to match the main structure of the house. First, I can use scale like we did earlier, but specify the axis I wish to change. The steps are as follows:

1. If necessary, switch to **Object Mode** and right-click on the cube to select it.
2. Go to **View** | **Front** to switch to the front view. Alternatively, you can hit *1* on your number pad as a shortcut.
3. Hit the *S* key on your keyboard to tell Blender to scale. Then type X to tell Blender you only want to adjust the dimension along the X (red) axis. Move the mouse toward the Object Origin to scale the cube smaller to match just the main structure. Left-click to apply. Because scaling works against the Object Origin, you may have to adjust the placement of the cube as it changes size:

Scaling the cube down to match just the main structure of the house

Another option for updating the size of the cube is to move the vertices themselves. The steps to move vertices to adjust our house height (the Z dimension) are as follows:

1. With our cube selected, switch to **Edit Mode**.
2. As a shortcut, click on the Face Select icon and right-click on the top face of our cube. This will automatically select all four vertices we wish to move:

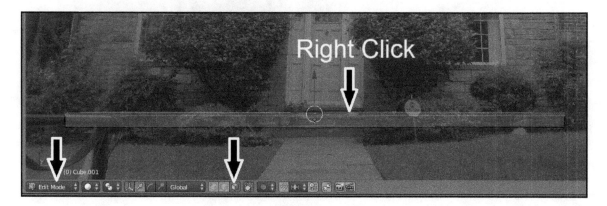

3. If necessary, go back to **View** | **Front** so you are viewing the front of the house.

4. Left-click and hold on the **Z** (blue) axis arrow and drag the face up to an appropriate spot based on the reference image. In this case, I'm going to stop where the roof begins. Release the left-click button to apply:

Sizing the along the Z axis.

You can switch to **View | Left** and use either technique to size the depth (Y dimension) of the house:

Scaling the Y dimension of the house.

Using Extrude and merging vertices

If necessary, you can temporarily turn off X-Ray mode and Transparency to get another assessment of your work. I have a rectangle appropriately shaped for the main structure of the house. Now I want to grow the top of my house up to start my roof:

The base of the house is done. Next up, the roof.

The same **Extrude** tool we used in `Chapter 3`, *Converting a Bezier Curve to a Properly Sized 3D Mesh,* to make our profile pendant can also be used on existing 3D objects. The steps to use Extrude to make the roof of my house are as follows:

1. If necessary, right-click on the cube to select it and switch to **Edit Mode**.
2. Click on the Face Select icon and right-click on the top face of our house to select it:

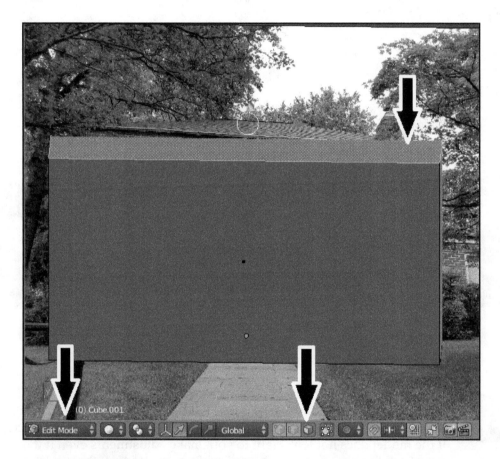

3. Go to the **View** | **Front** menu option or type *1* on the number pad to make sure you are viewing your object exactly from the front.

4. In the **Tool Shelf**, click on the **Tools** tab. Under **Mesh Tools**, click on the **Extrude Region** button. Move your mouse to adjust the height of the roof. Left-click to apply:

Using Extrude Region to start the roof

Reference images are just references

Reference images are subject to perspective and are not always accurate. For example, in my front photograph, the roof appears shorter than it is in real life. This is due to the angle I was standing at when taking the picture. If the model does not look right to you, make adjustments even if it does not match the photo you imported into Blender. You are the modeler, not the photograph.

Right now, my roof section is rectangular and not the triangular shape of the real roof:

The model has a square roof which does not match the real house.

If I go to the left or right side of the house, instead of the two points at the top, I would like to have one. Blender gives us the ability to merge or combine, vertices into a single point. There is a lot of flexibility for merging. One common option is to put the new, combined vertex in the center. This would be perfect to change our face into the desired triangle:

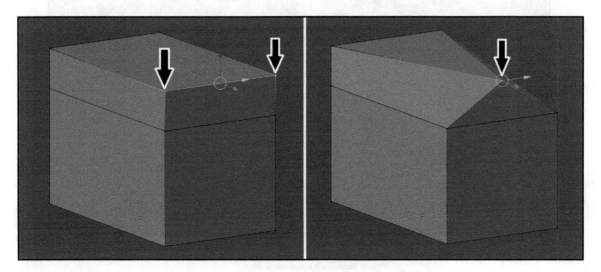

The impact of merging two vertices to the center.

The steps for merging the vertices are as follows:

1. If necessary, right-click on the cube to select it and switch to **Edit Mode**.
2. Go to **View | Right** or hit 3 on your number pad to view the right side of the house.
3. Click on the Vertex Select icon. Right-click on one of the top vertices to select it. Holding down the *Shift* key, right-click on the other top vertex to select it as well:

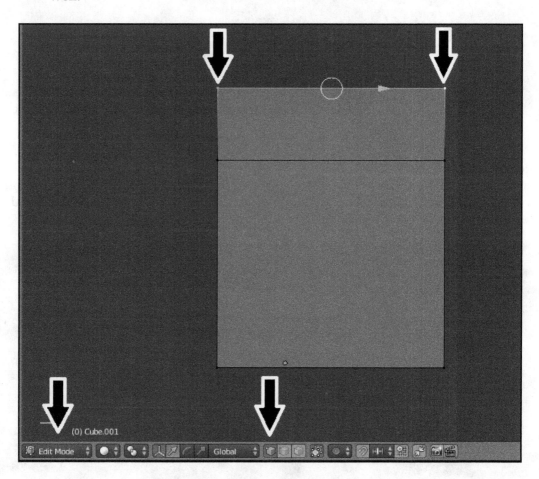

Selecting two side vertices to merge.

4. In the menu at the bottom of the screen, go to **Mesh** | **Vertices** | **Merge**. Alternatively, you can hold down the *Alt* and *M* keys together:

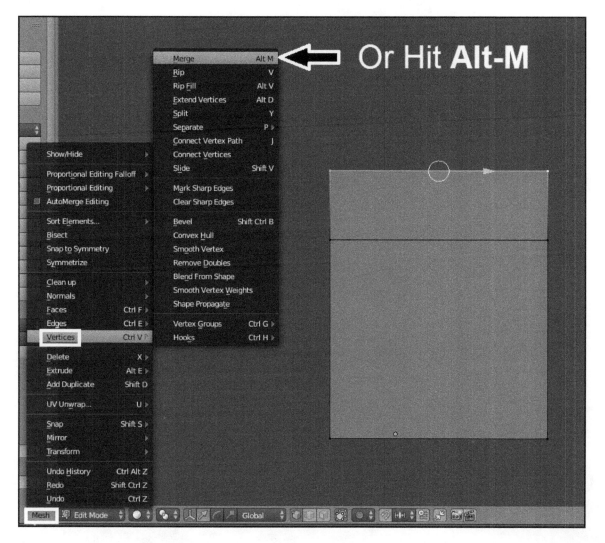

Choosing to merge the vertices

5. A pop-up menu asks you where you'd like the newly merged vertex to be placed. Select **At Center** to place it in the middle of our two selections:

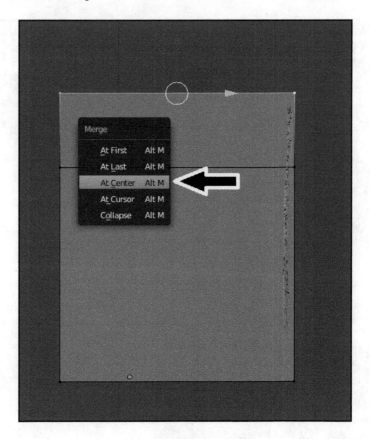

Telling Blender to merge at the center of the two selections.

Repeat the steps with the left side of the roof. When you are done, your cube is recognizably a house:

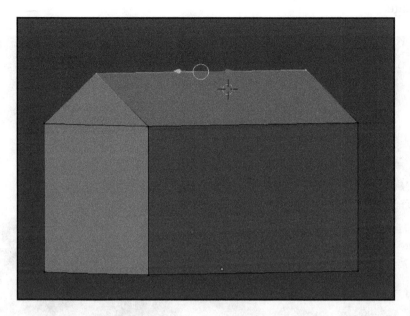

After merging the top vertices on both the left and the right side of the house, there is a nice roof shape.

For the particular house I am modeling, I do have one slight adjustment. In addition to the front and back, this roof is also angled on the left and right sides. To achieve that same effect in my model, I want the two top vertices of my roof to be closer to the center of my house, along the X (red) axis. In Blender, you can also use the **Scale** tool in **Edit Mode**. If you have more than one item selected, Scale can pull them closer together or push them further apart. The steps to use Scale to adjust the shape of my roof are as follows:

1. In **Edit Mode**, right-click on one of the top vertices to select it. Holding down *Shift*, right-click on the second vertex to select it as well.

2. Hit the *S* key and then the *X* key to tell Blender to scale only along the X axis. Use your mouse to adjust the placement of those points based on your reference image:

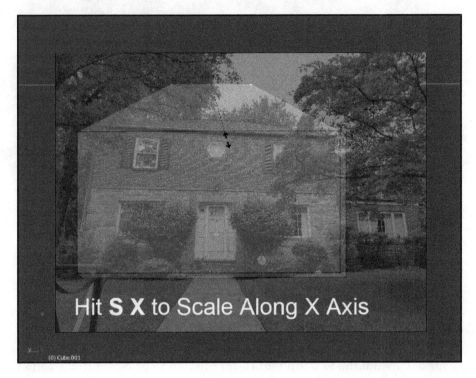

Adjusting the scale of the new roof

Using Loop Cut and Slide

Now I want to grow a little offshoot of my rectangle for the room on the right side of the house. I could select the rightmost face and extrude it to grow my house further to the right. However, if I do that, it grows the entire face, the entire right side of my house, which is too tall for my purposes. I also noted earlier that particular room is inset from the rest of the house's front:

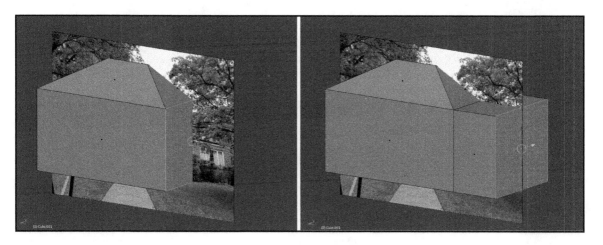

The Extrude tool can grow the side of the house, but it would be the wrong size.

What I'll want to do is strategically divide up that face, so I can pick just an appropriately sized section to extrude. One tool we can use is called **Loop Cut and Slide**. The Loop Cut and Slide tool will cut a ring of edges, a loop, in your object and will divide up the faces accordingly. This is very helpful with adding new vertices and edges to your existing model while preserving the shape and keeping the mesh clean and friendly for 3D printing.

When you first click on the **Loop Cut and Slide** button, you can hover your mouse over various points in your object and a purple cross-section line will illustrate your loop options. Hovering over different edges or parts of your model will produce different loops:

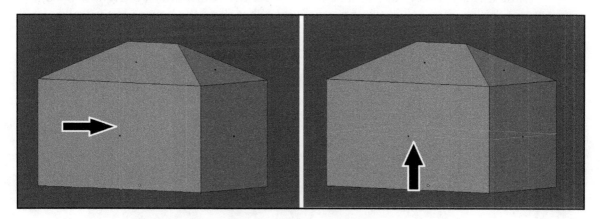

Loop Cut and Slide can produce different loops for cutting

When you left-click, you commit to that loop type and a yellow line gives you a preview of the cut. You can move your mouse to slide that cut to the right location. When you are satisfied, left-click will apply the cut and automatically adjust the faces, edges, and vertices of your model:

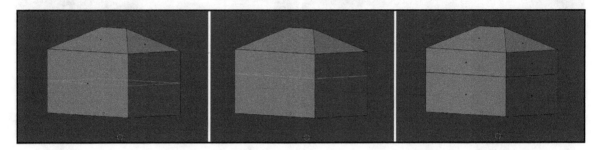

The three phases of Loop Cut and Slide: a purple line to preview the loop, a yellow line to place the cut, and the final edges and faces.

We can use **Loop Cut and Slide** to add some extra edges to make a face the right size for our side room. We'll add a cut to give that room a shorter height and we'll add a cut to give that room a slight inset from the front of the house. The steps are as follows:

1. If necessary, right-click to select the cube and switch to **Edit Mode**.
2. Go to **View** | **Front** or hit *1* on the number pad to view the house from the front.
3. In the **Tool Shelf** on the left side of the screen, click on the **Tools** tab. Under **Mesh Tools**, click on the **Loop Cut and Slide** button. Alternatively, you can hit the *Ctrl* and *R* keys at the same time. Hover over the leftmost or rightmost edge of the house to get a purple preview loop that slices the house up vertically, almost between floors. Left-click to commit to that loop:

The purple line gives you a preview of the cut.

4. The loop line is now yellow. Use your mouse to adjust the position of the loop based on the reference image. Left-click to apply the cut.

5. Go to **View** | **Right** or hit 3 on the number pad to view the right side of the house.

6. In the **Tool Shelf**, click on **Loop Cut and Slide** button or hit *Ctrl + R* again.

7. This time, hover over the bottommost edge of the house to get a purple preview loop that will slice the side of the house so we can give the room an inset. Left-click to commit to that loop and turn it yellow. Use your mouse to adjust the cut accordingly. Left-click to apply:

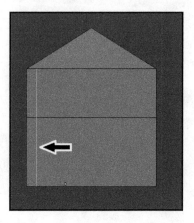

Moving the new loop to the desired spot

After those two Loop Cut and Slides, we now have a good sized face we can extrude out and complete the base of the house:

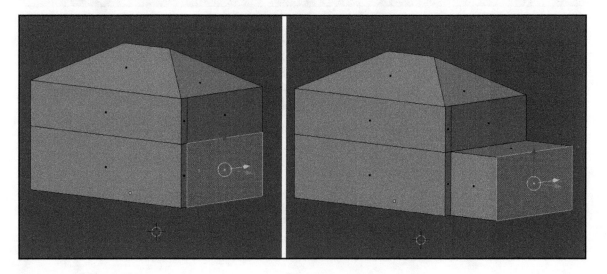

After Loop Cut and Slide, the Extrude tool can complete the side room of the house

Summary

In this chapter, you learned about the empty object and how it can be used to pull in reference images. You learned how to set Transparency and X-Ray Mode to assist with your modeling. You scaled your empty objects and adjusted for differences in photograph sizes. You got to practice mesh modeling techniques to build the base of the house figurine. You learned two ways to match the size of the cube to your house. You learned how to Extrude parts of an existing 3D object and how to merge vertices to make a roof. Finally, you learned about the Loop Cut and Slide tool and how it can add additional edges and faces to your object.

In Chapter 9, *Mesh Modeling and Positioning the Details*, you'll learn more mesh modeling techniques, such as Subdivide and Dissolve Edges, as you model the windows and doors of the house.

9
Mesh Modeling and Positioning the Details

In this chapter, we are going to add details to our house figurine by modeling the windows. The skills involved will include the following:

- Performing multiple cuts at once with Loop Cut and Slide
- Using the Subdivision tool to divide up existing faces and edges
- Dissolving unnecessary edges
- Using the Inset tool to create borders
- Renaming objects in the Outliner for better organization
- Positioning objects with the Snap during transform icon

Modeling windows

As I embark on adding details to the house, I do have some options for how to attack the modeling. Let's take the example of a window. I could continue to use the Loop Cut and Slide and Extrude tools to slice up new edges on the existing cube and make the windows part of the already existing mesh.

All my work would be contained in a single object, the cube:

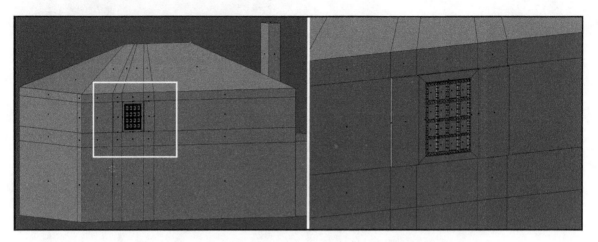

The existing cube could be cut up and the details, such as windows, could be modeled as part of the same mesh

Looking ahead, however, I can see that this particular window is a common element of the house. I can see it repeated not only on the front of the house but the other sides as well:

The same window is repeated throughout the house.

If I modeled the windows as a direct part of the existing cube, I would have to repeat my modeling steps for each window. That would not only add to my modeling time, but it also opens up the opportunity for slight variances in the sizing. Another option is to add a brand new cube and model a window as a separate object. Once satisfied, I could duplicate that window as many times as needed, saving work and ensuring consistency. Finally, because it is a separate object, I would be able to export just the window should I ever want to use it in another project.

Creating a window as a separate object

Starting the new window is as easy as adding a new cube and making it the proper size. The **X** and **Z** dimensions I will set based on the reference image. In regard to the Y dimension, this is going to reflect my detail height, how far off the main house the details will be raised. I think back to the considerations in `Chapter 1`, *Thinking about Design Requirements*, and and my printer's capabilities. I'm going to make most of my detailing 0.5 mm high.

The steps to add and size the new window are as follows:

1. If necessary, switch to **Object Mode** and left-click to move your 3D Cursor to roughly where you wish to add the new window
2. In the **Tool Shelf** on the left-hand side of the screen, look under the **Create** tab and click on **Cube**
3. Type s x and scale the length of the window to an appropriate size based on the reference image
4. Type s z and scale the height of the window to an appropriate size
5. In the **Properties Shelf** on the right-hand side of the screen, look under **Dimensions:** and type the desired detail height, in my case 0.5, for **Y:**

Creating the new cube, scaling it along the X and Z axes, and typing in the specific Y dimension

Adding shutters with a multi-cut Loop Cut and Slide

In Chapter 5, *Building a Base with Standard Meshes and a Mirror*, we used the Loop Cut and Slide tool to make strategic cuts in our house base. For my window, I'm going to want some extra edges to separate out the window from the shutters. One thing I'm concerned about is making sure both shutters are the same size. The Loop Cut and Slide tool has the ability to make multiple, equidistant cuts at the same time. When you get the purple preview line of the proposed loop, you can use your mouse scroll wheel to increase or decrease the number of cuts:

Using the scroll wheel on the mouse can increase the number of cuts with Loop Cut and Slide

As we've seen before, in Blender, there are many ways to approach this. I could make two cuts and scale or move those edges so they line up with the shutters. However, I happened to notice that if I make three cuts, the two outside cuts are right where I want them. For this particular window, I'm going to make three cuts and then use another Blender function to erase, or dissolve, the middle cut I don't need.

The steps are as follows:

1. If necessary, right-click on the cube to select it and switch to **Edit Mode**.
2. In the **Tool Shelf** on the left side of the screen, click on the **Tools** tab and, under **Mesh Tools:**, click on the **Loop Cut and Slide** button. Like in Chapter 8, *Using Empties to Model the Base of the House*, hover your mouse over the top or bottom edge of your window to get the purple cut preview line. Scroll up twice on the mouse scroll wheel to increase the cuts to three. Left-click to commit to the loop and immediately left-click again to apply the cuts as they are, without changing their placement.
3. If you inadvertently move the loops, hitting the *Esc* button will move them back their original centered placement:

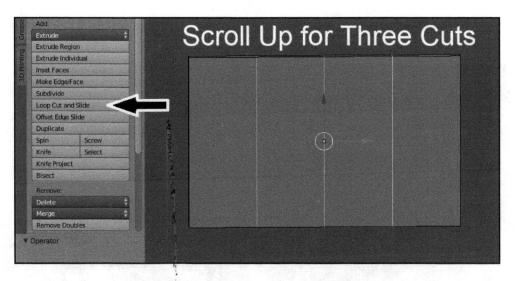

Scroll up for three cuts. Hitting Escape will return the centered placement

3. If necessary, click on the Edge Select icon. I also recommend turning off the Limit selection to visible icon. Go to **Select** | **Border Select** and draw a square over all the middle edges to select them:

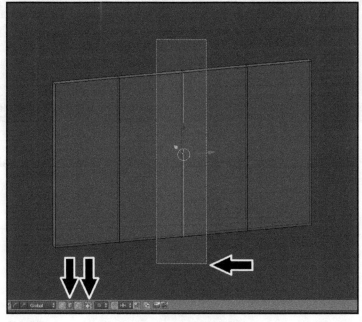

Selecting the two middle edges

4. Hit the **Delete** button. A popup will prompt for further details. Click on **Dissolve Edges**:

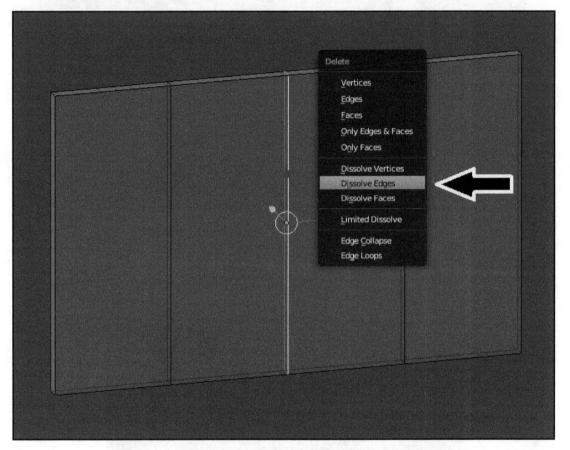

Dissolving the middle edges

At this point, the front and back of our window have three faces—two for shutters and one for the actual window:

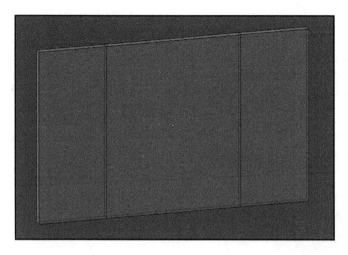

Three faces on the front of the window

Dissolve versus Delete

When you were removing the middle edges, you may have noticed you also have the option to **Delete**. When you dissolve an edge, Blender will try to automatically adjust any related faces and keep their appearance intact. When you delete an edge, any related faces are also deleted, leaving a hole in your model:

Deleting instead of dissolving would create a hole in the model

Starting window panes with Subdivide

Another handy mesh modeling tool in Blender is Subdivide. You can select faces or edges and tell Blender to cut it up into equal parts. Like Loop Cut and Slide, Blender will automatically adjust the geometry of your object to add any new faces, vertices, and edges.

By default, any edges are cut in half. If I select the front face of my window, a rectangle with four edges, and subdivide it, all four of those edges are cut in half. My single face becomes four. If I subdivide again, all the edges for those four faces are also cut in half and I end up with sixteen faces:

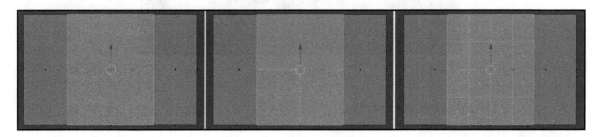

The impact of Subdivide on a four-edge face. The first click turns the face into four. The second click turns those four faces to sixteen

Already my window is starting to look like it is developing panes. If I'm being true to my grandfather's house, however, I'll want my window to have twelve panes, four rows of three panes each. I can achieve this thanks to two additional capabilities of the Subdivide feature.

Subdividing edges

Instead of selecting a face and subdividing that, I can pick specific edges to cut. In the case of my window, if I select just the top and bottom edges, Subdivide only cuts those two edges and leaves the left and right edges intact. My single face becomes two:

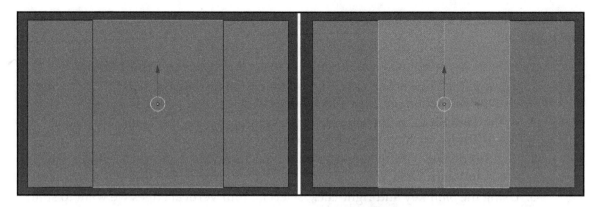

Subdividing edges instead of faces lets you control what gets divided

Controlling the number of cuts

When subdividing, Blender will add a **Subdivide** window underneath the Tool Shelf to help you further control the behavior. Just like Loop Cut and Slide, you can increase the number of cuts you make. In the window example, if I select the bottom and top edges, subdivide, and change **Number of Cuts** to 2, my face is divided into thirds:

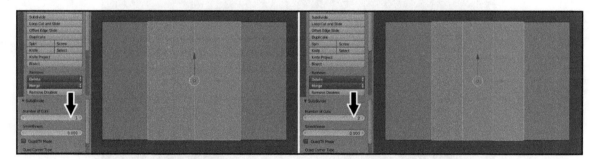

Blender allows you to change the number of cuts when subdividing

Pulling all this together, the steps for using the Subdivide tool to start twelve window panes are as follows:

1. If necessary, right-click on the cube to select it and switch to **Edit Mode**.
2. Click on the Edge Select icon. Right-click on the top edge to select it. *Shift* + right-click on the bottom edge to select that as well.
3. In the **Tool Shelf** on the left side of the screen, click on the **Tools** tab. Under **Mesh Tools:**, click on the **Subdivide** button.
4. The **Subdivide** window appears under the Tool Shelf with more options. Change the **Number of Cuts** to 2.
5. Using the *Shift* key and right-click, select all four vertical edges we want to split:

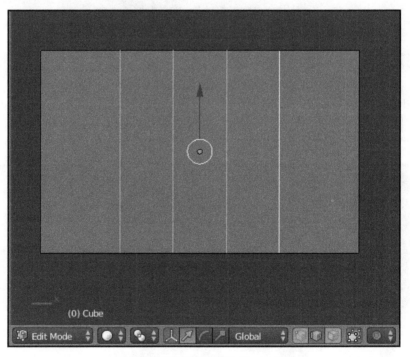

Selecting all four vertical edges

6. In the **Tool Shelf** on the left side of the screen, click on the **Subdivide** button again. This time, for **Number of Cuts**, pick 3:

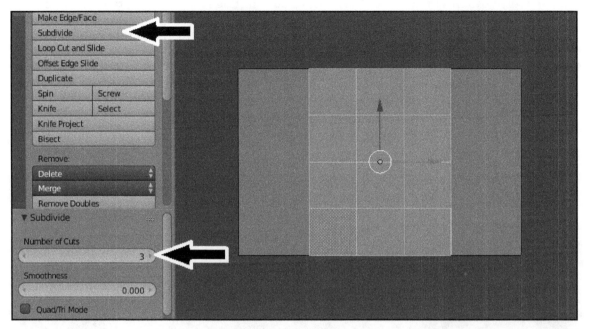

Telling Blender to make three cuts

What was once a single face is now twelve—four rows of three faces each to match the real window:

Both the real window and the modeled window have twelve panes

Finishing window panes with Inset

I have twelve squares in my model, which is just a starting point. To differentiate the border of the pane from the glass portion, I want a smaller rectangle inside each one of the existing pane faces. You can certainly achieve that with tools you are already familiar with, but it is also a great application for another tool in Blender called **Inset**.

The Inset tool will take the outline of the currently selected face(s) and allow you to make a larger or smaller copy. Again, Blender will automatically add all the necessary vertices, edges, and faces to adjust your model and keep it clean. With the example of a simple rectangular face such as a window pane, insetting makes a smaller rectangle inside it and all the necessary border faces around it:

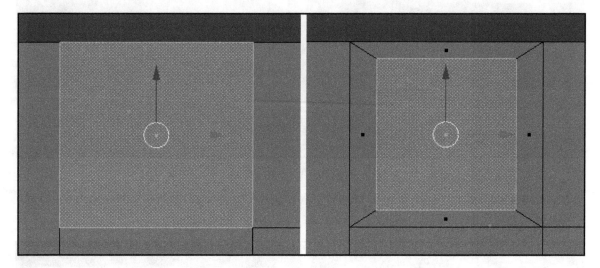

The impact of the Inset tool on a single face

As a heads-up, you may be tempted to select all twelve panes, thinking it would be a shortcut to inset them all at once. Since Blender is copying the outside edge of the selected faces, that'll only achieve a border around the entire group of panes:

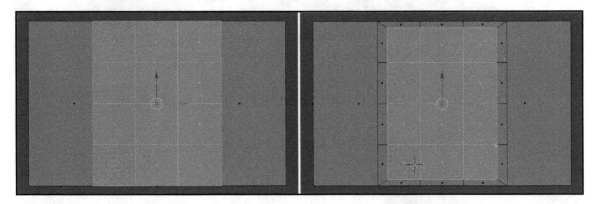

Insetting multiple faces once will make a border around all of them

Noting and applying exact thicknesses

When you are insetting a face, you can adjust the thickness by moving your mouse. It's very much like using the mouse to scale. If you move toward the origin of the selected face, the copied edges get smaller. If you move away, they get larger.

In lieu of using the mouse, you can also type in the desired thickness. For these window panes, it makes sense to type in a number so I can make sure each and every pane is identically sized. I can use trial and error to find the best size. Another option is to inset one pane and use the mouse to size it. As I work, Blender displays the current thickness at the bottom of the screen. This can help me get a feel for what thickness I'd like to use for all the panes.

I don't have to apply this inset. I can always hit the *Esc* button to cancel once I have the information I need:

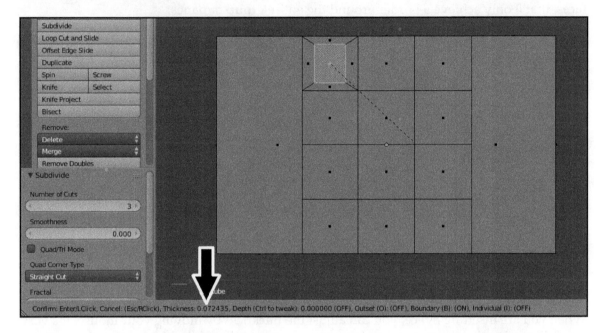

Blender will list the thickness of your inset at the bottom of the screen

After some investigation, I decide I want to inset each pane with a thickness of 0.05. The steps to apply that are as follows:

1. If necessary, right-click to select the cube and switch to **Edit Mode**. Click on the Face Select icon. Right-click on one of the faces to select it:

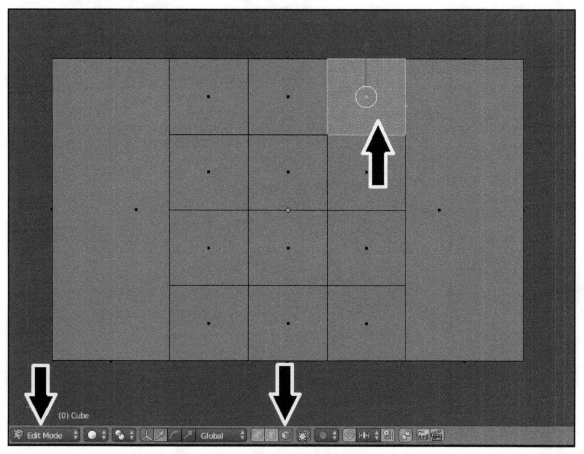

Right-clicking to select a face

2. In the **Mesh** menu at the bottom of the screen, click on **Faces** and then **Inset Faces**. Alternatively, you can press *I* on your keyboard as a shortcut:

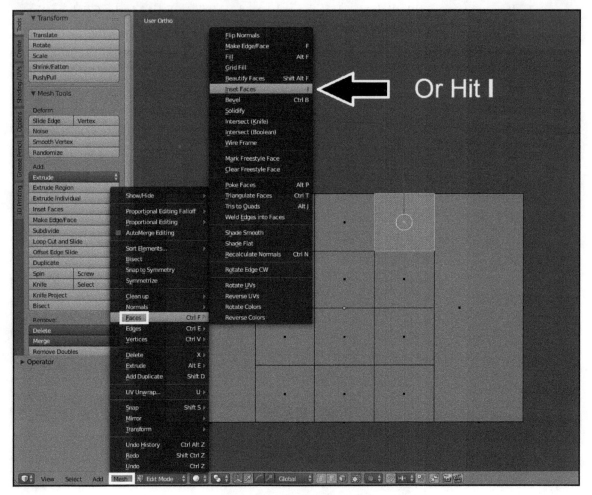

Starting the inset with the Mesh menu or hitting I

3. Type in the desired thickness. For my windows, I'm typing 0.05. Hit the *Enter* key to apply. Once you apply an Inset, an **Inset Faces** window appears under your **Tool Shelf** where you can review or adjust the **Thickness** further:

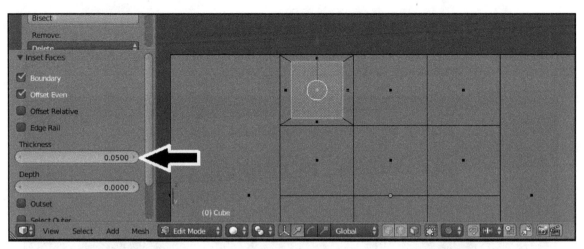

Thickness can be reviewed or adjusted in the Tool Shelf

4. Once you type in a specific thickness, Blender should remember it and use it as the default. Right-click to select the next face. Hit *I* on the keyboard and hit *Enter* to apply.

After I repeat step 4 for each pane, my window has borders around each piece of glass:

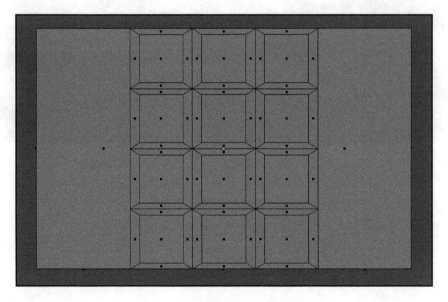

The window model after all the pane faces have been inset

Raising the details with Extrude

All our faces and edges are well defined. However, if we switch to **Object Mode**, the solid rendering of our window still looks like a plain rectangle:

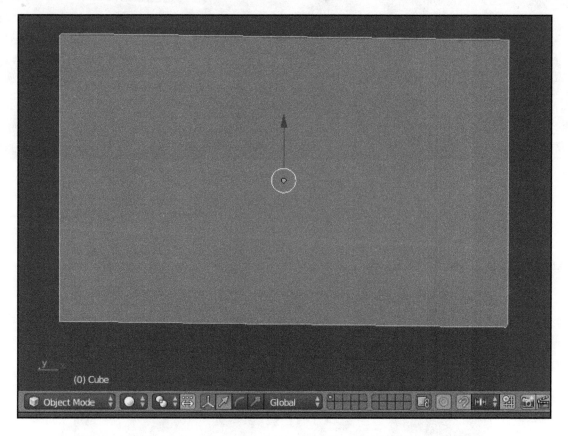

Since all edges and faces are the same height, our model still renders as a plain rectangle

Everything is at the same height right now, so there is no real differentiation between a window pane and a shutter. The 3D model and, more importantly, the final print won't reflect those details. If I am sending this out to a Service Bureau to do full-color printing, I do have the option of keeping everything flat and using colors to illustrate those details. Techniques for adding colors to your model and prints will be covered in Chapter 14, *Coloring Models with Materials and UV Maps*. My preference, even if I am using colors, is to give elements of the window different heights:

Two ways of making the details visible to the printer—changing colors (for full color Service Bureau printing) and placing the details at different heights

I'll keep all the borders of the window panes as they are, at 0.5 mm high. The shutters I'll raise to 0.6 mm, so they'll sit slightly higher than the rest of the window. In the photos, the actual glass of the windows looks flush with the pane borders. Here, I'll take an artistic liberty. I'll pull the glass part of the actual windows in closer to the rest of the house, so it is only 0.05 mm high and stands distinctly apart from the borders.

Thin walls apply to the final product

You may have noticed that the 0.05 mm thickness of the glass is well below the minimum wall thicknesses discussed in Chapter 1, *Thinking about Design Requirements*. That would be a legitimate concern if I were printing the window all by itself. However, this window will be lying flush to the base of our house. The printer will see it all as one object. This window won't be considered a thin wall because it has the entire thickness of the house behind it.

We can accomplish all these changes with the same Extrude tool we used with the profile pendant and making the base of our house. The steps are as follows:

1. If necessary, right-click on the cube to select it and switch to **Edit Mode**.
2. Click on the Face select icon. Right-click on one of the windows to select it. Holding down the *Shift* key, right-click on the remaining squares to select them:

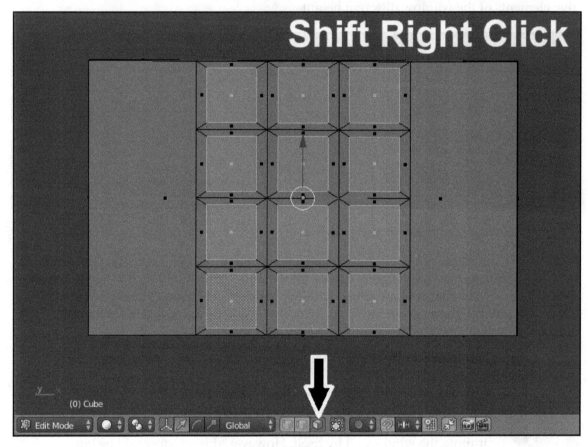

Selecting all the window faces

3. In the **Tool Shelf** on the left side of the screen, look under the **Tools** tab. Under **Mesh Tools:**, click **Extrude Region**. Type in -0.45. This moves the panes backward 0.45 mm, leaving the thickness of that section of the model as 0.05 mm:

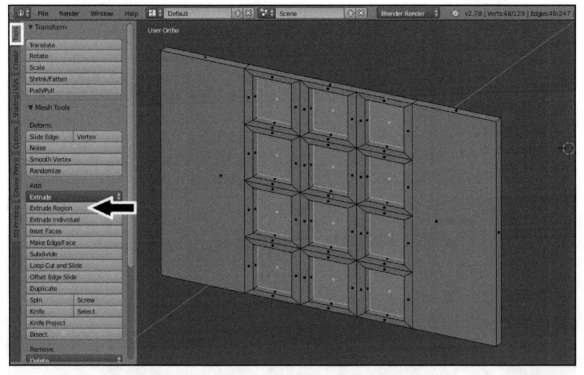

Extruding the faces down into the window

4. Right-click on one of the shutter faces to select it. *Shift* + right-click on the second shutter to select it.

5. In the **Tool Shelf** on the left side of the screen, click **Extrude Region** again. Type in `0.1`. This moves the shutters up an additional 0.1 mm, making the total thickness of that section 0.6 mm:

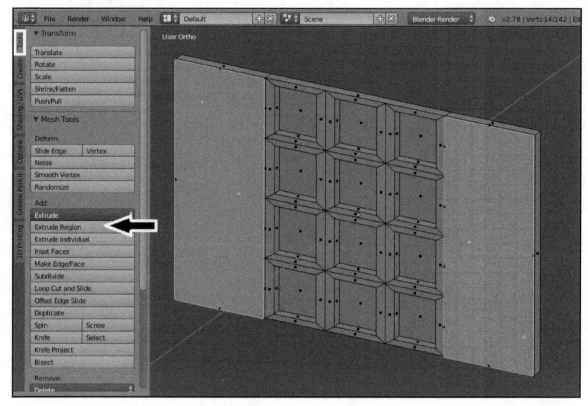

Extruding the shutters up higher than the rest of the window

Now that the details are at different heights, I can see the difference in **Object Mode**. My window looks like a window:

With the faces at different heights, the window detailing is visible in Object Mode

Renaming and copying windows

Once satisfied with the window, we can make copies to apply to the rest of the house. As we continue to add details to the project, the Outliner window is going to get quite a few objects in it. Blender assigns default names to each object based on what it is. For example, my project currently has two cubes named `Cube` and `Cube.001`:

The Outliner window with the default names of each object

It is helpful, particularly in large endeavors, to assign more meaningful names. It'll make it easier to select objects through the Outliner window and hide ones we don't want to see. The steps to rename an object are as follows:

1. In the **Outliner** window at the top right of the screen, right-click on the name you wish to update. A pop-up menu displays. Select **Rename**. Alternatively, you can double-click on the object's name:

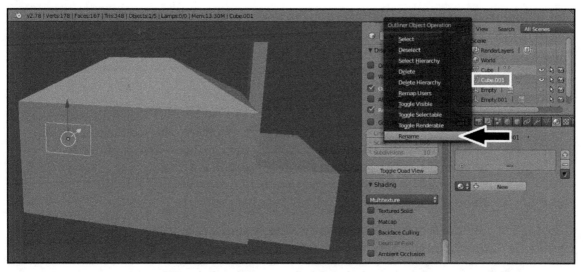

Asking Blender to rename an object

2. Type in the new name and hit *Enter* to apply:

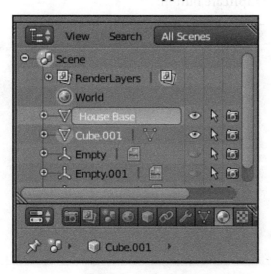

Typing in the new object name

This allows me to name one cube `House Base` and my other cube `Window`. Moving forward, Blender will assign names to any new copies by adding a number, so I'll get a `Window.001`, `Window.002`, and so on. I can always go back and rename those to be more meaningful as well, such as `Window - Alley Side` and `Window - Deck Side`.

Making backups

If you aren't sure of your direction with an object, you can make a backup of it by using the **Duplicate** button. In the Outliner window, I like to rename my backups with a `Backup -` prefix such as `Backup - Bay Window`. Click on the eye icon to hide it. Even though it is hidden, it is there if you ever need to refer to it or restore it.

Copying the window is easy. We can use the same **Duplicate** button we used in `Chapter 6`, *Cutting Half Circle Holes and Modifier Management*. The steps are as follows:

1. If necessary, switch to **Object Mode** and right-click on the object to select it.
2. In the **Tool Shelf** on the left side of the screen, look under the **Tools** tab. Under **Edit**, click the **Duplicate** button:

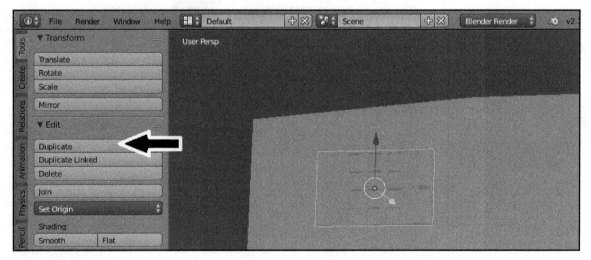

Clicking on the Duplicate button

3. Immediately, the copy is added and selected. Drag and drop to place it close to its final spot:

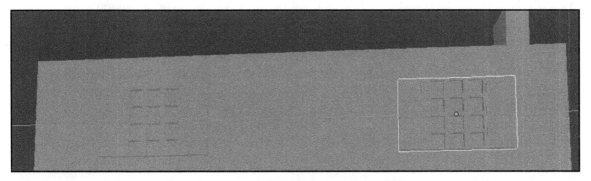

Moving the copy to its new spot

You will need to rotate some of the copies as you did with the torus in `Chapter 4`, *Flattening a Torus and Boolean Union*. With the house, we'll be rotating around the Z (blue) axis and usually an increment of 90 degrees. For a window on the left side of my house, I would rotate it -90 degrees (or 270); for a window on the right side of my house, 90 degrees:

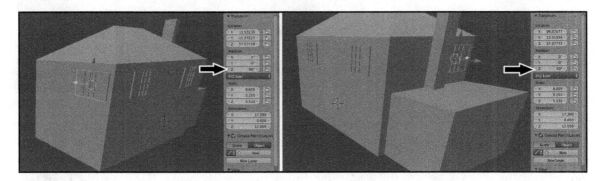

Rotation of copies for the left side and the right side of the house

The steps to rotate would be as follows:

1. In **Object Mode**, right-click on the window you wish to rotate
2. Hit the *R* key for rotate and the *Z* key to tell Blender to rotate around the Z axis
3. Type in the degree

Perfecting the positioning with Snap

As with the text on the coordinate bracelet, we do not want to cause confusion with overlapping geometry. We want our windows to line up exactly and lay flush to the house itself. In Chapter 7, *Customizing with Text*, we typed in the exact location coordinate to line the text up. You can still do that with the windows. The only catch is you'll first want to change the Object Origin to a specific vertex as we did in Chapter 5, *Building a Base with Standard Meshes and a Mirror*. Specifically, you want to move the Object Origin from the center of the window to a point you want to lie directly on the house. Once that is done, you match up the applicable coordinates. In the following example, I make sure the X coordinate of the window matches the X coordinate of a point on the left side of the house:

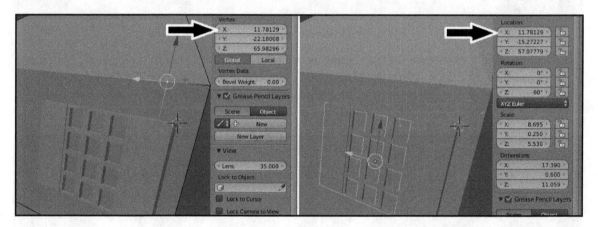

Windows can be lined up by changing the Object Origin to a specific vertex and making sure that Location matches a vertex on the house

Another option is to take advantage of the Snap during transform icon, which looks like a little magnet at the bottom of the screen. When this icon is on, you can tell Blender to automatically move objects to the closest landmark of your choosing. For example, I can tell Blender to snap to the nearest face. When I do that and move my window, Blender will line the window up to the face nearest to my mouse. The steps are as follows:

1. If necessary, switch to **Object Mode**.
2. At the bottom of your screen, click on the magnet icon so the magnet is shaded red and active. Click on the Snap element icon directly to the right of the magnet to display the **Snap Element** menu. Select **Face**:

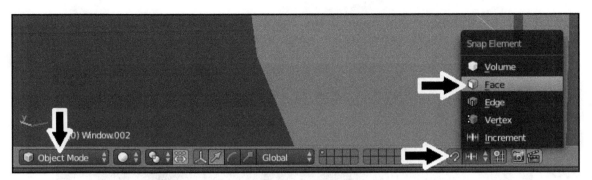

Telling Blender to snap to the nearest face

3. Right-click on your window to select it. Using the axis arrows and your mouse, drag and drop the window toward the house. You may notice the window making a dramatic hop to the nearest wall. A yellow circle helps identify what Blender will be snapping to. Release the mouse to apply:

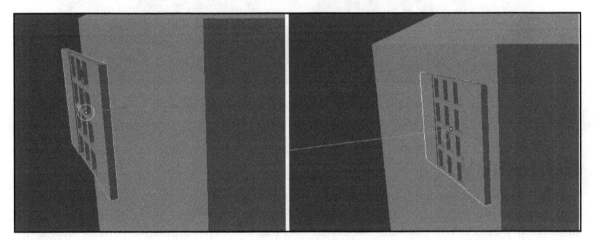

The window snaps into place

Without checking coordinates or changing Object Origins, my window lies flush on the house.

Armed with the techniques illustrated in this chapter, I can make and position the remaining windows, doors, and stairs for my grandfather's house:

Using the same techniques, more details are added to my grandfather's house

Summary

In this chapter, you got hands-on practice with mesh modeling techniques. You learned how to make multiple cuts with Loop Cut and Slide. You learned how to dissolve unnecessary edges. You used the Subdivide and Inset tools to emphasize your details. You got more practice extruding, duplicating, and rotating. You learned how to organize your work by renaming objects in the Outliner window. Finally, you learned about the Snap during transform icon and how it can expedite lining your objects up.

In the Chapter 10, *Making Textures with the Array Modifier and Scalable Vector Graphics*, you are going to learn two techniques to model textures. You'll learn about the Array Modifier for brickwork and how to import **Scalable Vector Graphic** (**SVG**) files to make stonework.

10
Making Textures with the Array Modifier and Scalable Vector Graphics

The windows and doors help make the house figurine recognizable. Adding textures, such as brickwork and stonework, will further elevate the piece and make it come alive. In this chapter, you will make large sheets of textures for use in `Chapter 11`, *Applying Textures with Boolean Intersection*. You will learn two techniques to make those textures. First, you will learn about the Array Modifier and how it can be used to make patterns such as brickwork. Secondly, you will learn how to build off an existing **Scalable Vector Graphics** (`.svg`) file to make stonework. The skills you will use include:

- Adding an Array Modifier
- Adjusting the size and offset of an array
- Considering scale and its impact on arrays
- Adding multiple Array Modifiers for more complex patterns
- Using the **File** | **Import** menu option to bring SVG files into your project
- Locating hidden objects by using the **Outliner** and the **Properties Shelf**

Making brickwork with the Array Modifier

My grandfather's house is mostly composed of bricks. A single brick is easy to model. It is simply a rectangle, a resized cube in Blender. The toughest part of modeling a brick is determining its size. For the X and the Z dimension, I'll pick sizes relative to the house itself and keep the general proportions you'd see in a real brick. For the Y dimension, my detail height, I'm going to make it slightly less pronounced than the detailing we made in Chapter 9, *Mesh Modeling and Positioning the Details*. The final sizes I decided on are:

Dimension	Size
X	1.5 mm
Y	0.4 mm
Z	0.6 mm

We'll start our brickwork with a single brick. The steps are:

1. If necessary, switch to **Object Mode** and left-click to move the 3D Cursor to where you want to create the brick. This does not need to be near or on the house yet.
2. In the **Tool Shelf** on the left-hand side of the screen, look under the **Create** tab, and under **Add Primitive** click **Cube**.
3. In the **Properties Shelf**, under **Transform**, type in the desired **Dimensions**. I type in 1.5 for **X**, 0.4 for **Y**, and 0.6 for **Z**.
4. In the **Outliner** window on the right side of the screen, double-click the new **cube** and type in a more meaningful name:

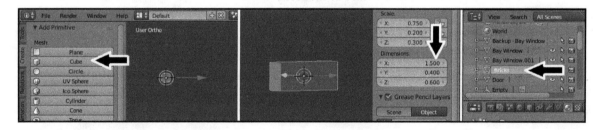

Making the first brick by adding, resizing, and renaming a cube.

Adding an Array Modifier

To change this single brick to an entire wall of bricks, we are going to use a tool called the **Array Modifier**. The Array Modifier can take a single object and make a repeating pattern:

The impact of Array Modifiers

Like the Mirror Modifier and the Boolean Modifier, Blender gives you a series of settings that can impact the behavior. The Array Modifier is quite powerful and has the ability to make complex patterns, even adding rotation and scaling into the mix. Today, we are going to only concentrate on a handful of properties.

Picking the Fit Type

The **Fit Type** is how Blender is going to determine how many times to copy your base object. The default is **Fixed Count** where you specifically type in how many objects you want. If I type in a **Count** of 5, for example, I will end up with five total bricks.

In the following example, I'm also adjusting the **Relative Offset** for the **X** dimension to **1.3**. Right now, this is for illustrative purposes to help you see the individual bricks. We'll dig more into spacing the bricks in the *Setting the Offset* section:

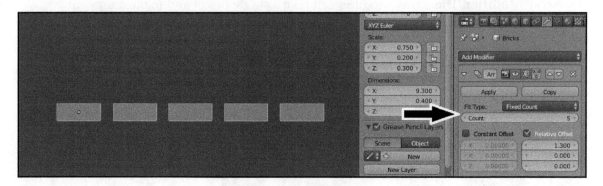

Array Modifier using a Fit Type of Fixed Count.

Another option pertinent to our brickwork is **Fixed Length**, where you tell Blender the final size you desire and it calculates how many objects you need. Let's take the example of 1.5mm bricks with 0.5mm gaps between each one. If I set the **Fixed Length** to **10**, Blender does all the math, and figures out that 5 bricks will be needed to fill that length:

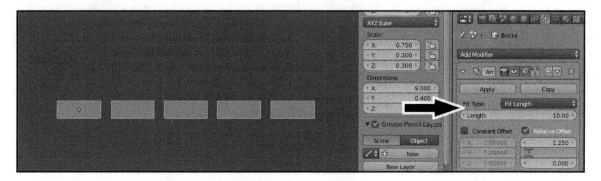

Array Modifier using a Fit Type of Fixed Length.

Ultimately, I want to make sure my sheet of bricks exceeds the dimensions of the largest wall of my house. I could use either the **Fixed Count** or the **Fixed Length** option, as long as I make sure the number of bricks will provide enough coverage. This may take some trial and error, particularly with the **Fixed Count**:

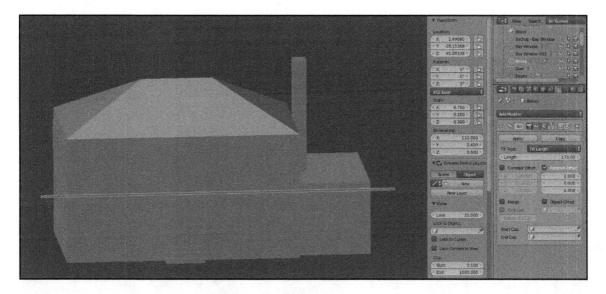

The ultimate goal is to have a row of bricks as long as the house.

Understanding the impact of scale on the Array Modifier

As you experiment with the Array Modifier and work with measurement settings, such as **Fixed Length** and **Constant Offset**, you may notice some unexpected results. The Array Modifier is set up to keep its proportions intact should you later resize and scale your original object. Blender achieves this by applying measurements such as **Fixed Length** to what the object would be at a perfect 1, 1, 1 scale. Blender will then multiply those numbers by the real, current scale of the object.

My brick started out as a 2 mm by 2 mm by 2 mm cube that I scaled to have the shape and size I wanted. The current scale along the X axis is 0.75. If I put in a **Fit Length** of **100**, the resulting row of bricks comes out smaller at **75.6**. When Blender adjusted the **Fit Length** for the current scale of the cube, it determined the resulting row of bricks needs to cover at least 75 mm *(100 * 0.75)* of space:

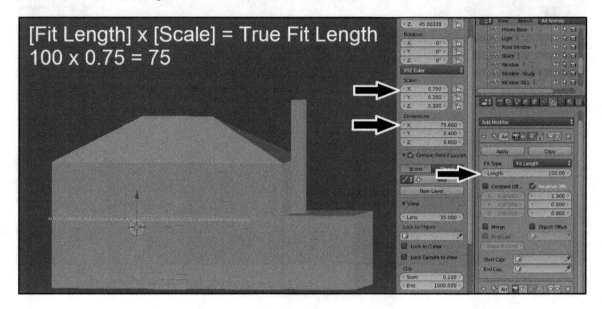

Fit Length multiplied by the appropriate Scale determines the true Fit Length.

This can be mitigated with trial and error or by adjusting your math. If the longest wall of my house is 114 mm and my brick is at a 0.75 scale, I want my **Fit Length** to be 152mm to get full coverage: *114 / 0.75 = 152*

Another option is to tell Blender to take a current snapshot of the object and its current sizing and make that the new scale of 1, 1, 1. The steps to apply the current scale of your brick are:

1. In **Object Mode**, right-click your object to select it
2. Under the **Object** menu at the bottom of the screen, go to **Apply** and click **Scale**:

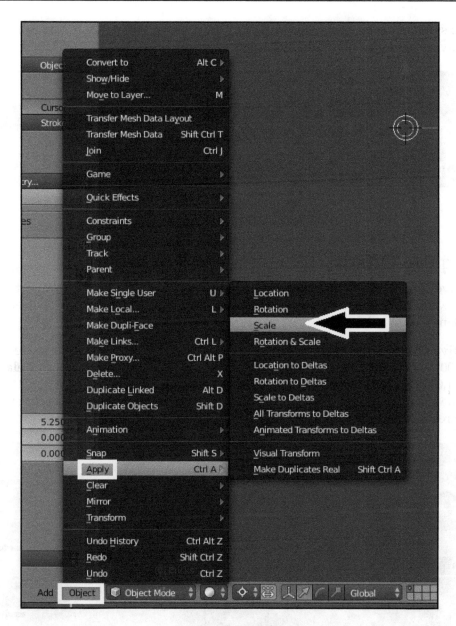

Applying the current scale

The dimensions of the brick stay the same, but the scale is now standardized to 1, 1, 1 making any future math substantially easier:

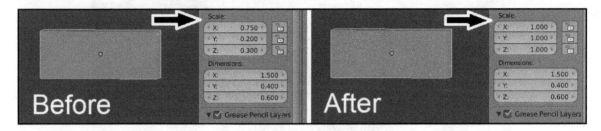

The impact of Apply I Scale on the brick.

Setting the Offset

Blender gives you many options to determine how far to space your copies apart. For our purposes, we'll focus on the **Relative Offset** and **Constant Offset** that can be used independently or together.

The **Relative Offset** defines the spacing based on a percentage of the object's size. 1.0 is the same as 100% of the object's original dimension. If my object is 1.5mm long, a **Relative Offset** of 1.0 would move the copy over exactly 1.5mm. The copy begins where the original ends. In the case of our brick, it would produce a large rectangle. Increasing that value would increase the gap between the bricks:

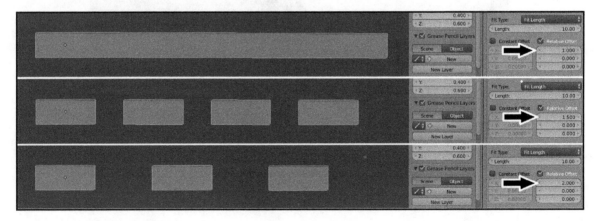

The impact of increasing the Relative Offset.

You could do all your spacing with **Relative Offset** if you wanted. For example, an **X** offset of **1.3** looks fitting for my bricks:

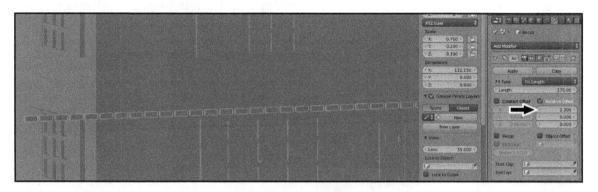

A row of bricks with a Relative Offset of 1.3.

Another option is to use the **Constant Offset**. The **Constant Offset** is actual Blender units (which we are using as millimeters) instead of a percentage. Like **Fixed Length**, this is the measurement when the object is at a perfect 1, 1, 1 scale. I am going to assume we have already applied the scale for simplified math (See *Understanding the Impact of Scale on the Array Modifier*). If my brick is 1.5 mm long and I want a gap of 0.5 mm between each brick, that would be a **Constant Offset** of *2.00 (1.5 + 0.5)*:

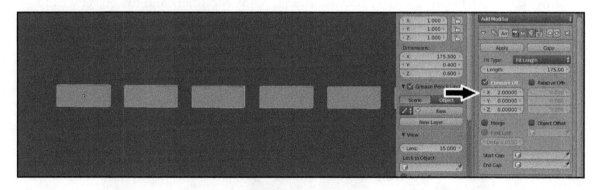

Spacing the bricks with just Constant Offset.

Finally, you can use both **Relative Offset** and **Constant Offset** together. Blender will apply the **Relative Offset** first and then apply the **Constant Offset**. As mentioned before, a **Relative Offset** of 1.0 will move 100% of the item's current length/height/depth on that axis. If I set a **Relative Offset** of 1.0 and a **Constant Offset** of 0.5 (again assuming the scale of the object is 1, 1, 1), then Blender will move the copy the full length of the object plus an additional 0.5 mm:

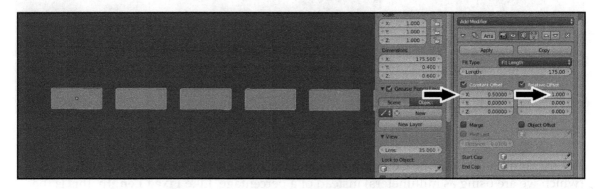

Spacing the bricks with Constant Offset and Relative Offset together.

Using **Relative Offset** and **Constant Offset** together allows you to concentrate on the gap you want and not have to know or think about the current length of your object. This becomes particularly helpful as we add additional Array Modifiers and the object we are using to make the pattern becomes more complex.

Nesting Array Modifiers

You can add more than one Array Modifier to build off the existing pattern. Once we have a row of bricks, for example, we can add another Array Modifier, set the **Z** offset, and easily make additional rows. However, in real life the bricks are staggered and alternate between every row:

Real life bricks are staggered.

A solution is three total Array Modifiers:

- One to copy the single brick to make a row of bricks
- One to copy that row just once and offset it so they are staggered with the first
- One to copy our pair of staggered rows so they alternate back and forth:

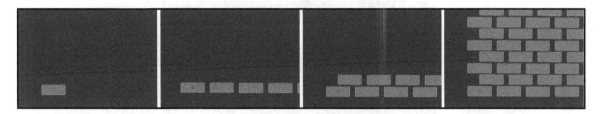

The original brick and the impact of successive Array Modifiers.

My desired effect can be achieved solely with **Relative Offset**, solely with **Constant Offset**, or with a combination of the two. I decide to aim for a gap of 0.3 mm between each brick and to use a combination of offsets for all three Array Modifiers. The steps I take are:

1. If necessary switch to **Object Mode** and right-click your object to select it.
2. For easier math, go to the **Object | Apply | Scale** menu option to make the current sizing the 1, 1, 1 scale.
3. In the **Properties Window**, click the wrench icon to access your **Modifiers**. Click the **Add Modifier** drop-down and then select **Array**:

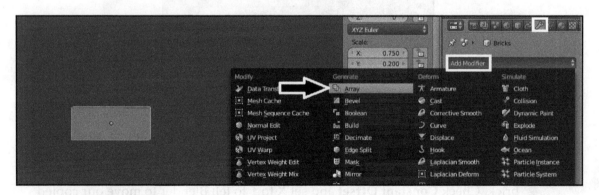

Adding a new Array Modifier

4. Set the **Fit Type** to **Fit Length** and type in a value to match or exceed the longest wall of the house. In my case, I type 114. Set the **Relative Offset** for **X** to 1.0 tell Blender to move over the entire length of the brick. Check **Constant Offset** and for **X** type 0.3 to tell Blender to move the copied bricks an additional 0.3 mm:

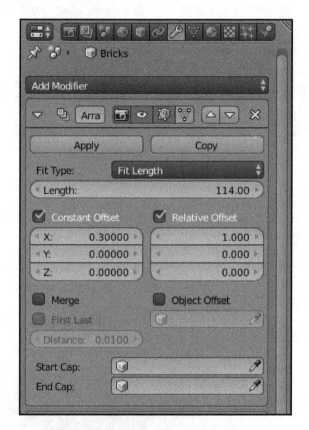

Setting a Relative Offset of 1 and a Constant Offset of 0.3

5. Click the **Add Modifier** drop-down and select **Array**.
6. This time, keep the **Fit Type** to **Fixed Count** and set the **Count** to 2. Blender will only make one additional row of bricks. For the **Relative Offset,** set **X** to 0 and set **Z** to 1 to tell Blender to move copies of the row up the exact height of the brick. Check **Constant Offset** and set **X** to 1 to tell Blender to move our copied row over 1 mm along the *X* axis to offset it with the previous row. Set **Z** to 0.3 to make a gap of 0.3mm between the two rows:

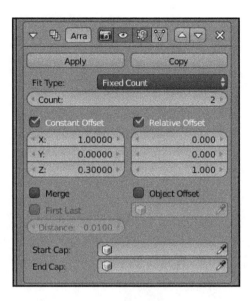

Setting the offsets of the second array

3. Click the **Add Modifier** drop-down and select **Array**.

4. Set the **Fit Type** to **Fit Length** and type in a value to match or exceed the highest wall of the house. In my case, I type 70. For **Relative Offset**, set **X** to 0 and set **Z** to 1 to tell Blender to move copies of the pair of staggered rows up their exact height. Check **Constant Offset** and set **Z** to 0.3 to put a gap of 0.3mm between the pair of brick rows:

Setting the offsets of the final array

3. Preview your work. When satisfied, click the **Apply** button for each Array Modifier in the order they were added, from top to bottom:

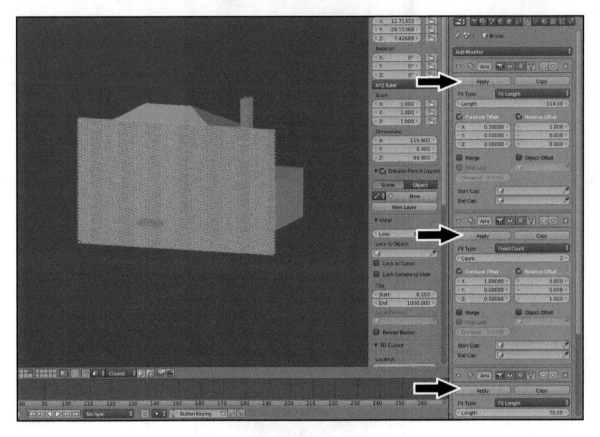

Applying the arrays in order

When you are done, you have a nice sheet of bricks you can use in Chapter 11, *Applying Textures with Boolean Intersection,* to add brickwork to the house figurine.

The Array Modifier can help with detailing

The Array Modifier can help with any repeating or patterned portion of your model. One example is the railing for a deck:

Railing is another good use of the Array Modifier

Importing a Scalable Vector Graphics file for stonework

You don't necessarily have to recreate the wheel and model your texture templates from scratch. As you have seen with the reference images, Blender has the ability to import external files to help further your work. Another helpful file format is SVG files. Rather than using pixels, vector files build their images out of shapes and paths, allowing them to change sizes without pixelation or deforming like straight image files would. The path nature of SVG files translate well to Bezier curves.

If I were to model the stonework from scratch, I would likely start with a series of Bezier curves, like we did in Chapter 2, *Using a Background Image and Bezier Curves*, and use them to trace out the individual stones. However, if I make or find an SVG file of a pattern I like, I can import that into Blender rather than modeling the stones from scratch. Once imported, I have all the capabilities of normal Bezier curves without the work of setting up control points and handles.

Making Your Own SVG Files

If you have an image, drawing, or logo you'd like to incorporate into your 3D models, there are tools to help you turn it into an SVG file. One example is the open source vector graphics editor, Inkscape. It has a learning curve comparable to Blender's. If you can learn Blender, you can learn Inkscape. Inkscape is free and has the ability to trace paths of regular images and save them as Plain SVG files. More information can be found at https://inkscape.org.

In my case, I have an existing SVG file of stonework I think will look nice on my model:

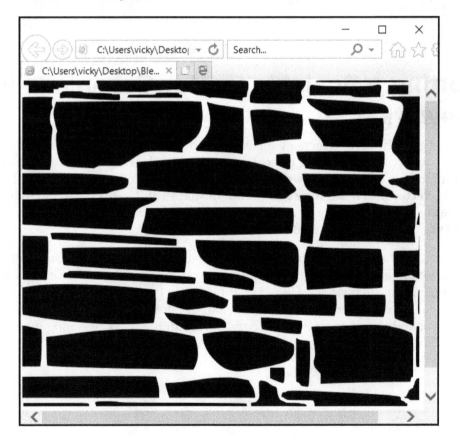

An example of an SVG file in a web browser.

The steps to import an SVG file into Blender are:

1. In the top menu, go to **File | Import** and pick **Scalable Vector Graphics (.svg)**:

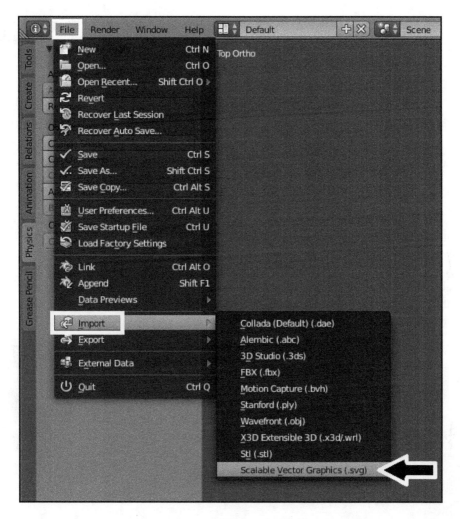

Telling Blender to import a SVG file

2. Using the white arrow and folder icons, browse your computer's file system to find where you downloaded or saved the SVG file. Select the file and click **Import SVG**:

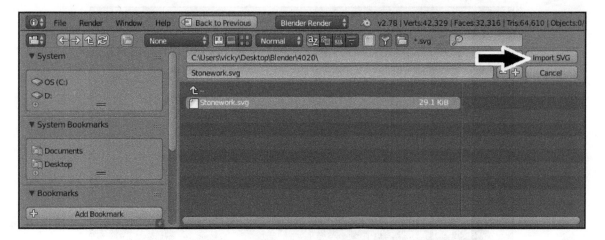

Picking the SVG file to import

Immediately, you'll see at least one new "Curve" in your **Outliner**. At first glance, you may not see that curve in your 3D View. Newly imported curves are often very small compared to the other objects you've been modeling:

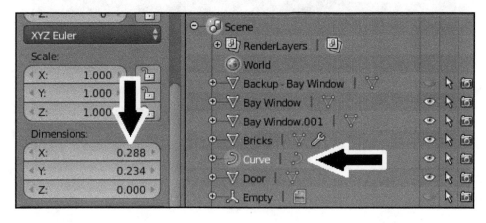

SVG files imported as new Bezier curves are often quite small

You can always use the mouse scroll wheel to zoom in and find your newly imported curve. However, it may be faster just resize it.

Using the Outliner and Properties Shelf to find objects

You can hit the *S* key and scale the newly imported curve with your mouse. I find it easier, particularly with the small-sized SVG files, to type in a new **Scale** in the **Properties Shelf**. The steps are:

1. By default, newly imported SVG files should be already selected. If not, make sure you are in **Object Mode** and in the **Outliner** window, you can left-click the object to select it even if you can't see it in the 3D View window:

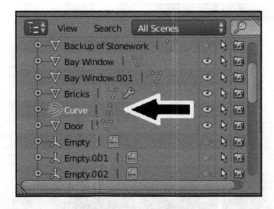

Clicking objects in the Outliner will select them

2. In the **Properties Shelf**, under **Transform**, change the **Scale** for **X**, **Y**, and **Z** to equally large numbers. I type in 50 for each axis:

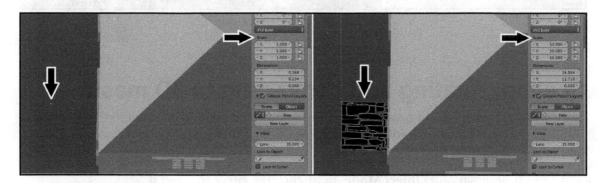

Scaled larger, the imported SVG file is visible

If the curve still alludes you, try switching to the Top viewpoint as imported SVG files are added to the X-Y plane. Another helpful technique is setting the Object Origin to the middle of the imported design, and then use the **Location** section of the **Properties Shelf** to move it to predictable spot like **0,0,0**. The steps are:

1. In **Object Mode** with the curve selected, go to the **Object | Transform | Origin to Center of Mass**.

2. In the **Properties Shelf** on the right side of the screen, adjust the **Location** coordinates to a predictable spot. In my case, I set **X** to 0, **Y** to 0, and **Z** to 0. I then know to look for my curve at the intersection of the three axis lines:

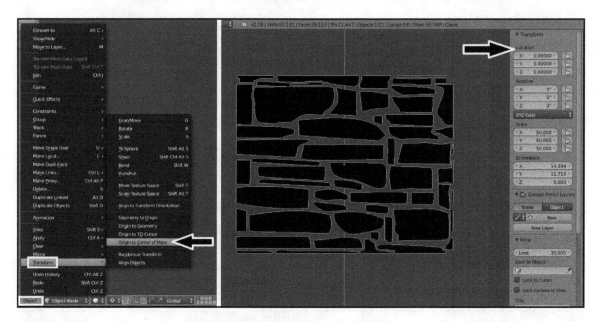

Setting the Object Origin to the center and giving it an easy-to-find position.

Scaling, rotating and converting to 3D mesh

Once located, I recommend rotating the curve so it can be better compared to the house's walls. In my case, I decide to rotate it 90 degrees along the X (red) axis so it matches up to the front of the house. The steps are:

1. If necessary, in **Object Mode**, right-click the curve to select it.

2. In the **Properties Shelf** on the right-hand side of the screen, type in a **Rotation** value for **X**. I type in 90. Alternatively, you can type *R* on the keyboard for rotate, X to tell Blender to rotate over the X axis, and then type 90:

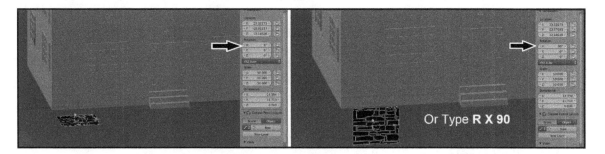

Rotate the imported SVG file for better comparison.

You can move the imported stonework closer to the house and, if necessary, scale it to a more desirable size:

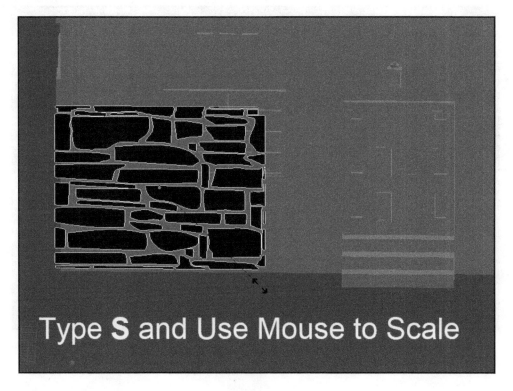

Scaling with the mouse to a desired size.

At this point, we are in familiar territory. We have a Bezier curve we want to convert to a 3D mesh and then we'll want to use the Extrude tool to set it to our decided detail height. Staying consistent with the bricks, I will set that to 0.4 mm. The process is identical to the Profile Pendant in `Chapter 3`, *Converting a Bezier Curve to a Properly Sized 3D Mesh*. A summary of the steps are:

1. In **Object Mode**, right-click the curve to select it
2. On the menu at the bottom of the screen go to **Object | Convert to | Mesh from Curve/Meta/Surf/Text** to convert it to a 3D mesh
3. Switch to **Edit Mode** and if necessary, click the Vertex Select icon
4. Hit *A* to select all vertices
5. In the **Tool Shelf** on the left side of the screen, look under the **Tools** tab and click the **Extrude Region** button
6. Type in the desired height. In my case, I type `0.4`

When complete, I have a 3D mesh of my stonework:

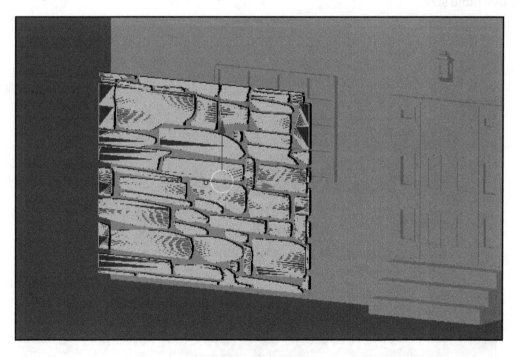

Stonework is now a 3D mesh.

Why is my SVG mesh colored?

Your imported SVG file may not be the usual grey you are used to with your other Blender objects. That is because it imported in with a **material** that gives it color. More on materials and colors will be discussed in `Chapter 14`, *Coloring Models with Materials and UV Maps*.

Combining with the Array Modifier

Like other Blender objects, the stonework can be combined with the Array Modifier. In my case, the SVG file was just a small tile of stone. By adding two Array Modifiers, I can make it a large sheet.

A summary of the steps are:

1. In **Object Mode**, right-click the curve to select it.
2. In the **Properties Window**, click the wrench icon to access your Modifiers. Click the **Add Modifier** dropdown and then select **Array**.
3. Under **Relative Offset**, keep the **X** set to 1. This ensures each new tile of the pattern starts where the last one left off. Keep the **Fit Type** as **Fixed Count** and increase the **Count** as needed.
4. Click the **Add Modifier** dropdown again and then select **Array**.

5. Under **Relative Offset**, set the **X** to 0 and the **Y** to 1. Keep the **Fit Type** as **Fixed Count** and increase the **Count** as needed:

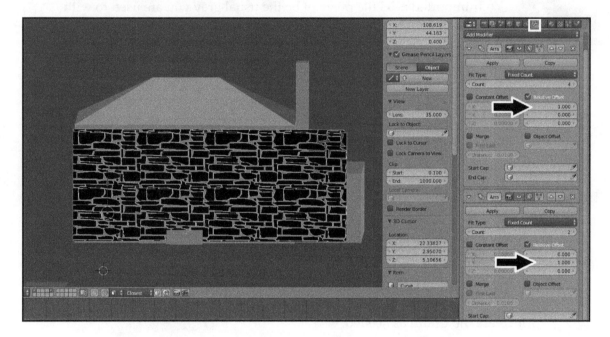

Combining the Array Modifier with an imported SVG files produces a larger sheet of stonework.

6. Once satisfied with the sizing, click **Apply** for both Array Modifiers:

With the completed sheet of stonework joining the bricks, we now have two sheets of textures and are ready to start applying them to the house:

Stonework and brickwork

Summary

In this chapter, you practiced two ways of making sheets of texture. You learned how the Array Modifier can take something as simple as a cube and transform it into a sheet of patterned bricks. You learned how to control the size and spacing of your pattern with Fit Type and offsets. You learned how an object's scale can impact the Array Modifier. For stonework, you imported an SVG file and converted it to a 3D mesh. Finally, you learned that both techniques can be combined and that the Array Modifier can be used with SVG files.

In Chapter 11, *Applying Textures with Boolean Intersection*, you'll learn about the third and final operation of the Boolean Modifier, the Intersection, and how it can be used to turn our large sheets of texture into the right sizes and shapes for the house.

11
Applying Textures with Boolean Intersection

In this chapter, you will embellish the house figurine by adding textures to the walls and chimney. By using Boolean Intersection, you'll turn the large sheets of brickwork and stonework from Chapter 10, *Making Textures with the Array Modifier and Scalable Vector Graphics*, into appropriate shapes for each wall of the house. In addition, you'll get hands-on experience with more mesh modeling techniques. The skills covered in this chapter include:

- Duplicating vertices
- Using the Separate function to move selected vertices, edges, and faces to a new object
- Joining multiple groups of vertices into a single object
- Adjusting vertex coordinates with scale and the Properties Shelf
- Drawing new edges from scratch
- Using Fill to make new faces
- Adding a Boolean Intersection Modifier

Making template shapes

You have seen how the Boolean Modifier can combine, or make a union of, two objects. You have also seen how it can subtract one object from another to get the difference. In this chapter, you will use the final capability of the Boolean Modifier, the ability to evaluate two objects and take the overlap, the intersection, of the two.

You can think of the intersection like the middle part of a Venn diagram. If I had a Venn diagram with one circle illustrating **3D Modeling Software** and another illustrating **Free Software**, Blender would be in the middle, in the intersection of the two:

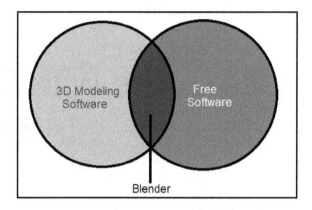

A Venn diagram on software. Blender would be in the middle overlap

Similarly, if we had two cylinders in Blender and we took the intersection, we would be left with just the eye-shaped piece where both cylinders overlapped:

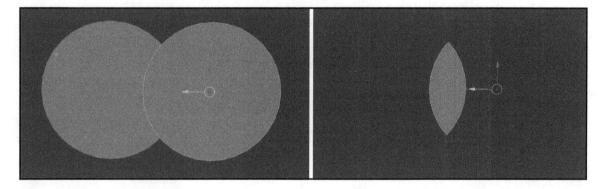

Two cylinders and their intersection

The Boolean Intersection is going to be a key tool as we apply the stonework and brickwork from Chapter 10, *Making Textures with the Array Modifier and Scalable Vector Graphics*, to our house. We are going to start by making templates of where we want the texture. These will not be mere copies of the walls. Since we don't want brickwork on places like our windows, we'll want cutouts for all the places we don't want texture. Once we have our template, we can pull in our texture and get the intersection of the two objects:

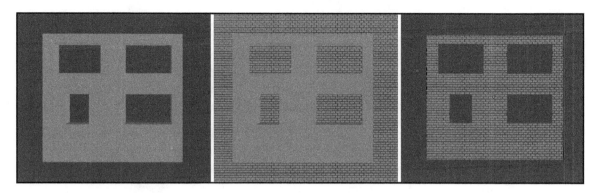

We start with a template with cutouts for windows and doors. After taking an intersection with the sheet of bricks, we get a brick wall.

We'll be left with the texture we can apply flush to the original face of the house and be assured that the other detailing, such as windows, doors, and stairs will still be visible:

The brickwork allows for the window detailing to show through

We begin by making those starting templates.

Duplicating and separating vertices

One of the surest ways to ensure your cutouts and outlines are perfectly sized for the house is to use the exact same vertex placement. The **Duplicate** feature we used earlier to copy windows also works in **Edit Mode** on vertices, edges, and faces. We don't need to copy every vertex, just enough to make the new templates we need.

Let's look at the stonework for the front of the house. It is only on the bottom of the house, which currently houses two windows, a door, some stairs, and the bottom of an outside light. To make a template for where I will want the stonework, I will ultimately need copies of:

- Four outside corners of the bottom front of the house
- Four outside corners of the two windows
- Since the stairs and door are so close and we don't need stonework between them, the two top corners of the door and the two bottom corners of the stairs
- Since the outside light only partially extends into the stonework, only the four vertices that will be inside the stonework:

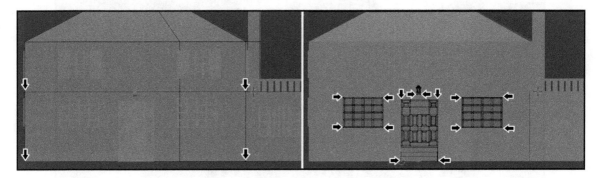

Vertices that will make up our the stonework template

When selecting vertices from the detailing, such as windows and doors, it is ideal to pick a point flush with the house itself to ensure all points on the new template are all on the same plane, as shown in the following image. If small mistakes are made, we can use Blender's scale feature (steps will follow) to make corrections:

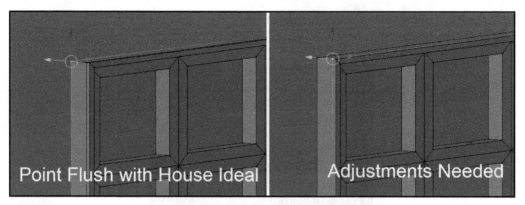

It is ideal to pick a point flush with the base of the house.

For each item, we'll use the multi-select capabilities described in Chapter 6, *Cutting Half Circle Holes and Modifier Management*, to select each applicable vertex. We'll duplicate those vertices and then immediately use another Blender function to separate the copied vertices into a new object. The steps are as follows:

1. In **Object Mode**, right-click on the object to select it. Initially, select the house base. Later, you may be selecting a window or door object.
2. Switch to **Edit Mode** and make sure you are in **Vertex Select** mode.
3. Right-click on the first applicable vertex to select it. Holding down the *Shift* key, right-click on the remaining required vertices:

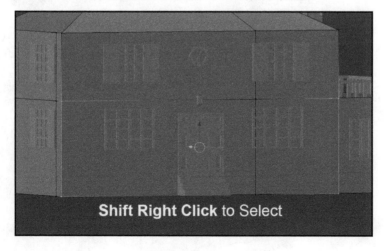

Selecting key vertices to copy.

4. In the **Tool Shelf** on the left side of the screen, look under the **Tools** tab, and click on **Duplicate**. Blender creates copies of each selected vertex:

Hitting the Duplicate button to make a copy.

5. The new copies are selected by default. To tell Blender to separate them, go to the **Mesh** menu at the bottom of the screen. Next, go to **Vertices | Separate | Selection**:

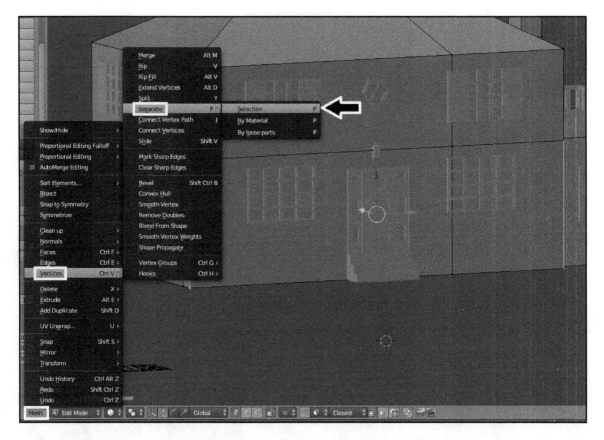

The Mesh | Vertices | Separate | Selection menu will move the selection to a new object.

There is now a new object in the Outliner window containing just those copied vertices. Since it is perfectly aligned with the existing vertices, it may be hard to see. You can turn off the visibility of the original object to get a better look:

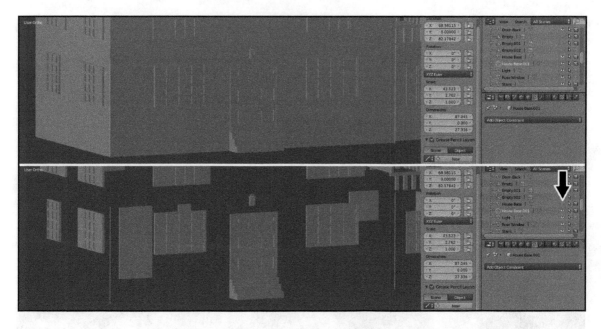

Turning off the visibility of the original object helps you to evaluate your work

I can repeat these steps for the details I will want to cut out, such as the windows and the outdoor light:

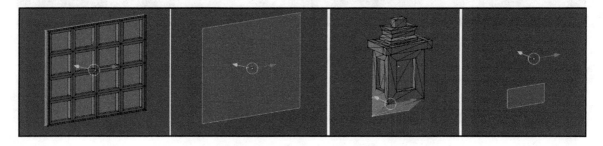

Repeating steps by duplicating and separating vertices from a window and a light

Joining and separating objects as a shortcut

In Chapter 4, *Flattening a Torus and Boolean Union*, we compared the **Object** | **Join** feature with the Boolean Union. In the profile pendant project, the pendant and the hook overlapped, leading to some confusing extra vertices and edges left inside when **Object** | **Join** was used.

This project presents us with a solid and safe use case for **Object** | **Join**. The windows and doors of the house do not overlap with each other. This allows them to be joined and later they can be separated back out using the same **Mesh** | **Vertices** | **Separate** function we have been using.

You could use this to help expedite your work of copying vertices for the cutouts. You could join all the detail objects you want to cut out from this particular section of house. This would allow you to select and copy all the cutout vertices at once and would minimize the back-and-forth between **Object Mode** and **Edit Mode**.

These steps are certainly not required. Should you wish to join your details, the steps are as follows:

1. In **Object Mode**, right-click on the first detail object to select it. Holding down the *Shift* key, right-click on the remaining detail objects to select them as well.

2. In the **Object** menu at the bottom of the screen, select **Join**:

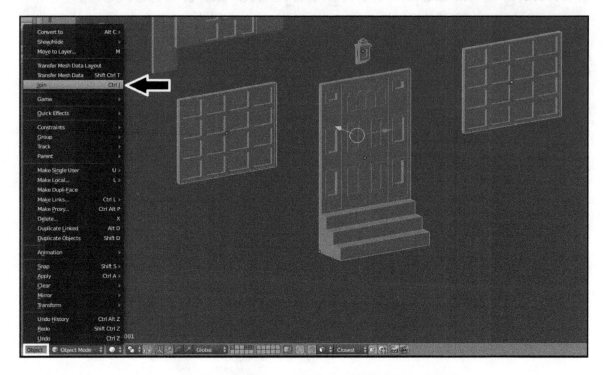

Individual objects can be combined into one with Object | Join

The selected objects are now considered one object. As a result, all their vertices are available for selection in **Edit Mode** and can be duplicated and separated in one trip:

With Object | Join, all vertices can be duplicated and separated at once

At this point in this project, there is really no need to have these objects separate. There is no harm in leaving them joined for the remainder of the project. If you do need to manipulate a single object, the joined items can be separated back out with the following steps:

1. In **Object Mode**, right-click on the joined object you wish to break out into parts.
2. Switch to **Edit Mode**.
3. In the **Mesh** menu at the bottom of the screen, select **Vertices | Separate | By loose parts**. This tells Blender to find all the individual parts and separate them that way:

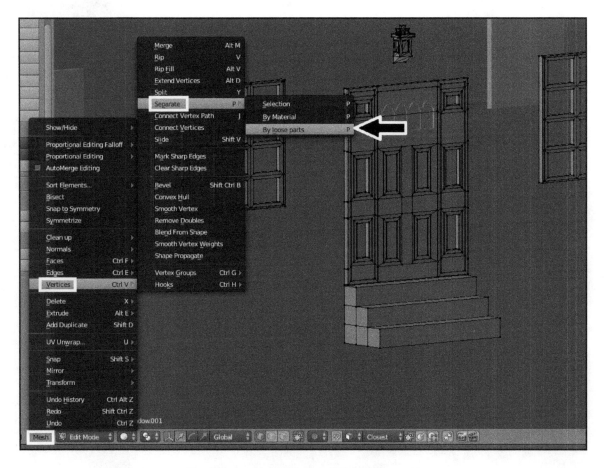

Grouped objects can be separated back out with Separate | By loose parts.

Your original detail objects are separated back out into individual objects.

Downsides of joining and separating

There are some downsides to joining and separating. When you join objects, they are consolidated under a single name. When you separate them back out, they do not regain their original names. After this process, for example, what was once named **Stairs** may now be named **Bay Window.001**. This can be corrected by renaming them in the Outliner if desired:

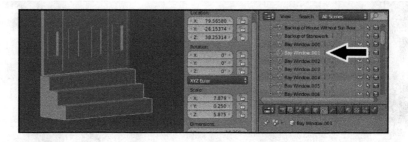

Separated objects are named after their parent

In addition, separated objects don't regain their original Object Origin. The Object Origin for the newly-separated objects may not even be on the object itself. The Object Origin of the door, for example, is now far off to the right in the center of one of the windows, as shown here. This can be corrected by using the **Object | Transform | Origin to Center of Mass** menu option:

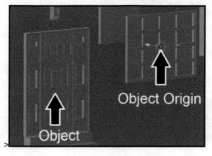

Separated objects may have unexpected Object Origins

Joining and making new faces

Once all the vertices we need for the template are copied, we'll want to join them together into a single object. The steps are as follows:

1. If necessary, switch to **Object Mode**.
2. It might be helpful to temporarily hide the original objects. In the **Outliner** window on the right side of the screen, click on the eye icon to the right of any object to toggle its visibility.
3. Right-click on one of the objects with copied vertices to select it. Holding down the *Shift* key, right-click on the remaining copied objects to select them.
4. In the **Object** menu at the bottom of the screen, click **Join** to make the selections into a single object:

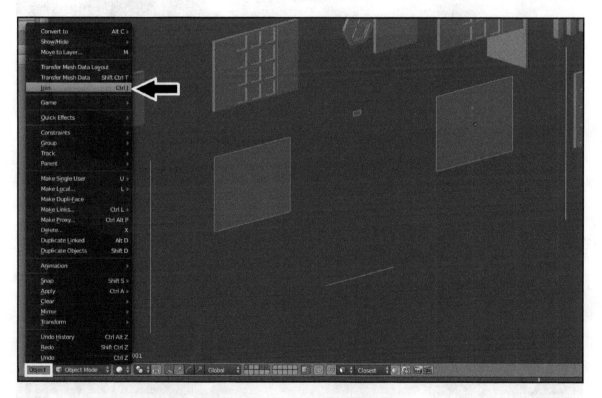

Using Join to consolidate all our selections into a single object.

Once all the vertices needed for the new template are joined into a single object, the next task is to put together new edges and faces.

Deleting unnecessary faces and edges

Depending on the copied vertices, some faces may have copied over too. You can see an example of that with the two windows. Square faces for the windows copied over, but since you don't want stonework over your windows, you want those sections to be holes or cutouts. You first need to delete the unnecessary faces. The steps are as follows:

1. If necessary, in **Object Mode**, right-click on the object to select it and switch to **Edit Mode**.
2. Click on the Face Select icon and right-click on the face you wish to remove to select it:

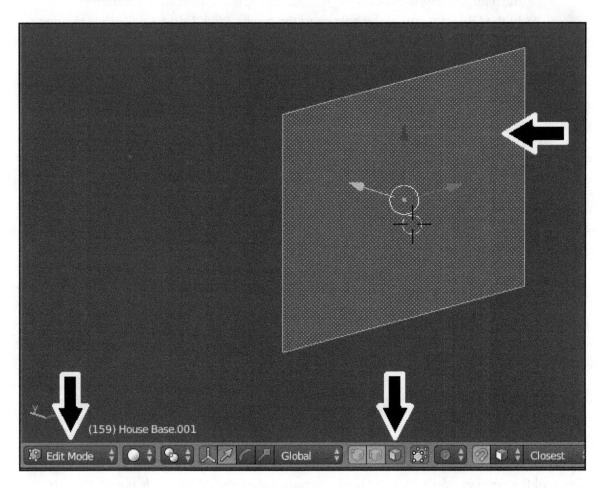

Selecting a face to remove

3. Click the *Delete* key on your keyboard. A menu prompt will ask you for more specifics. Select **Only Faces** to delete just the faces and leave the edges and vertices in place:

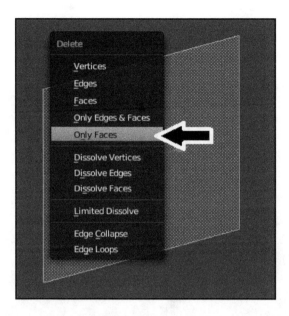

Telling Blender to only delete the faces

It is also possible unwanted edges were copied over. An example of this is the part of the outdoor light you copied. After you delete the two unwanted faces, there is still a diagonal edge remaining in the desired cutout. Since this will be a small divot at the top of your template, you can remove the top edge as well.

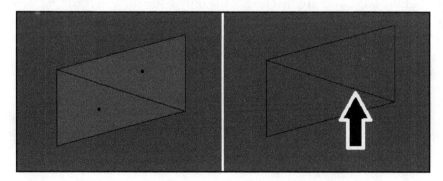

After deleting faces, an unwanted edge remains

The steps to delete any unwanted edges are as follows:

1. In **Edit Mode**, click on the Edge Select icon. Right-click on the unwanted edge to select it.
2. Hit the *Delete* key. If the vertices you wish to create are used by other edges, go ahead and pick **Edges** to delete just the edge. Because they are used elsewhere, the vertices will remain:

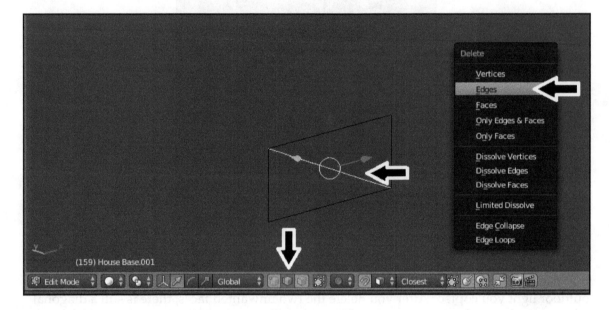

Deleting the extra edge.

In the event that the edge you are deleting is the only edge for a vertex, that vertex will also be removed. If you would like to preserve those vertices, choose the **Only Edges & Faces** option instead:

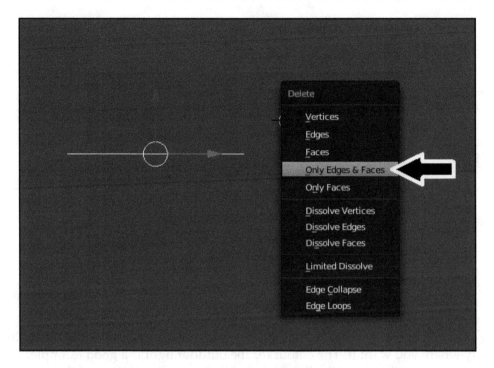

To keep the vertices in tact, choose Only Edges & Faces instead.

Adjusting vertex coordinates

There may be cases where adjusting the position of specific vertices may be necessary. One case is the situation where the vertices are not lined up on a flat plane. For example, perhaps you picked a corner of a shutter that was raised up and not flush with the base of the house. You could correct that situation quickly by using the Scale 0 process we used in `Chapter 4`, *Flattening a Torus and Boolean Union*. For a template based on the front of my house, I would want to make sure all the vertices are perfectly aligned and flat along the Y axis. The steps to make corrections are as follows:

1. In **Edit Mode,** click on the Vertex Select icon. Hit *A* to select all vertices.

2. Type S for scale, Y for along the Y axis, and **0** to make all the Y coordinates identical:

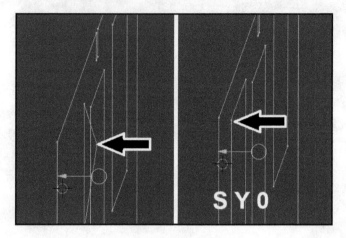

Vertices can be aligned by scaling to 0

Another situation is that perhaps detailing vertices are very close to the border outline, but not exactly where you want it. The cutout for the outdoor light is a good example. The vertices you have for the top of the light are slightly lower than the top of the outline. To achieve a perfectly horizontal line, you need to move those vertices up. One way you can accomplish that is to simply copy the Z position of a good vertex and paste it to the troubled one. The steps are as follows:

1. In **Edit Mode**, click on the Vertex Select icon. Right-click on a vertex with the desired position. In this case, I right-click on the top left corner of my face outline. In the **Properties Shelf**, under **Transform**, click on the **Vertex** coordinate you wish to copy. In this situation, click on the **Z** box. Hit *Ctrl + C* to copy that value:

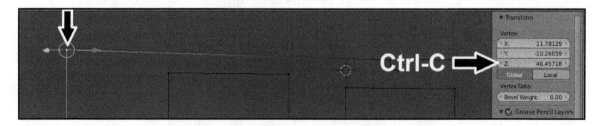

Copying the Z coordinate from a good vertex.

2. Right-click to select the vertex you wish to adjust. In the **Properties Shelf**, click on the **Vertex** coordinate you want to correct. Hit *Ctrl + V* to paste in the new value:

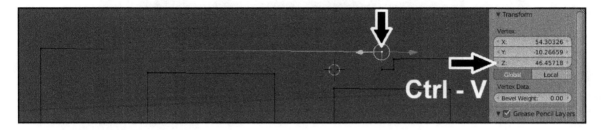

Pasting the desired Z coordinate in to move the vertex.

Creating new edges and filling faces

The next step is to add any missing edges we'll need for our outline. The steps to make new edges are as follows:

1. In **Edit Mode**, click on the Vertex Select icon and right-click on the first vertex of your new edge. Holding down the *Shift* key, right-click on the second vertex.
2. Hit *F* on the keyboard to make a new edge. Alternatively, you could also use the **Mesh | Faces | Make Edge/Face** menu option:

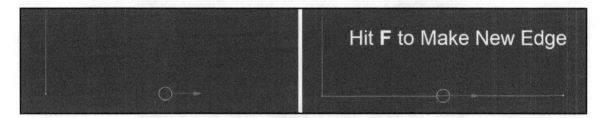

A new edge can be added between two vertices by hitting F

Repeat with any other missing edges. At the end of this process, the template is really starting to take shape and should be recognizable:

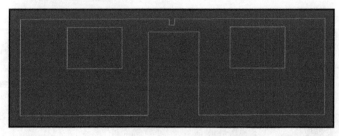

The new edges outline the shape of our template

In Chapter 3, *Converting a Bezier Curve to a Properly Sized 3D Mesh*, we used the **Make Edge/Face** option, with a keyboard shortcut of *F*, to make a new face. That feature worked great for the profile pendant. However, it does not account for holes in the new face. As a result, if we used it on our template, the new face would cover the holes for the windows:

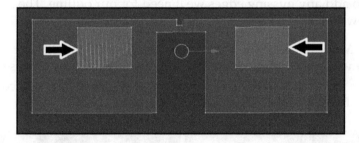

The normal Make Edge/Face feature will cover the holes for the windows

Blender also has an option called **Fill**. When used, Blender will create a series of triangular faces to fill the outline. That feature will adjust for holes:

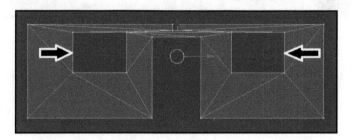

The Fill face feature supports holes

The steps to fill faces are as follows:

1. If necessary, in **Edit Mode**, click on the Vertex Select icon
2. Hit the *A* key to select all vertices
3. Under the **Mesh | Faces** menu option, click on **Fill**. Alternatively, you can hold down the *Alt + F* keys at the same time:

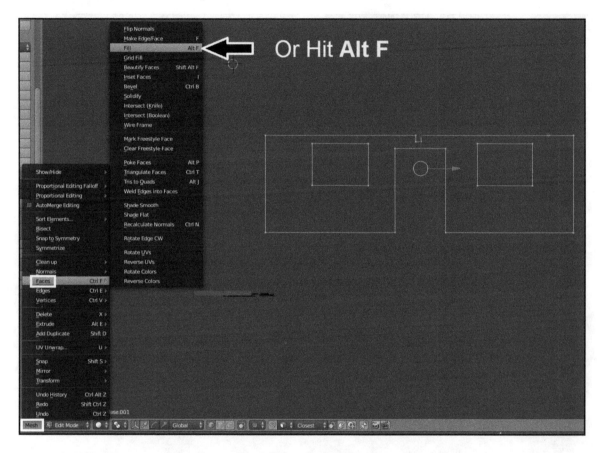

Using the Fill feature to make new faces

If you ever don't like the results you get with **Fill** and would prefer to have more control over the faces, you can always create your own extra edges. Using the multi-select techniques from Chapter 6, *Cutting Half Circle Holes and Modifier Management*, and the standard **Make Edge/Face** function, you can create the desired faces from scratch. For example, you can add some extra edges to the template and manually make five faces to preserve the window cutouts:

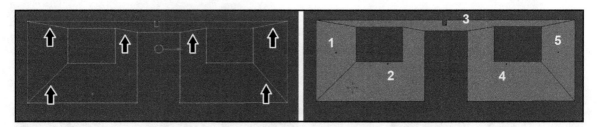

Extra edges can be added to have more control over the final faces

However you choose to make the faces, once you are satisfied, you will want to use **Extrude Region** to make them 3D. In the past, we have been very specific about how far we are extruding, often guided by the minimum wall thickness and the Design Requirements. In this case, we have the luxury of not having to worry about the specific height. We just have to make it thicker than the stonework we made in Chapter 10, *Making Textures with the Array Modifier and Scalable Vector Graphics*. Since we are taking an intersection, our final object is going to adopt the smaller height of the two, the height set up for the stonework.

The steps to extrude your new faces are:

1. In **Edit Mode**, click *A* to select all items (vertices, edges, or faces will all work)
2. In the **Tool Shelf**, on the left side of the screen, look under the **Tools** tab and click on **Extrude Region**

3. Use the mouse to size the template as you see fit and left-click or hit *Enter* to apply:

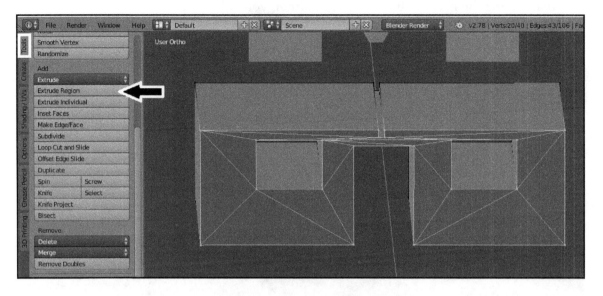

Extrude Region gives the wall some thickness.

Now that the faces are extruded, we have two objects we are ready to take an intersection of:

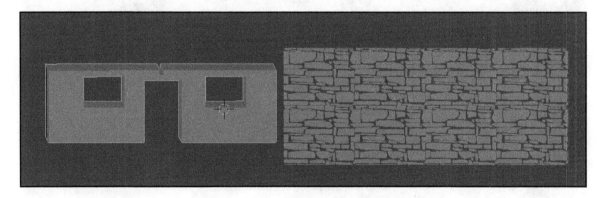

The new template and the stonework are ready for Boolean Intersection

Taking an intersection

Before applying the Boolean Intersection Modifier, you will want to make sure the two objects actually intersect. If they aren't touching each other at all, the intersection would be nothing. To put it into specifics for this project, we'll want to make sure the stonework is inside the new template mesh. Thanks to the copied vertices, we are assured that our new template object is aligned with the front of the house. It is ideal to keep that template in place and move the stonework to it. The steps are as follows:

1. If necessary, in the **Outliner**, click on the eye icon to make the stonework visible. Make sure you are in **Object Mode** and right-click on the stonework to select it.
2. Left-click and hold either the white circle or one of the axis arrows. Drag and drop the stonework so it overlaps the new template. In some cases, you may also have to rotate the stonework. That can be done by typing R and typing in the degrees, such as 90:

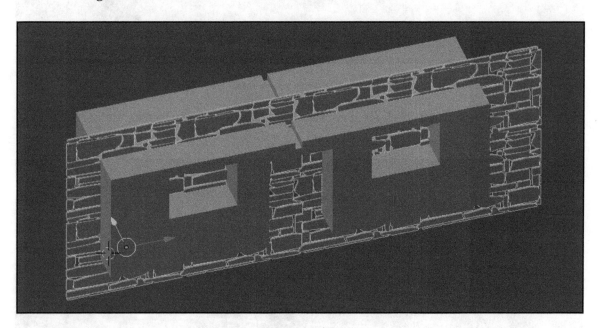

Moving the stonework so it lays inside the wall template

Adding a Boolean Intersection Modifier

The Boolean Intersection Modifier is added and edited the same way you did with the Boolean Union and Boolean Difference. As a reminder, the object the modifier is being applied to is the one that is going to be changed. We want to preserve the textures we built in `Chapter 10`, *Making Textures with the Array Modifier and Scalable Vector Graphics*, so they can be reused for other walls. This is particularly important with the brickwork that is prevalent in my grandfather's house. The shape template we made earlier in this chapter only needs to be used once. It is okay if that object permanently changes. That means we want to add the modifier to our template shape, and not to the sheet of stonework. The steps are:

1. If necessary, switch to **Object Mode** and right-click on the object you wish to change. In this case, select the shape template.
2. In the **Properties Window**, on the right-hand side of the screen, click on the wrench icon to access Modifiers. Under the **Add Modifier** dropdown, select **Boolean**:

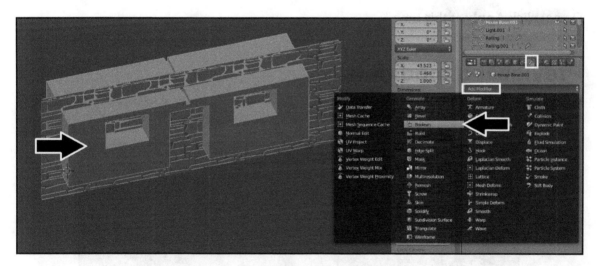

Adding a new Boolean modifier.

3. Leave the **Operation** as **Intersect**. For **Object**, select the object you would like to intersect with. In this case, select the stonework. Finally, for **Solver**, select **Carve**:

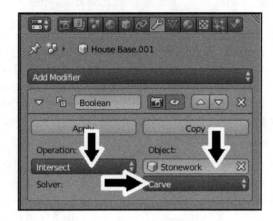

Picking the Intersect Operation, the Object, and the Solver.

Do not click **Apply** at this time.

Previewing modifiers

Before applying the modifier, it is beneficial to preview the results. As soon as you define the intersection, the yellow outline of your object will give you an idea of your work:

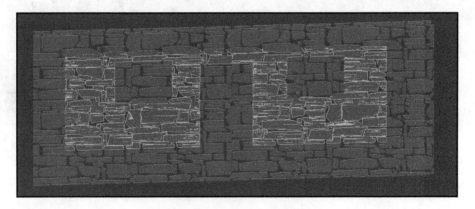

Object Mode previews the changes of the intersection

There are a couple of additional techniques to get a better view.

Switching viewport shading to wireframe

Just as you can change your viewport and viewing perspective, you can also tell Blender how to shade the objects on the screen by changing the **viewport shading**. By default, we have been working in **Solid** mode. The objects are displayed as solids with simple shading. Blender also has a **Wireframe** mode that only displays the vertices and edges. Without the faces and shading, you can often get a clearer view to evaluate your work:

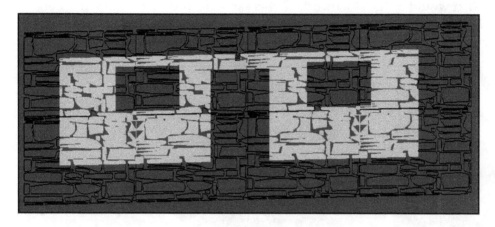

The intersection in Wireframe mode

You can change the viewport shading by:

1. In either **Edit Mode** or **Object Mode**, click on the icon directly to the right of the Interaction Mode dropdown. Select **Wireframe**. Alternatively, you can hit the Z key to toggle between the **Solid** and **Wireframe** modes:

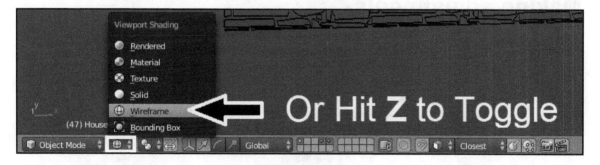

Switching to Wireframe mode

2. When you are ready to switch back, you can use the same dropdown and select **Solid** or hit *Z* again.

Hiding the supporting object

Another way to preview the intersection is to hide the supporting object that doesn't change. That would be the stonework, in this example. Just like we did in Chapter 6, *Cutting Half Circle Holes and Modifier Management*, you simply turn off the eye icon in the **Outliner** window. Hiding the stonework provides a better look at our changed object:

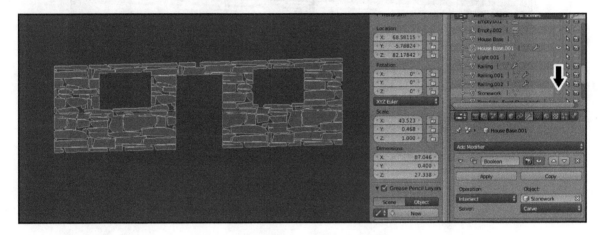

Hiding the stonework permits a better view of the new object

Making adjustments

Since you have not yet applied the modifier, you have the ability to make adjustments. If you don't like the placement of the stones, for example, you can scale or move the sheet of stonework until you get a look you like.

As you make adjustments to either object, Blender will recalculate the intersection in real time. This can be an intensive operation for Blender and cause delays or lags in your interface. You can better control when Blender makes those recalculations by turning the visibility of the modifier off during adjustments. The steps are as follows:

1. In **Object Mode**, right-click on the object with the modifier. With the current example, this is the template we made earlier in the chapter.

2. In the **Properties Window**, if necessary, click on the wrench icon to view Modifiers. Click on the eye icon above the modifier to turn it off. Blender will refresh the window showing the template's original shape:

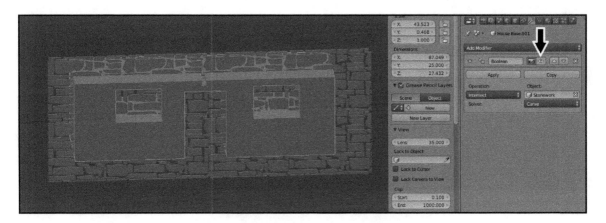

Turning off the eye icon will hide the effects of the intersection

3. Right-click on the object you wish to move to select it. In this case, you want to preserve the template's placement as it is already lined up with the rest of the house. You will want to move the sheet of stone texture instead. Use the white circle or the axis arrows to move the object as needed:

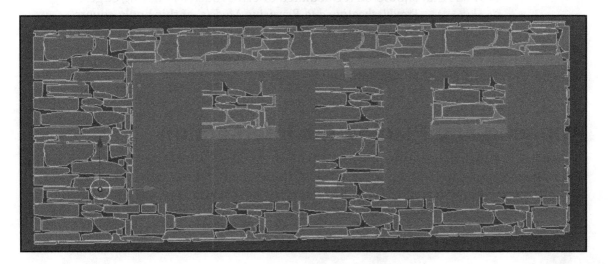

Moving the stonework

4. Right-click on the object with the modifier. Click on the eye icon above the modifier to turn it back on. Blender will recalculate and display the revised intersection:

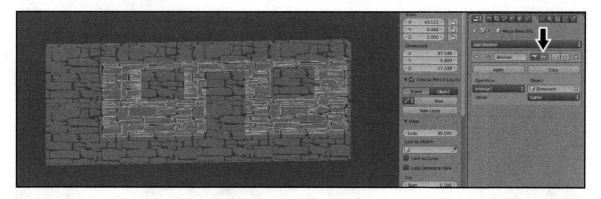

Turning the Boolean Modifier back on.

Boolean modifiers are picky

Like 3D printers, Blender's Boolean Modifier relies on face normals to determine the inside and outside of an object. If you get unexpected results with your intersection, it could be an indication your mesh has bad normals that should be recalculated or errors such as missing edges. Chapter 15, *Troubleshooting and Repairing Models*, of this book, covers troubleshooting and fixing those types of issues.

I can review my new work by hiding the stonework or switching to Wireframe mode. If necessary, I can make further adjustments.

Applying and Placing the Intersection

Once you are satisfied, you can apply the modifier. By taking advantage of the Snap during transform icon you used in Chapter 9, *Mesh Modeling and Positioning the Details*, you can then move the texture to be flush with the rest of the house. Since you directly copied vertices, your newly-textured template should already be lined up with the front of the house along the X and Z axes. You will only have to adjust the *y* axis.

The steps are:

1. In **Object Mode**, right-click to select the object with the modifier. In the **Properties Window**, under the wrench icon, click the **Apply** button:

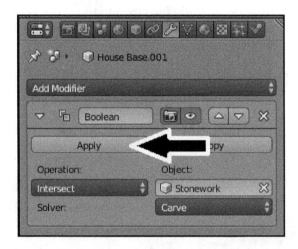

Applying the intersection and making the changes permanent.

2. In the Outliner window, turn off the visibility of the sheet of stonework so it is out of the way. If necessary, turn on the visibility of the base of the house:

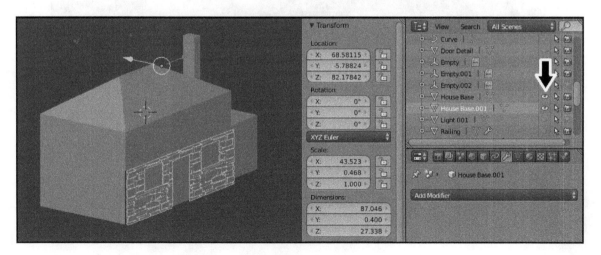

Hiding the sheet of stonework

3. Right-click on your newly-textured shape to select it. It may have an odd Object Origin that could make it difficult to move. If needed, reset the Object Origin by picking the **Object | Transform | Origin to Center of Mass** menu option.

4. At the bottom of the screen, click on the magnet icon to turn on Snap during the transform. If necessary, pick the face icon to the right. For more exact placement, move alone only the axis you need to adjust. In this case, left-click on the Y axis (green) arrow and move it to the front face of the house:

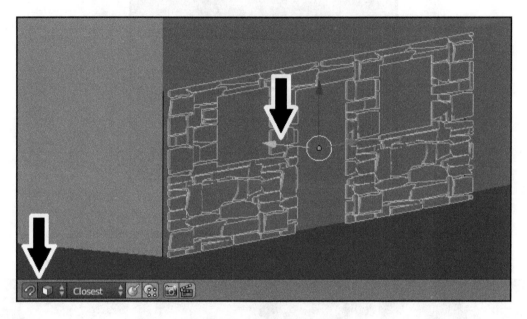

Using Snap during transform to position the stonework.

The front of the house is now sporting some lovely stonework that allows the windows and other details to show through:

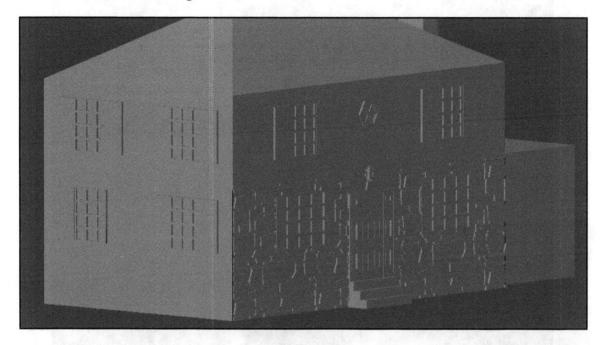

The stonework in its final position

Finalizing and exporting the house

The steps outlined in this chapter can be repeated with the bricks and the rest of the house. Once you have made and placed all the textures, you'll want to export your work to an STL file for 3D printing. The steps are as follows:

1. In the **Outliner**, turn on the visibility of all the components of your house. This includes the base, detailing such as windows, and the new textured shapes. Turn off visibility for anything that isn't a part of the final product, such as the original sheets of brick and stonework.
2. In the menu at the bottom of the screen, go to **Select | Border Select** and **draw a square** around the whole house to highlight everything.
3. In the top menu, go to **File | Export | STL (.stl)**. Make sure to check the **Selection Only** box. Pick a filename and hit **Export STL**.

At this point, the replica of my grandfather's house is ready for its inaugural print:

The final model with all the detailing and textures in place

Summary

In this chapter, you learned how to make new meshes by copying and separating vertices from other objects. You removed unnecessary faces and edges and learned how to create new ones. You got more practice at extruding 3D meshes. You learned about Boolean Intersection and how to preview the results to make sure they are satisfactory. Finally, you placed the newly-created texture shapes in their proper place on the house. You have finished your third 3D printing project.

The projects so far have been inorganic shapes: jewelry pieces and a house. Chapter 12, *Making Organic Shapes with the Subdivision Surface Modifier,* will illustrate how Blender can also model organic shapes. You'll begin modeling a human hand.

12
Making Organic Shapes with the Subdivision Surface Modifier

The projects so far have been very geometric, with precise measurements. In this next section of the book, you will work with a more fluid and artistic project. You'll learn how the Subdivision Surface Modifier can be combined with mesh modeling to make more organic shapes. In this chapter, we'll start modeling a human hand. The skills include the following:

- Thinking ahead about finger placement and print overhangs
- Starting the model from either a cube or a plane
- Filling out the hands and fingers with Loop Cut and Slide, Extrude, and Scale
- Rotating specific faces
- Adding a Subdivision Surface Modifier and adjusting its View property

Thinking about overhangs and flat bases

This project will present fewer challenges in regard to wall thickness and detail height. Nonetheless, we will still want to take a moment to think about design considerations, particularly if we are expecting to print this at home on an FFF/FDM or SLA printer. First, you'll want to reflect on how this model will be oriented on the printer. As we discussed in Chapter 1, *Thinking About Design Requirements*, flat bases are optimal for FFF/FDM printers.

Looking over pictures of my youngest son's hand, I think the best place to plan on a flat base is the cross-section at the wrist. That'll mean the print will start at the wrist and grow upward toward the tips of the fingers:

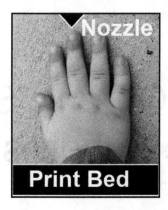

The wrist will print directly on the bed and the hand will grow upward.

Once you know where bottom of the print is, you can think about the overhangs and how they relate to your printing process. If I model my son's fingers straight up like they are in the picture, I should be all set without much worry. The finger positions are well within the 45 degree overhang capabilities of my printer.

If, however, my son had his fingers curled, that would present some substantial overhangs:

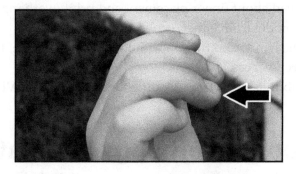

Curled fingers would create challenging overhangs for the printer.

If that was the case, I could do one of three things:

- Consider a different orientation for the print so those overhangs would not be as severe. Perhaps choosing a different bottom of the print would work out better:

Positioning the hand differently would give better overhangs for printing.

- Adjust the angles of the fingers during modeling. I could make them more upright so they would have friendlier overhangs for my printer. I could also curl the fingers in more so they were touching and getting natural support from the palm of the hand.
- Finally, model the fingers as they are and let the slicer add in extra supports to assist with the print.

Modeling additional objects for support

Pinshape has a wonderful article on techniques to avoid printing extra supports with 3D modeling. One example is borrowing from the marble sculptors of the past. If a neoclassical sculptor had a section that could not support its own weight, the artist would add in another detail to assist—a wall, a staff, another person, or a pillow. Read the full Pinshape article at `https://pinshape.com/blog/dotm-fantasy-graph-3d-printer-support-structures/`.

Making a low-poly hand

In this chapter, we'll build off familiar mesh modeling techniques to construct what is called a **low-poly model**. A low-poly model is one with a relatively small number of polygons or faces. It's simple in nature and easy to edit. Once we have a low-poly model, we'll use the Subdivision Surface Modifier to smooth it out and give it a more realistic feel:

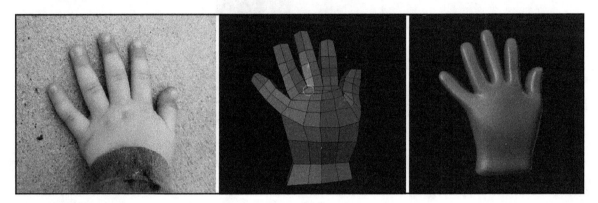

Reference photo, low-poly model, and the results of the Subdivision Surface Modifier.

Adding in reference images

Once you decide how you want to position the hand and fingers, I recommend pulling in reference images to assist with your work. You can do this with a background image like we did in Chapter 2, *Using a Background Image and Bezier Curves*, with the profile pendant. My preference is to use empty objects like we did in Chapter 8, *Using Empties to Model the Base of the House*, with the house figurine. This will allow me to rotate around my object without losing visibility of my reference image. Here is a recap of the steps:

1. In **Object Mode**, left-click to move the 3D Cursor where you would like to add the empty.
2. In the **Tool Shelf** on the left side of the screen, click on the **Create** tab. Look under **Other** and click on **Empty**.
3. In the **Properties Window** on the right side of the screen, click on the axes icon to get to the Empty properties. Change **Display** to **Image**.
4. Click the **Open** button. Using the white arrow and the folder icons, browse to the image you wish to add and click on the **Open Image** button.

If desired, you can adjust the X-Ray and Transparency settings like we did in `Chapter 8`, *Using Empties to Model the Base of the House*. You can also rotate the reference image. Since my image is of the top of the hand, I'm going to leave the empty flat on the X-Y plane. This will keep the **View** | **Top** viewpoint synced up with what I consider the top of the hand:

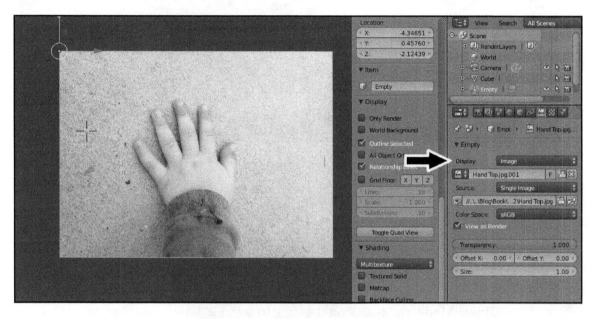

Adding in a reference image via an Empty to help with modeling.

Out of all the projects, this final one will be the most subjective and the steps can vary according to personal taste. Even from the very beginning, you have a choice of how to start. You can decide to use a cube as the base of your hand, working with a 3D object from the get-go. You could also opt to do the initial modeling with a 2D plane and make it 3D at the end. It may be tempting to trace the hand out as a Bezier curve.

I do not recommend that option, however, as it makes subsequent modeling with the Loop Cut and Slide tool difficult:

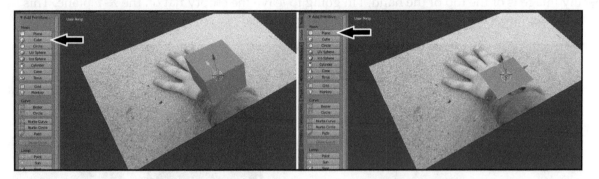

From the very first step, you have choices on how to attack the model. For example, you can start with a cube or a plane.

Modeling a low-poly hand from a cube

Following the same process as the house figurine, you can start by scaling the default cube to an appropriate size. In my case, I'm going use the cube as the wrist of my hand. The steps are as follows:

1. In **Object Mode**, right-click on the cube to select it. If necessary, move it to its proper spot. In my case, I move the cube to the wrist.
2. Hit *S* to tell Blender to scale and then hit *Z* to scale along the Z axis. Use the mouse to shape the cube to an appropriate thickness for a wrist:

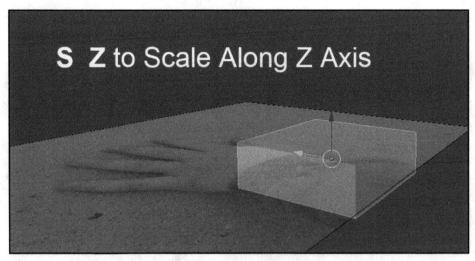

Scaling the height of the hand.

3. Repeat with *S* and *Y* and *S* and *X* to get a good fit for the wrist.

Planning ahead for fingers with Loop Cut and Slide

At this point, I have another choice. I could start to use the Extrude tool to model the shape of the hand. Later, I could use Loop Cut and Slide to add more edges and placeholders for my fingers. I decide to go ahead and get all those extra vertices and edges right now and do a multi-cut Loop Cut and Slide like we did with the shutters in Chapter 9, *Mesh Modeling and Positioning the Details*. The steps are as follows:

1. With the cube selected, switch to **Edit Mode**.
2. In the **Tool Shelf** on the left side of the screen, under the **Tools** tab, click on **Loop Cut and Slide**.

3. The purple preview line appears. Scroll the mouse wheel up to increase the cuts. In this case, I decide to go with four cuts so I have a sliver for each digit:

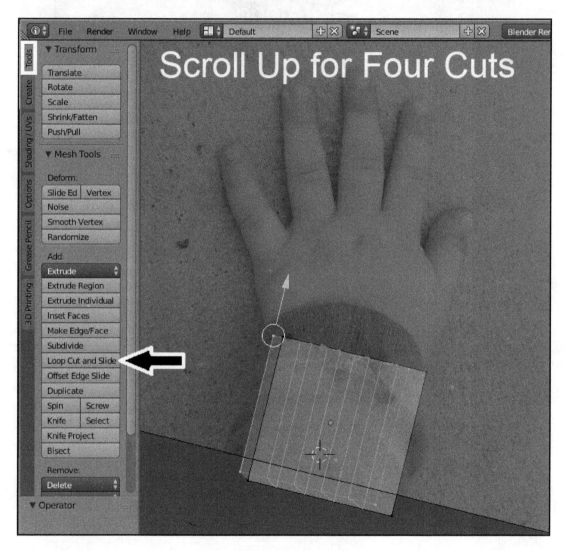

Making four cuts with Loop Cut and Slide.

4. Left-click to approve those cuts. Left-click again to apply the cuts.

Shaping with Extrude and Scale

Most of the low-poly hand can be built with a combination of two tools—**Extrude** and **Scale**. The steps I use to get started are as follows:

1. In **Edit Mode**, click on the Face Select icon. Right-click on one of the corner faces at the back of the cube, one of the faces that will become the rest of the hand. Holding down *Ctrl*, right-click on the other corner face at the back of the cube. All the faces in between should be selected as well:

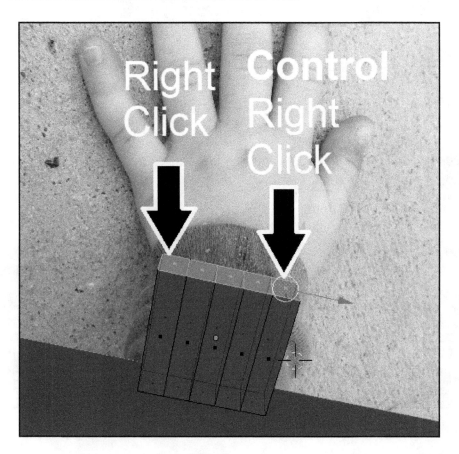

Selecting faces to extrude.

2. In the **Tool Shelf** on the left side of the screen, make sure you are on the **Tools** tab. Click the **Extrude Region** button. Alternatively, you can hit *E* on the keyboard. Using the reference image as a guide, move the mouse to control the size of the extrusion. In this case, I move it up just a little bit as I want to capture the curvature of the hand:

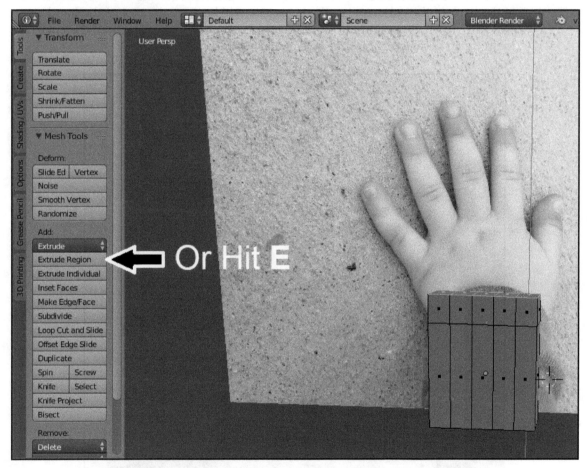

The initial extrusion to start shaping the hand.

Next, hit *S* to scale and use your mouse to resize the new faces. You do have the ability to scale a specific axis at a time. Since the hand is naturally thicker and wider than the wrist, I go ahead and scale everything at once:

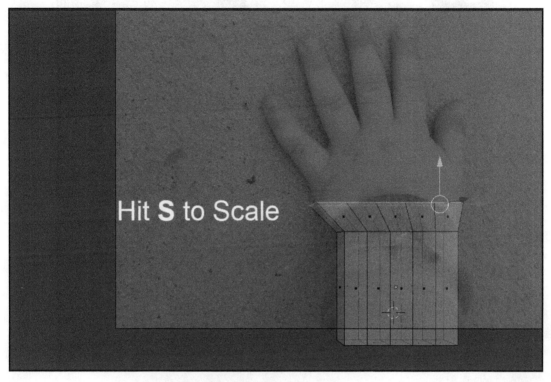

Scaling the new extrusion to make it wider.

I can repeat these steps to built up the shape of the hand:

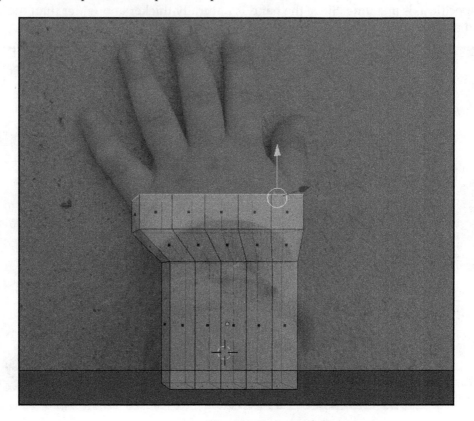

Extruding and scaling can build up the shape of the hand.

Rotating faces and making manual adjustments

Another thing you can do is rotate individual faces so they are pointing the right way. An example is the face that is going to lead to the pinky finger. I can rotate just that face so it is at a better orientation. The steps are as follows:

1. In **Edit Mode,** make sure the Face Select icon is picked. Right-click on the face to select it.

2. Hit *R* for rotate and then *Z* to tell Blender you want to rotate around the Z axis. Use the mouse to point the face in a better direction:

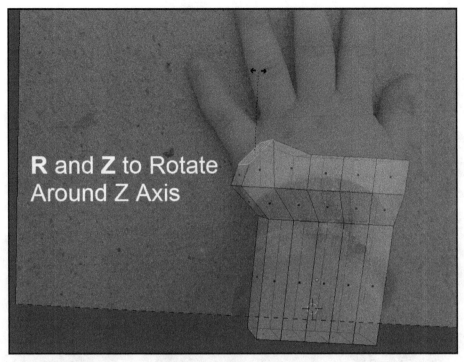

Rotating a single face around the Z axis.

You can also adjust specific edges as you work for a more appropriate shape. The steps are as follows:

1. In **Edit Mode**, click on the Edge Select icon
2. Right-click on the edge you'd like to move to select it

3. Use any of the moving techniques (hitting *G* on the keyboard, left-clicking on the white circle, or left-clicking on a specific axis) to move the edge to an appropriate spot:

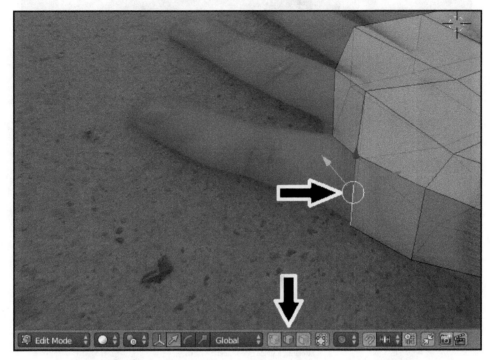

Individual edges can be moved and adjusted.

Why not move vertices?

You can edit specific vertices as well. In fact, vertex movement will be prevalent in Chapter 13, *Trial and Error – Topology Edits*. For making the general hand shape, however, it is helpful to keep the vertices on the bottom of the hand synced up with the vertices on the top. If you do edit by vertices, you may want to make sure the Limited selection to visible icon is turned off and use **Border Select** to make sure you select both vertices you would like to move.

Extruding and scaling fingers

When a tadpole becomes a frog, a little nub protrudes out of the main body. It slowly grows longer to become a leg. The process of making fingers in Blender is very similar. You'll select a single face and extrude that out. That initial nub will continue to be extruded to become a finger. Since fingers are smaller than the hand itself, I'll also scale the new extrusions down. The fingers do not have to be perfect. We'll be working on topology edits in Chapter 13, *Trial and Error – Topology Edits*, to refine the shape. The steps I take to make a pinky finger are as follows:

1. In **Edit Mode**, make sure the Face Select icon is picked. Right-click to select the face you wish to extrude. I pick the one at the base of the pinky finger.
2. In the **Tool Shelf** on the left side of the screen, look under the **Tools** tab and click the **Extrude Region** button. Alternatively, you can hit *E* on the keyboard. Use the reference image as a guide for how far to Extrude:

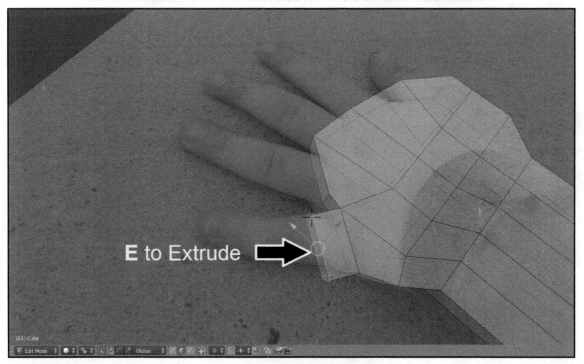

Starting the pinky finger.

3. With the new face still selected, hit *S* and scale that section of the finger slightly smaller:

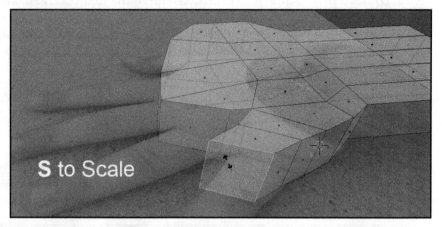

Scaling the finger down.

4. Repeat to grow the digit. Rotate any faces or adjust edges as needed. The very tip is just another example of an extruded face that is scaled small:

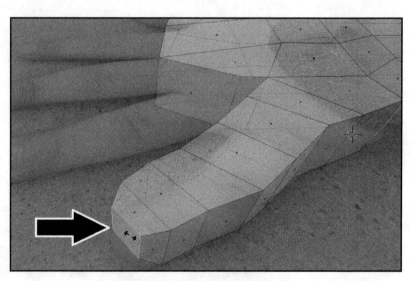

The tip of the finger is another scaled down face.

The same process can be repeated for the other fingers and the thumb until you have a full hand:

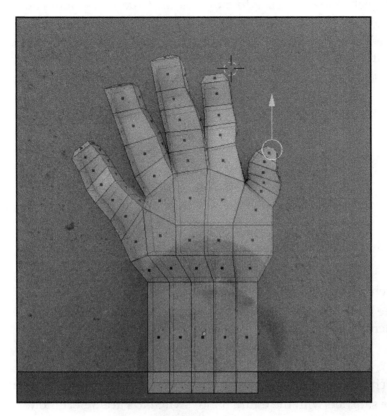

A low-poly hand made using Extrude and Scale.

Modeling a low-poly hand from a plane

If it is easier, you can also choose to model the shape of the hand in 2D form by starting with a plane. You can go through all the same steps of Loop Cut and Slide, Extrude Region, and scaling. The difference is, your work would be simplified and limited to 2D. You can scale without worrying about messing up the thickness of fingers. You can move vertices without worrying about another one on the bottom getting left behind. Once you have faces for the shape of your hand, you could extrude them all at once to make the shape 3D.

Here is a summary of the steps:

1. In **Object Mode**, left-click to move the 3D Cursor to where you want to add the new plane.
2. In the **Tool Shelf** on the left side of the screen, click on the **Create** tab. Under **Add Primitive**, click **Plane**:

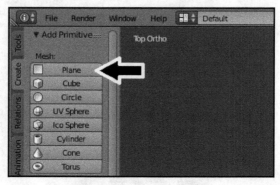

Adding a new plane.

3. Switch to **Edit Mode**.
4. In the **Tool Shelf**, under **Tools**, click on **Loop Cut and Slide**. Use the scroll wheel to increase to four cuts. Left-click twice to apply.
5. Using a combination of **Extrude Region** and **Scale**, start shaping additional faces to lay out the rest of the hand.
6. Switch to **Vertex Select** mode and adjust individual vertices if needed.
7. Once satisfied with the entire hand, switch to **Face Select** mode. Hit *A* to select all the faces.
8. In the **Tool Shelf**, look under the **Tools** tab and click on **Extrude Region**. Alternatively, you can hit *E* on the keyboard. Use the mouse to pick an appropriate height.

This will give everything a consistent thickness. You can make adjustments, such as making fingers thinner, with the topology edits in Chapter 13, *Trial and Error – Topology Edits*:

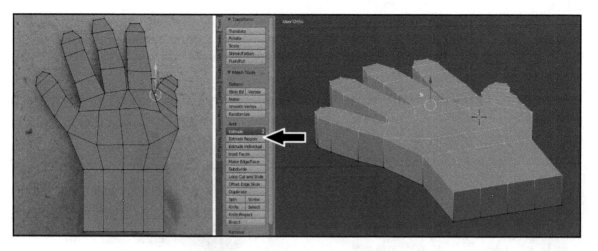

Another option is to lay out the hand shape in a plane and then extrude that work to make it 3D.

Adding a Subdivision Surface Modifier

The Subdivision Surface Modifier takes an existing object, rounds it out, and makes it smoother. It does this by dramatically increasing the number of vertices, edges, and faces. At the top of Blender, to the right of all the menu options, some metrics are displayed. These are statistics for the entire project when you are in Object Mode. When you add a Subdivision Surface Modifier and increase the number of subdivisions, you can see your object getting smoother. You can also see the number of vertices and faces go up:

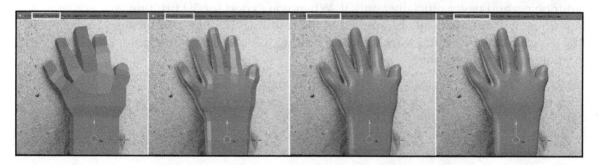

As the hand gets smoother with the Subdivision Surface Modifier, the vertex and face count goes up as well.

When you apply the Subdivision Surface Modifier, those new vertices, edges, and faces become a permanent part of the object. As you can imagine from the following figure, the hand on the left with the original faces would be much easier to edit and tweak than the one on the right:

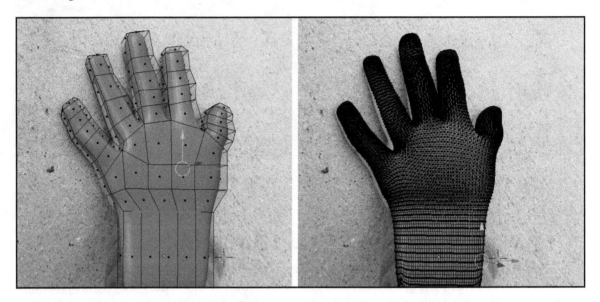

Original faces, and faces after the Subdivision Surface Modifier is applied.

In previous chapters, we have seen how you don't have to apply the modifiers to see and export their effect. This is also true for the Subdivision Surface Modifier. You can add it to your object and never officially apply it. When you export for 3D printing, any active modifiers will automatically be applied to the resulting STL file. This means you can keep the simplified vertex framework intact for editing, yet still export the more complex, organic model for printing.

The steps for adding a Subdivision Surface Modifier are as follows:

1. In **Object Mode**, right-click on the object you wish to add the modifier to.
2. In the **Properties Window** on the right-hand side of the screen, click on the wrench icon. Click on the **Add Modifier** drop-down menu and select **Subdivision Surface**:

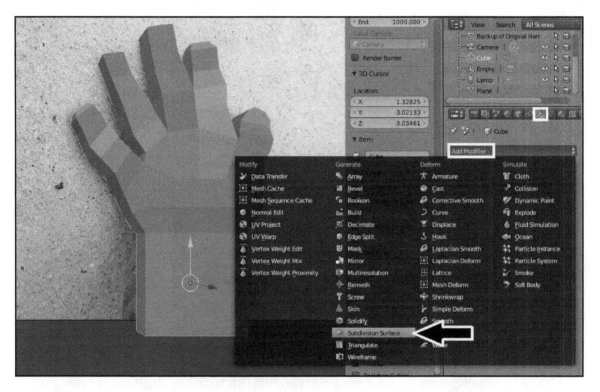

Adding a new Subdivision Surface modifier.

3. Keep the type of surface to **Catmull-Clark**. Increase the **View** number to the smoothness you are looking for. Keep in mind that the higher you go, the longer it can take Blender to refresh your 3D View window:

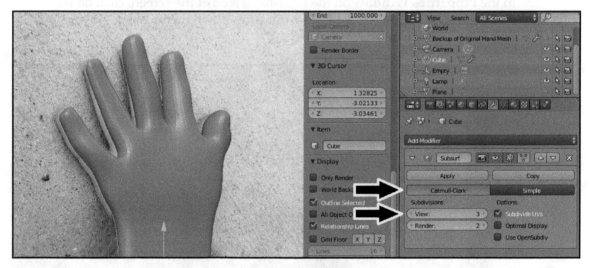

Changing the number of Subdivisions.

Do not click **Apply** at this time as we'll be improving the shape of the hand and adding additional details in Chapter 13, *Trial and Error – Topology Edits*.

View not Render for 3D printing

Typically, modelers are encouraged to make sure the Render subdivision count is higher than the View subdivision count. They do not want to be misled by the 3D View (impacted by the **View** setting) having a higher quality than the final rendered product (impacted by the **Render** setting). That is not a concern for our purposes. When exporting a model for 3D printing, Blender applies the View subdivision count to the final 3D model.

After adding the Subdivision Surface Modifier, your handiwork has become less blocky and appears more organic. You may also see room for improvement and areas you'd like to adjust. Both are great opportunities to learn about topology edits:

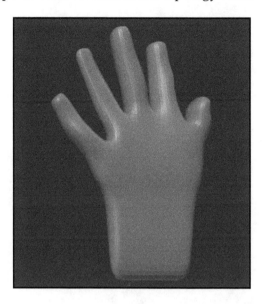

Not perfect, but the hand is identifiable as a hand.

Summary

In this chapter, you extended your experience with mesh modeling by creating a low-poly human hand. You imported a reference image. Starting with either a cube or plane, you used tools such as Loop Cut and Slide, Extrude Region, and Scale to fill out the shape of the hand and fingers. You learned how you could rotate faces and move specific edges to get a better shape. You saw how the Subdivision Surface Modifier could take that low-poly hand and make it look more realistic by smoothing the shape and adding more faces.

In Chapter 13, *Trial and Error – Topology Edits*, we'll improve the shape of our hand with topology edits and add some key detailing such as fingernails and wrinkles.

13
Trial and Error – Topology Edits

In this chapter, you'll see how moving and adding edges and vertices affects the appearance of your hand. You'll add extra edges to round out surfaces, outline new details, and control the sharpness of other edges. You'll learn new editing techniques to help streamline your process. The chapter will cover the following topics:

- Learning about the advantages of quad faces over triangles
- Using the Loop Cut and Slide tool to better shape the hand
- Creating extra edge loops to flatten the base
- Selecting a whole edge loop at once
- Using Edge Slide to move existing edges
- Changing Blender's Pivot Point to better control rotation
- Editing groups of vertices with Blender's Proportional Editing tool

Preparing yourself mentally

Shaping the hand will be difficult to relay in step-by-step instructions. Real hands vary from person to person. Our modeled hands will certainly vary, as will our tastes and aesthetic preferences. This chapter will provide you with tools, strategies, and considerations as you embark on your journey of fine-tuning your hand. I have two thoughts before you even make your first mouse click.

Embracing failure

My first piece of advice is to not strive for perfection. Allow yourself to make mistakes. This type of modeling is one where you are going to have to pay your dues and practice. Accept that your hand is not going to be perfect right away. Accept that you will become intimately familiar with the *Ctrl* and *Z* keys on your keyboard as you undo changes that don't work. Accept that you'll get everything looking great from the top, then you'll change perspective and discover it looks all wrong from the side.

Be tenacious. Don't give up. Finally, celebrate the fact that you are making a model for 3D printing. Our colleagues using Blender for animation have many more considerations and opportunities for failure. Whereas they will have to master face flow, poles, and how different areas will deform with movement, our ultimate consideration is "Does the model look the way I want?"

Aiming for quads

Next, I would recommend as much as possible to keep your faces as **quads**, or faces with four vertices. Thanks to our combination of Loop Cut and Slide and Extrude, all the faces in our hand should already be quads. As we make additional edits, particularly if we are tempted to merge vertices or use the Knife tool, we'll want to be conscious of trying to stick to quads. The advantage of quads becomes clear as you continue to use the Loop Cut and Slide tool to add additional edges. Loop Cut and Slide knows how to navigate quads. If I wanted to add another edge loop down the ring finger, that loop could successfully circle the entire hand:

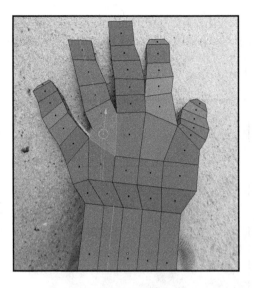

Loop Cut and Slide can navigate quads

If I merged two vertices together to make one of the faces a triangle instead, it is a different story. The Loop Cut and Slide tool will dead-end at that triangle and not continue any further:

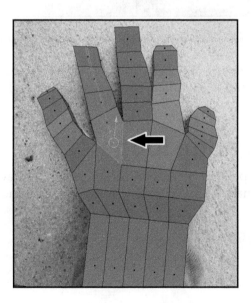

Loop Cut and Slide dead-ends at a triangle

The same thing would happen if I changed that quad face into a *n-gon*, a face with more than four vertices. The Loop Cut and Slide tool would also dead-end. You can think of it dead-ending because there is a triangle hiding in that n-gon. The following pentagon could also be made out of a quad and, you've guessed it, a triangle:

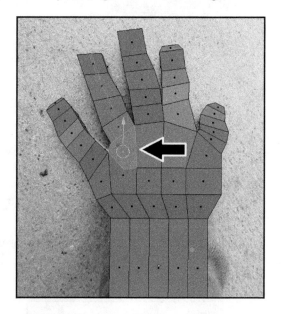

An n-gon, in this case a pentagon, could also cause dead ends with your edge loops

Triangles and n-gons may not be noticeable in the final slice and 3D print. Nonetheless, it is a good practice to stick to and it will make later edits substantially easier.

Adding extra edge loops

As you begin to better shape your hand, you will most likely be adding additional edge loops. A few common scenarios are controlling rounding, shaping details, and flattening the base.

Controlling rounding

As we have seen, the Subdivision Surface Modifier rounds and smooths things out. There are cases, however, where we would like to have better control of the rounding. An example in this model is the right side of my hand. It initially has a very flat feel. Doing a Loop Cut and Slide down the cross-section of the entire hand gives me extra control to start to round those areas out:

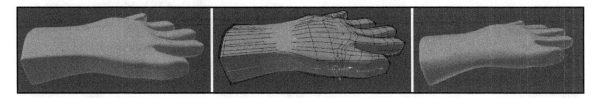

Adding an extra edge loop provides extra vertices to round out the side of the hand

I also add extra edge loops down the center of each finger for the same purpose. Those new finger edge loops can also help define tendons further down the hand:

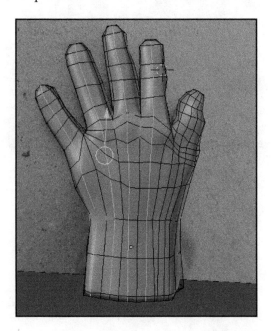

Extra edge loops down the center of each finger will help define rounding and tendon detail in the hand.

Shaping details

Edge loops are also crucial in shaping and outlining details. In this model, extra edge loops between the thumb and the pointer finger follow the muscle to shape the base of the thumb:

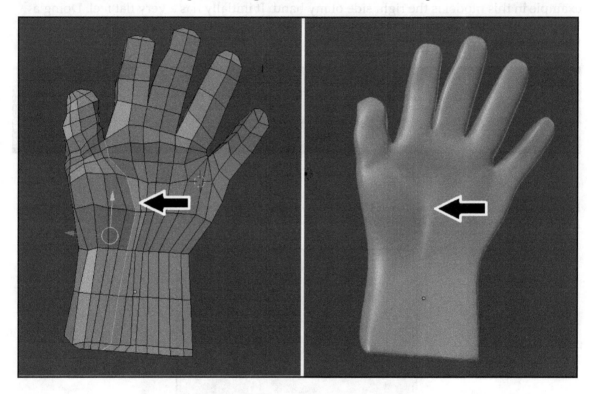

Extra edge loops can help shape the musculature of the thumb.

Another example is the knuckles. Extra edge loops near the base of the fingers give us the opportunity to bring out some subtle definition of the knuckles:

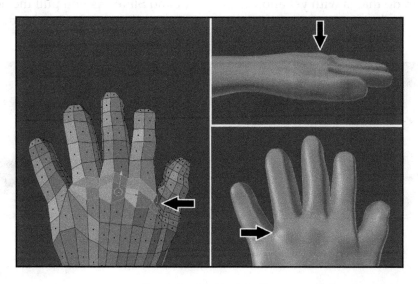

Extra edge loops help define the knuckles.

Flattening the base

By default, the cross-section of the wrist is going to be rounded like everything else. In Chapter 12, *Making Organic Shapes with the Subdivision Surface Modifier*, I decided I would like that to be the base of my print. It is best if I flatten out that section:

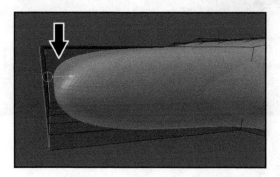

The rounded wrist is not going to be a good base for the print.

Flattening with Loop Cut and Slide

One way I can do that is with yet another Loop Cut and Slide. As you pull the new edge loop closer to the base, you can see the impact on the Subdivision Surface Modifier. The closer you get to the existing edge, the flatter the base gets:

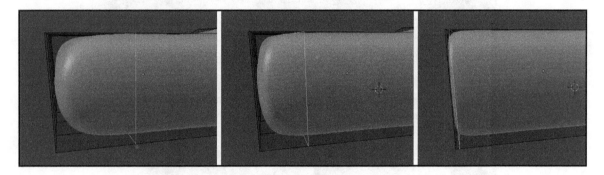

The new edge loop's placement has a direct impact on the curvature of the base.

Flattening with Mean Crease

Another option is to select all the edges around the wrist and set the **Mean Crease** property to `1.00`. The Mean Crease setting can be found in the **Properties Shelf** under **Transform** in the **Edges Data** section. Changes to the Mean Crease will export to both STL and X3D (a 3D printing file format that saves color information). In the following screenshot, you can see the impact of moving the Mean Crease from 0.00 to 1.00:

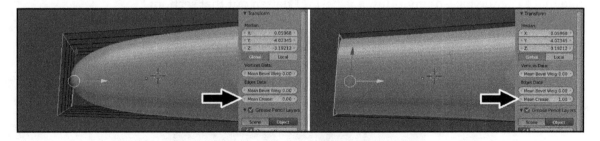

Mean Crease of 0.00 and Mean Crease of 1.00.

Moving vertices and edge loops

You should touch every single vertex in your model. Whenever you add another edge loop, you should expect to tweak all the new vertices it adds. It may sound tedious, but that effort is exactly what is going to make your model look more real and organic. As you work, you will be naturally reinforcing lessons and techniques from previous chapters:

Technique	Chapter
Switching viewpoint to evaluate work from different angles	Chapter 2, *Using a Background Image and Bezier Curves*
Turning Limit selection to visible on and off to see hidden vertices	Chapter 4, *Flattening a Torus and Boolean Union*
Using Border Select to pick multiple vertices at once	Chapter 4, *Flattening a Torus and Boolean Union*
Using the white circle, axis arrows, or the G hotkey to drag and drop vertices, edges, and faces	Chapter 4, *Flattening a Torus and Boolean Union*
Using the Shift and Ctrl keys with the right mouse button to multi-select	Chapter 6, *Cutting Half Circle Holes and Modifier Management*
Switching to Wireframe Mode to see obscured vertices and edges	Chapter 11, *Applying Textures with Boolean Intersection*
Turning on and off a Modifier (such as the Subdivision Surface Modifier)	Chapter 11, *Applying Textures with Boolean Intersection*

There are a couple of new features and shortcuts that will assist with your editing process.

Selecting edge loops

There may be a situation where you want to move or scale an entire ring of edges. Perhaps the Subdivision Surface Modifier shrunk my fingers and I want to scale them back up, or perhaps I have an edge loop I want to align with the actual joint of the finger. I could use the *Ctrl* and *Shift* keys to multi-select the edges I want. Blender also has the ability to select an entire edge loop in a single click.

The steps are as follows:

1. In **Edit Mode**, make sure you are in **Edge Select** mode.
2. Right-click on one edge in the ring you wish to select. Under the **Mesh** menu, go to **Edges** and select **Edge Loops**. Alternatively, you can hold down the *Alt* key and right-click on an edge in the ring:

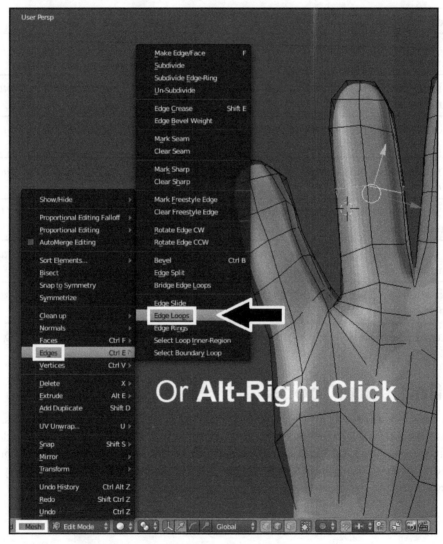

Blender allows you to select entire edge loops at once via the menu or hitting Alt + right-click.

Blender will automatically select all the edges in that ring. This is particularly helpful with the longer edge loops running down the length of the hand:

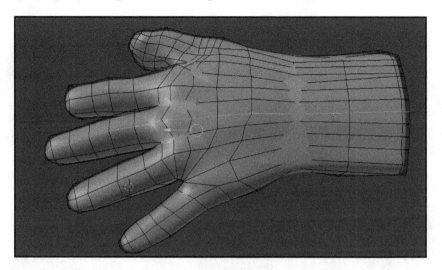

Alt + right-click can select longer, more complex edge loops such as one going lengthwise down the hand

Sliding edges

Once I have an edge loop selected, there may be a situation where I want to move it and have it adapt to the shape that is already established. An example is one of the edge loops in my fingers. I would like that to be better aligned with the actual joint. If I were to move that edge loop in a normal manner, the edges would keep their exact lengths and angles as they travel. In my case, it is deforming the finger and I'd like to keep my adjustments to a minimum.

Blender also has an Edge Slide feature. By default, Edge Slide adjusts the edges and their angles based on the distance to the next edge. This brings less distortion to the original shape:

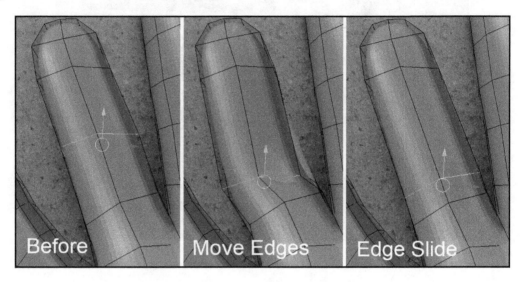

The difference between just moving edges and doing an Edge Slide

The steps to perform an Edge Slide are as follows:

1. In **Edit Mode**, make sure you are in **Edge Select** mode. Select the edges you would like to adjust. In my example, I use *Alt* + right-click to pick an edge loop on the ring finger.
2. In the **Mesh** menu at the bottom of the screen, go to **Edges** and select **Edge Slide**. Alternatively, you can hit the *G* key twice on the keyboard:

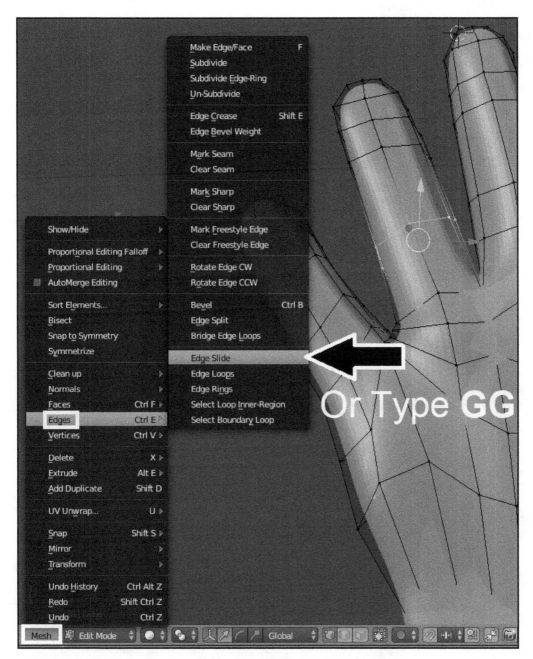

Use the menu or hit GG to do an edge slide

3. Use the mouse to adjust the position and left-click or hit *Enter* to apply.

Rotating around the 3D Cursor

As I took a closer look at my hand, I found that I had inadvertently created the thumb at an unintended angle. It was sticking up above the rest of the fingers:

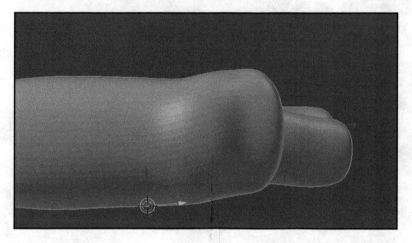

Crooked thumb

I could adjust all the edges and vertices manually, but I am happy with the current shape. I just want to rotate everything I already have. Blender allows us to do that, by giving us the power to change our Pivot Point. The steps I take to adjust my thumb are as follows:

1. In **Edit Mode**, switch to **Vertex Select** mode and turn off Limit selection to visible. Select all the vertices you wish to rotate. In my case, I use **Select | Border Select**:

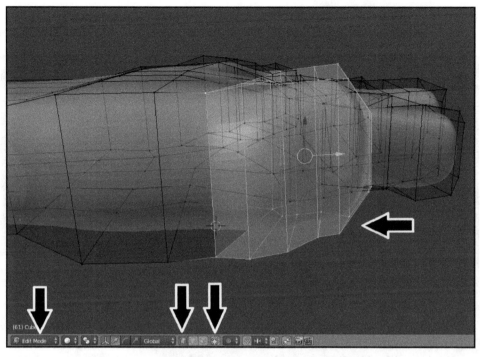

Selecting the vertices that need to be adjusted

2. Left-click at the point you would like to rotate around. The 3D Cursor moves to that point:

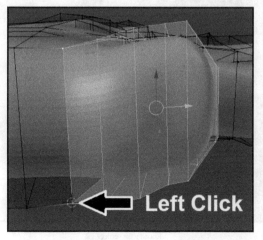

Left-click to move the 3D Cursor to where you want to rotate around

3. At the bottom of the screen, there is a **Pivot Point** drop-down menu (to the right of Viewport shading). Click on that drop-down menu and select **3D Cursor**:

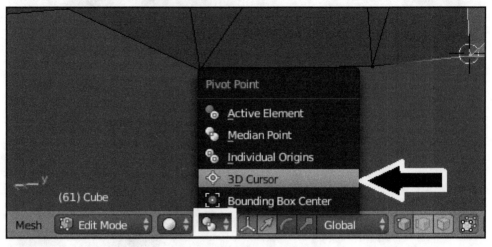

Changing Blender's Pivot Point

4. Adjust your viewpoint so you are looking perpendicular to the direction you wish to rotate. In my case, I want to rotate the thumb down, so I look at it from the right side. Hit *R* as normal to rotate, and move your mouse to adjust the rotation. Blender is rotating specifically around the 3D Cursor instead of the normal Object Origin:

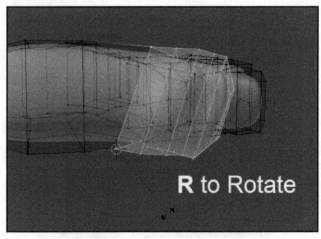

Rotating the vertices

5. When satisfied, left-click or hit **Enter** to apply. Switch the **Pivot Point** back to **Median Point**:

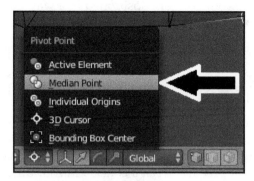

Returning the Pivot Point to Median Point

When I am done, my thumb is in a better position in relation to the other fingers:

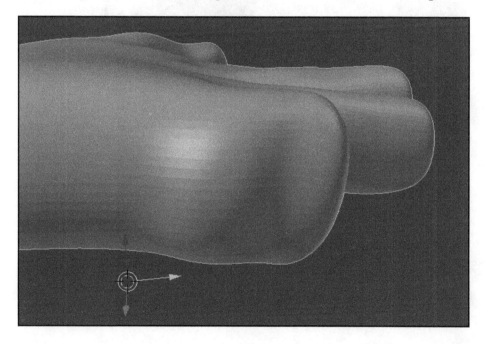

Rotated thumb

Rotating can help adjust overhangs

If you do have some fingers positioned in a way that will be challenging for your printer, you can use Rotate to give them a more print-friendly position.

Using Proportional Editing

Another way to adjust multiple vertices at once is to use Blender's Proportional Editing feature. It allows related or nearby vertices to be adjusted at the same time. An example application of Proportional Editing may be the top of my wrist. As is, the vertices are all pretty flat and I would like to give the wrist a consistent rounding:

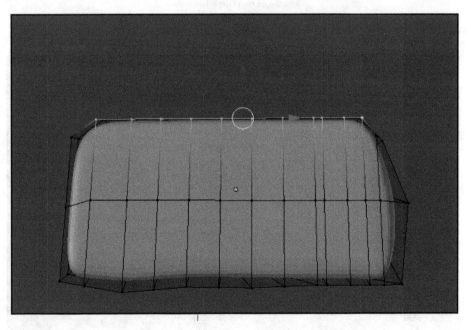

The top of the wrist is flat and does not have the desired rounding shape.

Instead of individually tweaking each vertex, I could use Proportional Editing to get a head start with my adjustments. With Proportional Editing disabled, only the selected item is changed. When Proportional Editing is enabled, however, you can impact nearby or connected vertices in a specified pattern. Blender refers to the pattern options as the Falloff. Picking Constant for the Falloff, for example, will raise the other vertices the same amount as the selected one. Linear will adjust the other vertex positions to keep a straight line. Root will produce a nice curvature. There are numerous other options to help fit your needs:

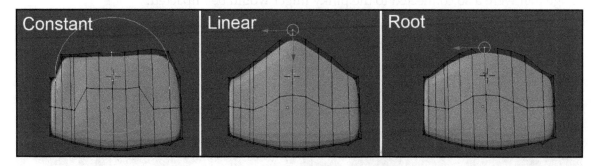

Just three of the Falloff options for the Proportional Editing tool.

You can also tell Blender how many vertices will be impacted by specifying the influence range. When Proportional Editing is turned on, you can adjust a circle that will define the impact area:

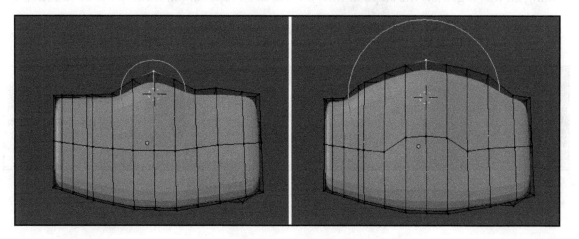

The difference of increasing the influence range for Proportional Editing.

Blender also lets you decide whether you want to adjust any item within the influence range or only adjust the items that are connected to the one being moved. A practical application of using Connected mode would be if you wanted to edit a single finger. The fingers themselves are quite close together. If you simply had Proportional Editing enabled, you would impact anything within the influence range, including other fingers. If I was working with the pinky finger, for example, vertices in the ring finger may be adjusted as well. Using Connected mode would circumvent that problem. Only vertices within the range that were also connected to the pinky finger would be impacted:

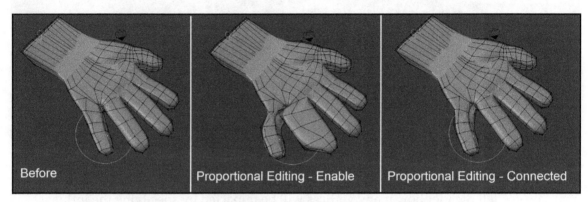

Enabling Proportional Editing alters the ring finger. Using Connected, one only adjusts the pinky finger.

Pulling all this together, the steps to turn on and use Proportional Editing are as follows:

1. In **Edit Mode**, click on the Proportional Editing icon. It is directly to the right of the Limit selection to visible icon:

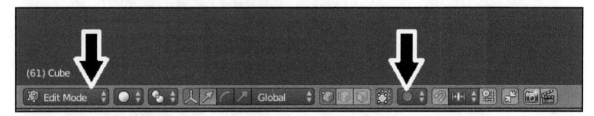

In Edit Mode, you can see the Proportional Editing icon.

2. Pick whether you want to **Enable** the **Proportional Editing** or use it in **Connected** mode. For my wrist, I select **Enable**:

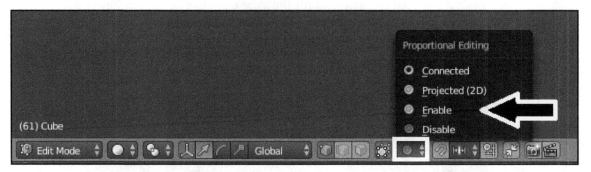

Pick Enable to turn on Proportional Editing.

3. A new drop-down menu appears to the right. Click on it to pick your **Proportional Editing Falloff** pattern. In my case, I pick **Inverse Square**:

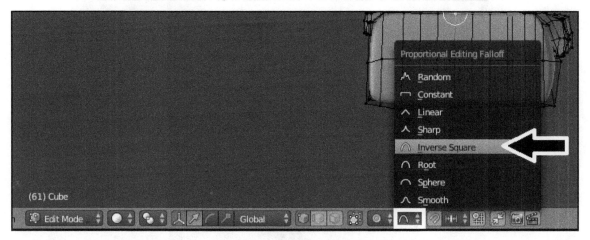

Picking the Falloff pattern.

5. If necessary, right-click on the item(s) you wish to adjust. I pick a single vertex in the middle of my wrist.

6. Left-click in the white circle or hit *G* for grab. The white circle now indicates your influence range. Scroll up on the mouse wheel to increase the radius and down to decrease. Alternatively, you can hit the *Page Up* and *Page Down* keys on the keyboard. In my case, I increase it just large enough to select all my top vertices, but small enough to leave the bottom ones alone:

Scroll up on the mouse wheel to increase the influence range.

7. Move your selection. If you don't like what you are seeing, hit *Esc* and try a different Falloff or Influence Radius. Otherwise, hit *Enter* or left-click to apply:

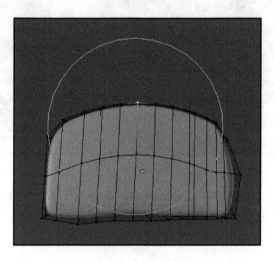

You can preview the changes as you work.

8. When you are done, click on the Proportional Editing icon again and select **Disable** to turn it off for future edits.

This will not be the end of my vertex adjustments for the wrist, but I did give myself a good head start with a nice rounded shape:

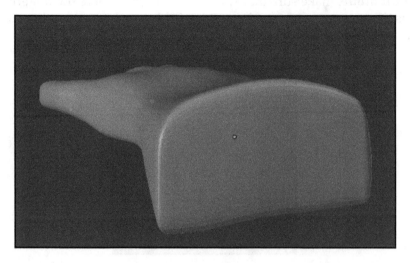

The top of the wrist is rounded thanks to Proportional Editing.

Modeling fingernails and wrinkles

Depending on the size and the detail of your print, you may want to add additional details such as fingernails and wrinkles. As with most things in this book, there are many options in Blender. If you were going to print this model in Full Color Sandstone from one of the 3D Printing Service Bureaus, one option is to add that detailing by coloring your model. Adding colors and UV maps will be covered in Chapter 14, *Coloring Models with Materials and UV Maps*. If you are using a single color printer, you would want to convey those details in the model itself. It is best to save modeling such details for last when you are satisfied with the rest of the work.

Using Inset and Extrude for fingernails

For the fingernail, I want a slight curve inward going down before the fingernail itself emerges. I'm going to do this with a combination of Inset and Extrude.

The steps are as follows:

1. In **Edit Mode**, make sure there are edges roughly where the fingernail begins and ends. If necessary, you can do an **Edge Slide** to move an existing edge or a **Loop Cut and Slide** to add another:

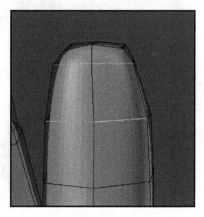

Position the edge loops for fingernails.

2. Make any initial adjustments for the shape. In my case, I pull the middle vertices away from each other to prepare for a more rounded look:

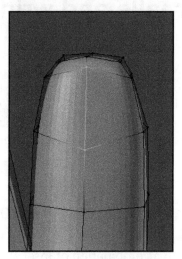

Make any preliminary adjustments to shape by moving vertices.

3. Switch to **Face Select** mode and right-click and *Shift* + right-click to pick the two fingernail faces. Hit *I* and inset the faces slightly. This will be a border of finger around the fingernail:

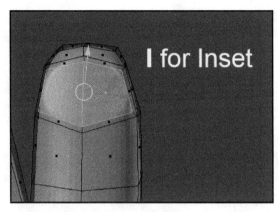

Insetting for a cuticle.

4. Hit *I* again to create another inset. This will be the cuticle and help with the curvature around the fingernail itself:

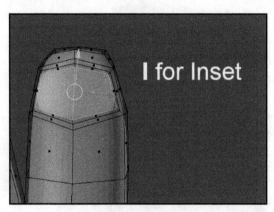

Insetting again for the actual fingernail.

5. Left-click on the Z (blue) axis arrow and pull the two new faces into the finger. This creates an impression. In my case, I also scale the faces down to get a better curve:

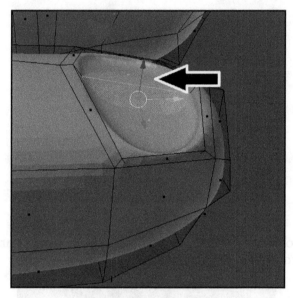

Pulling the fingernail nail for a divot.

6. In the **Tool Shelf** on the left side of the screen, look under the **Tools** tab and hit **Extrude Region**. Alternatively, hit *E* on the keyboard. **Extrude** back up above the finger:

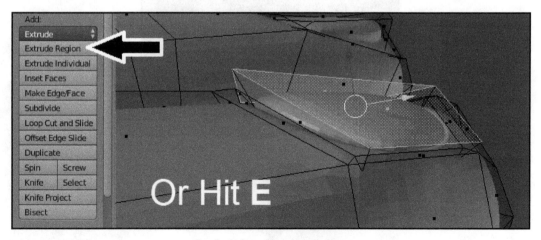

Extruding the fingernail back up over the finger.

7. Adjust, adjust, and adjust until you get the look you want. Make sure you check your work from different viewpoints. In my case, the steps are as follows:

    1. Hit *S* to scale the newly extruded faces larger

    2. Pull the back faces in tighter with the cuticle

    3. Pull the front faces out to shape the fingernail over the tip of the finger

    4. Adjust the side vertices to give the fingernail a better shape

Selecting a hard-to-reach vertex with Edge Select

You already have a few ways to select hidden vertices. You can switch to **Wireframe Mode**, turn off the Limit selection to visible icon, and temporarily turn off the **Subdivision Surface Modifier**. If you can see the edge the vertex is on, another technique is to switch to **Edge Select** mode and **select the edge**. Then switch back the **Vertex Select** mode, hold down the *Shift* key and unselect the visible vertex. The hidden one is still selected and you can make your adjustments:

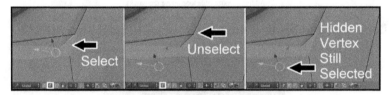

Using unselect to get a hidden vertex.

Using edge loops for wrinkles

One way you could incorporate wrinkles is by leveraging the skills you already have and adding additional edge loops. Earlier in the chapter, you saw how the base of the wrist sharpened as a new loop was placed closer to it. The same is true for wrinkles. As a result, for each wrinkle, I want three edge loops: one for the wrinkle itself and one on either side to help sharpen that detail. An example is adding a crease to a finger. I decide I want an existing edge at one of the joints to become a crease.

The steps are as follows:

1. In **Edit Mode**, click on **Loop Cut and Slide** and add an additional loop directly above the existing edge:

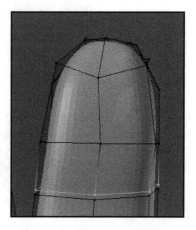

Adding an extra edge loop above the wrinkle

2. Use **Loop Cut and Slide** again to add an additional loop directly:

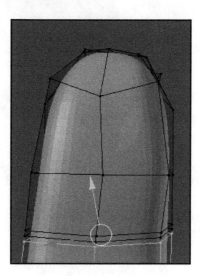

Adding an extra edge loop below the wrinkle

3. Right-click on the leftmost vertex in the original edge. Holding down *Shift*, right-click on the rightmost vertex. Hit *S* to scale them closer together:

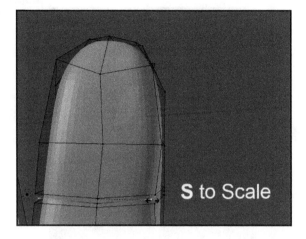

Scaling two vertices from the wrinkle closer together

4. With those two vertices still selected, click on the Z (blue) axis arrow and pull them into the finger.
5. Adjust vertices as needed to get the look you want.

When you are done, your finger will now have a crease:

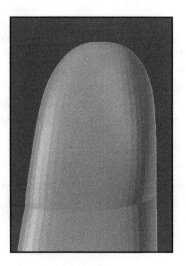

New crease in finger

With additional details such as fingernails and creases, your hand starts to become more alive:

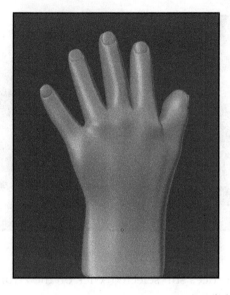

Hand with fingernails

Summary

In this chapter, you did a lot of adjusting to fine-tune the shape of your hand. You learned how extra edge loops could be used to control rounding, shape large details such as muscles and tendons, and flatten the base of your piece. You learned how to select entire edge loops at once and how to slide them without distorting your shape. You learned how to correct a poorly positioned thumb by rotating vertices around the 3D Cursor. Finally, you learned about Blender's Proportional Editing tool and how it can adjust multiple items at once.

The 3D Printing Service Bureaus support full color printing. In Chapter 14, *Coloring Models with Materials and UV Maps,* you will learn how to take advantage of that by adding colors to your 3D model.

14

Coloring Models with Materials and UV Maps

In this chapter, you will learn how to add colors to your model for full-color printing at a 3D Printing Service Bureau. The skills include:

- Adding new materials and setting their colors
- Assigning materials to specific faces
- Adding a new Editor Panel to Blender's interface
- Unwrapping your model for more advanced coloring
- Using Blender's Fill and draw brushes for painting
- Exporting your work to X3D format and uploading to a Service Bureau

Using materials

For most printing processes, the color you put on your model in Blender has no impact on the color of the final print. For the FFF/FDM printers, the color of your print is going to be the color of the filament(s) you have loaded into the machine. SLA will be dictated by the resin being used. For the 3D Printing Service Bureaus, you may be picking a dye color when you order your prints.

The exception is the full-color printing 3D Printing Service Bureaus offer in Sandstone (gypsum powder) and now Plastic. Those printers need color information. In Blender, one way you can add color is by adding and assigning single-colored materials to your objects and faces.

Adding a material to the whole object

The steps to add a material and color to your entire object are as follows:

1. In **Object Mode**, right-click your object to select it.
2. In the **Properties Window** on the right-hand side of the screen, click the sphere icon to access materials:

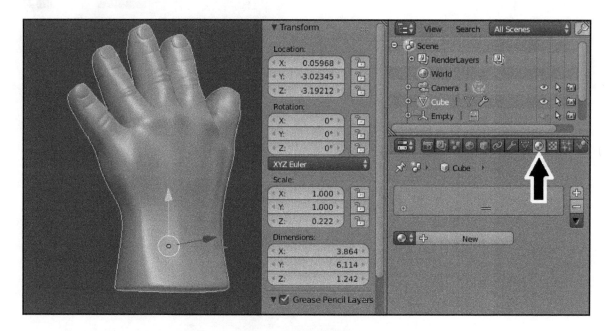

3. Click the **New** button to add a new material:

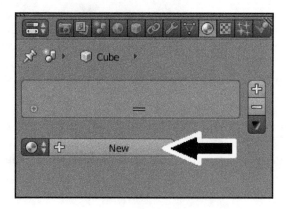

4. The new material is added and a number of new properties display. By default, the color will be white. Look for the **Diffuse** heading and click the box directly underneath:

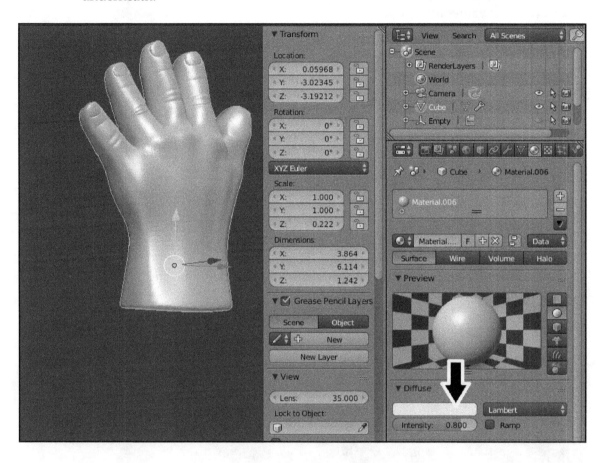

5. A pop-up screen displays a color wheel. Click inside the color wheel to designate your base color. You can control the shade by clicking the gradient bar along the right. Alternatively, you can type in specific **R** (for red), **G** (for green), and **B** (for blue) values at the bottom:

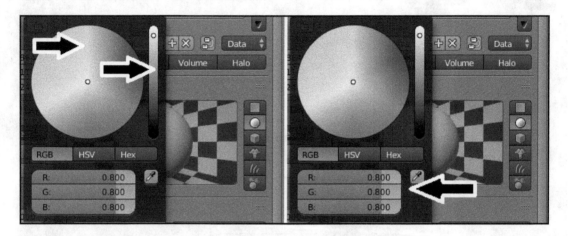

Once a color is picked, the model is updated to reflect the new coloring:

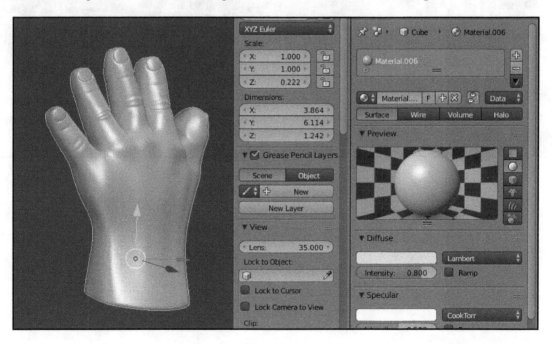

Updated color for the hand model

Adding a material to specific faces

Once you have an initial material defined for the object, you can customize specific faces so they have a different material and, therefore, a different color. In our hand model, an example would be the fingernails. I could assign just those faces a different color. The steps are as follows:

1. In **Edit Mode**, switch to Face select mode. Press *Shift* + right-click to select all the faces you want to change the color for. In my example, I selected all the faces involved with a fingernail:

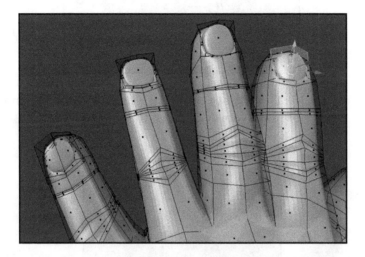

2. In the **Properties Window**, click the sphere icon to access materials. There is already one material listed, the skin color that was added earlier. Click the + icon to add a new slot for a new material:

3. Click the **New** button to fill that spot with a new material:

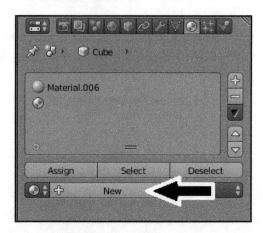

4. As before, click the **Diffuse** box and select the new color. When you are satisfied, click the **Assign** button to apply it to just the selected faces:

The majority of the hand stays the skin color. The selected faces are now the second color:

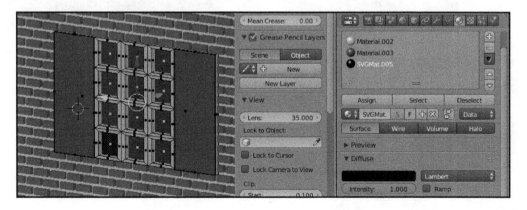

The nail for the index finger is now a darker color

Another example application of this technique would be the windows in the house figurine. By assigning faces different materials, the shutters, the panes, and the glass can all be different colors:

Another usage of coloring by assigning different materials to specific faces

Selecting extra faces with the Subdivision Surface Modifier

We have seen how the Subdivision Surface Modifier rounds things out. This will impact how the coloration works on your faces. If I select just the top face of my fingernail, the new color does not cover the full nail. That's because, with the subdivision Surface Modifier, the side faces are also contributing to the shape of the nail. If I make sure to select those faces as well and assign the color to them, I'll find the color extends to the full nail:

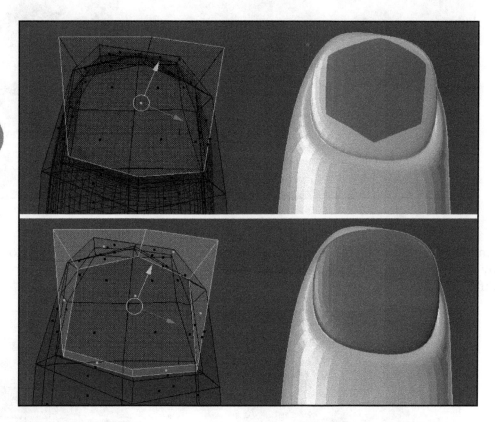

Reusing existing materials

Materials are available for any other object or face in the same Blender project. This can help keep colors consistent. For example, in the house figurine, I don't have to worry about slight variations in the brickwork. Each panel would be assigned the same material and would be using the exact same color. This will also save you work. Rather than entering the same R, G, B, colors or having the find the right color on the color wheel, you simply select what is already there.

Regardless of whether you are adding a material to a whole object or assigning a material to a specific face, the process is roughly the same:

1. Instead of clicking the **New** button to add a new material, click the sphere icon to the left of the button. A drop-down menu will show you a listing of all the materials defined in this Blender project. Click the one you want to use:

Another advantage of reusing materials surfaces when changes are necessary is that, if you highlight the material and update the **Diffuse** color, that change will automatically trickle down to all the faces and objects using that same material. An example is if I want to change the fingernail color. I don't have to reselect and update all the fingernail faces again. I can change the material in one place:

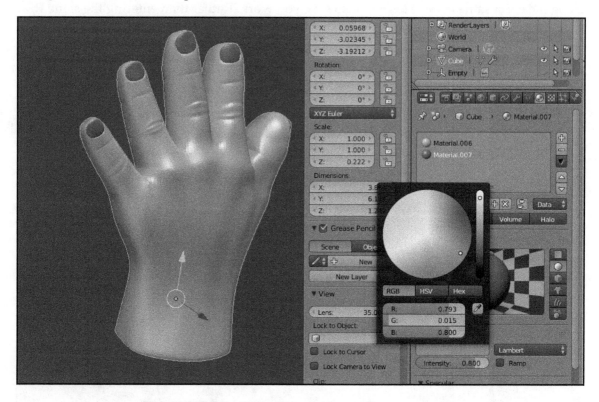

Changing the Diffuse color of the material will change all the places assigned that same material

If you are happy with this approach to coloring and it meets your needs, you can skip ahead to section *Exporting and Uploading X3D Files*. For a more in-depth option of coloring, you can have Blender create what is called a UV Map.

Coloring with UV Maps

Another technique for adding colors to your model is to **unwrap** your object to make a flat 2D representation of the surfaces, which is called a UV Map. That 2D image can be colored and decorated. Your colors would not be limited to specific faces. UV Maps give you the ability to add very specific details and shading to your object. You can color the image inside Blender with a process called **texture painting**. You can also work with an image editing software you are already familiar and comfortable with. In either case, the very first step would be making the UV Map to color.

Adding a new panel to Blender

When working with UV Maps, it is helpful to add another panel to Blender. This will give you visibility to your object in **Object Mode** or **Edit Mode** as well as the ability to see the related UV Map at the same time. The steps to add another Blender panel are:

1. In the upper right-hand corner of your **3D View** panel, there is a small icon of three 45 degree lines. If you have your **Properties Shelf** displayed, those lines will be in the upper right-hand corner of the **Properties Shelf** instead:

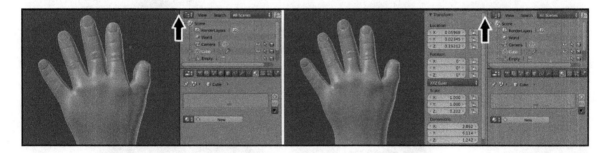

2. Hover your mouse over that area until your cursor changes to a little white cross. Left-click and drag that area to the left. As you do, you open up another working screen. Release the mouse button when you're satisfied with the placement:

3. At the bottom left of the new panel, click the cube icon. You are given an **Editor Type** list. Select **UV/Image Editor**:

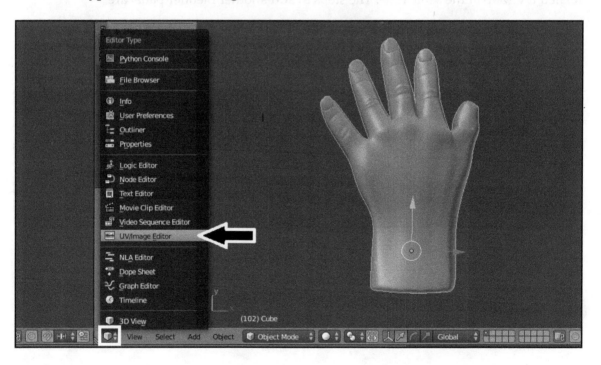

When you are done, you have two editing panels—one showing the normal 3D View and the other showing the new **UV/Image Editor** screen:

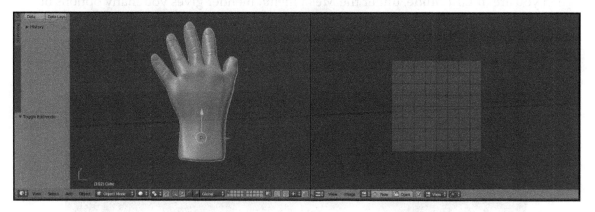

Blender with two editing panels showing the hand in Object Mode and showing the UV/Image Editor

Removing the extra panel

If you ever want to get rid of the extra panel, left-click the three white lines in the upper right-hand corner of your original **3D View** window. As you drag that to the right, you'll see a large grey arrow appear over your new panel. **Release** the mouse and your 3D View window will be restored over the extra panel:

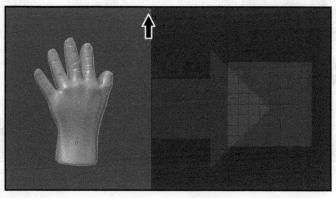

Dragging the corner over the original panel will remove the new one

Unwrapping an object into a UV Map

When you are in **Edit Mode**, under the **Mesh** menu, Blender gives you many options of how to unwrap your 3D object into a 2D UV Map. The **UV Smart Project** option is a good one to get acclimated to the process. The steps are:

1. In **Edit Mode**, switch to Face select mode and press *A* to select all the faces:

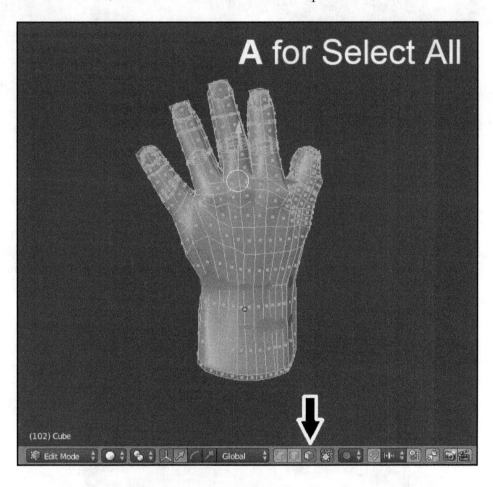

2. Under the **Mesh** menu, select **UV Unwrap...** and **Smart UV Project**:

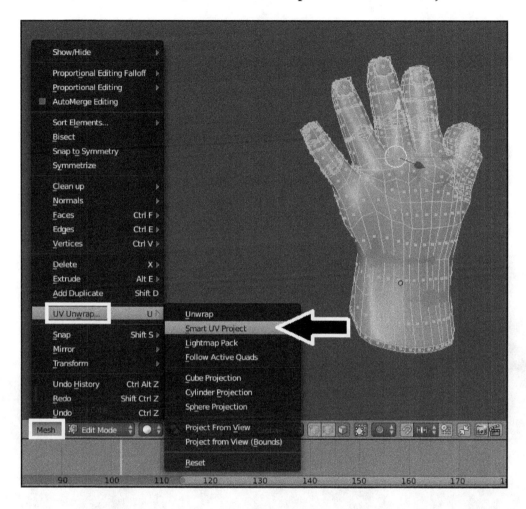

3. A menu option appears with settings. Keep the default options and hit **OK**:

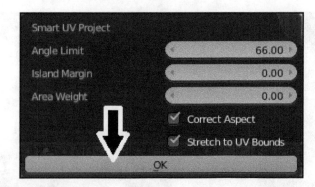

In your **UV/Image Editor** panel, you will see how all the faces from your hand have been flattened out and are displayed:

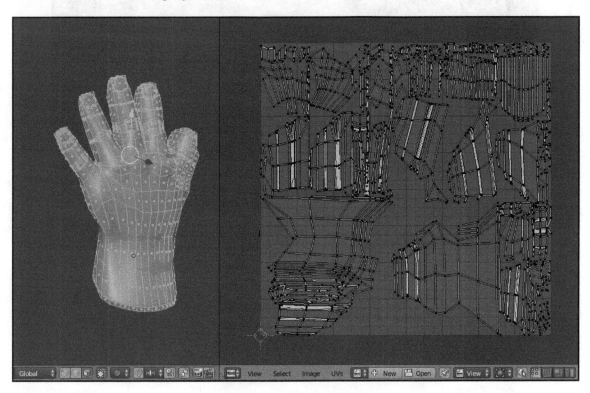

In the UV/Image Editor panel, all the flattened faces are displayed

The UV/Image Editor only displays the currently selected items. If I were to only select my knuckles, those flattened faces would be the only ones displayed:

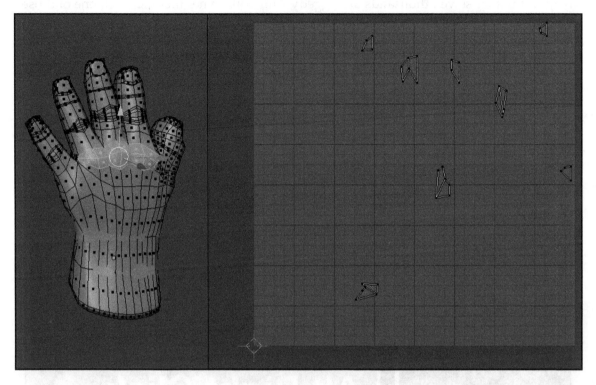

Only selected faces are displayed on the UV Map

Sometimes, the faces are put in unexpected places by the **Smart UV Project**. In the preceding example, adjacent faces in the knuckles are not adjacent in the UV Map. This may not be of concern if you are going to use Blender's built-in Texture Painting. If you'd like to edit in an outside graphics program, however, you may want to have a little more control over the appearance of your UV Map by telling Blender specifically how you want to cut up your model.

Marking and clearing seams

My grandmother sewed thousands of Raggedy Ann dolls in her lifetime. Each one of those dolls started out as flat pieces of fabric. They came together to make the 3D doll by carefully placed seams. In Blender, you can control how your faces are cut up and flattened by defining your own seams in your 3D model. To illustrate that, let's look at the process of cutting the hand into a top piece and a bottom piece. The steps are:

1. In **Edit Mode**, switch to **Edge select mode**.
2. Hold down the *Alt* key and right-click on an edge to select an entire edge loop. In my case, I select the edge loop that divides the hand into a top and a bottom:

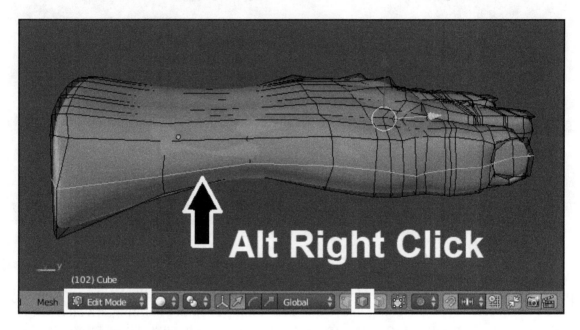

3. In the **Mesh** menu at the bottom of the screen, choose **Edges** and then **Mark Seam**. Alternatively, in the **Tool Shelf** on the left side of the screen, look under the **Shading/UVs** tab and click the **Mark Seam** button:

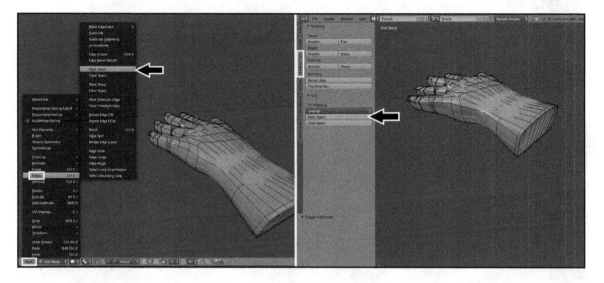

The selected edges are now shaded red to indicate they are a seam. To see those seams in action, we'll want to remake our UV Map, this time using plain **Unwrap**. The steps are:

1. In **Edit Mode**, switch to **Face Select** mode. Hit *A* to select all the faces.
2. Under the **Mesh** menu go to **UV Unwrap...** and select **Unwrap**:

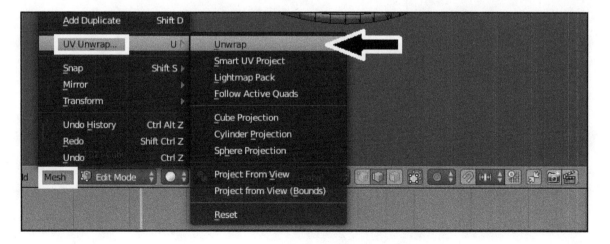

The resulting UV Map looks different. The faces were cut along the seams. I have a section for the front of my hand and another one for the back:

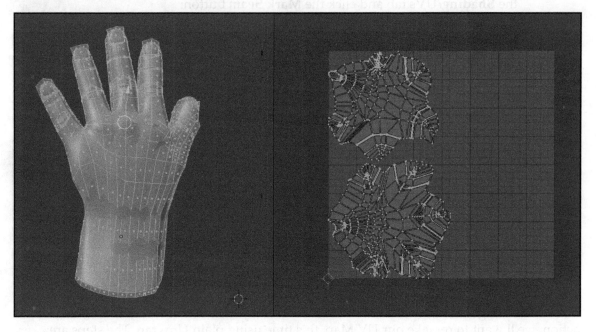

Seams cut the hand along the sides and produce a different UV Map

In addition, you'll find the faces may be in a more intuitive spot. When I select my knuckle faces now, they are all adjacent in my UV Map:

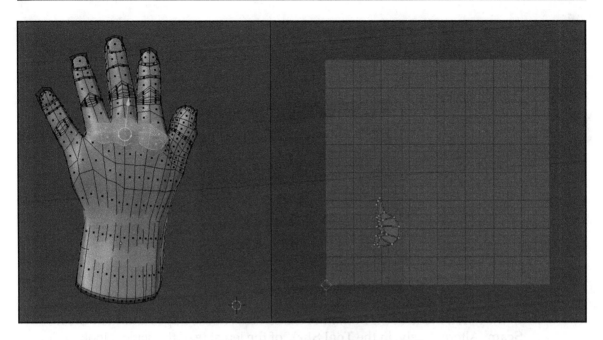

By using seams, faces may be more intuitive positioned in the resulting UV Map

In my grandmother's case, she would make sure the seams were in inconspicuous spots. She would want a seam to run down the side of the doll instead of right smack down its face. In 3D modeling, our seams are not going to leave a visible souvenir on our work. For our purposes, we would want to put seams around areas we want to easily identify and decorate. I know I want to style the fingernails, so I add additional seams around each fingernail as well. In my case, I would also have to remove a seam going through the thumbnail.

The steps to remove, or clear, seams are as follows:

1. In **Edit Mode**, hold down the *Shift* key and right-click the edges you would like to remove as seams:

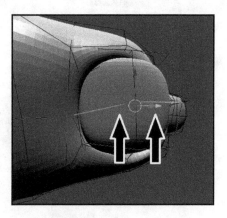

2. In the **Mesh** menu at the bottom of the screen, choose **Edges** and then **Clear Seam**. Alternatively, in the **Tool Shelf** of the left side of the screen, look under the **Shading/UVs** tab and click the **Clear Seam** button:

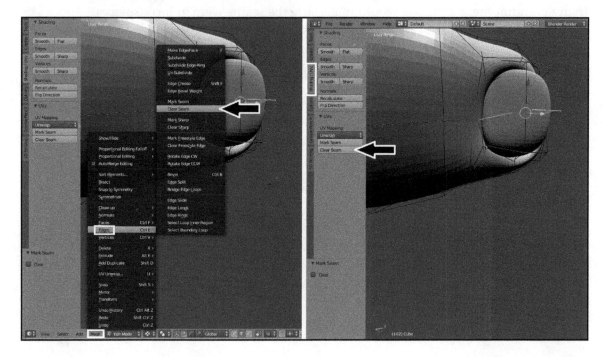

3. When you make seam changes, you'll need to unwrap again for your changes to take effect. In the **Mesh** menu, go to **UV Unwrap...** and select **Unwrap**.

4. It may be helpful to space the individual sections away from each other. At the bottom left hand of the screen there is a new **Unwrap** section. Increasing the **Margin** number will increase the space between islands. In my case, I set it to **0.10** to make sure my fingernail sections aren't touching the hand:

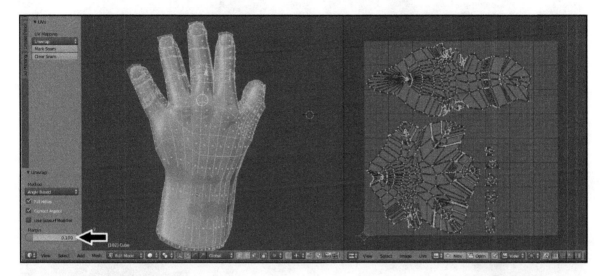

When I finish, I have my unwrapped hand with the fingernails cut out and set aside.

Preparing to Texture Paint

Blender gives you the ability to decorate and color your UV Map within its interface. It has tools very similar to other image editing tools such as Photoshop, Microsoft Paint, or GIMP. It has a **Fill** tool, for example, that will allow you to color a whole section at once. Before you begin, you have to assign a material to your object and set up an image to save the design.

The steps are as follows:

1. Change the **Object Mode** to **Texture Paint**:

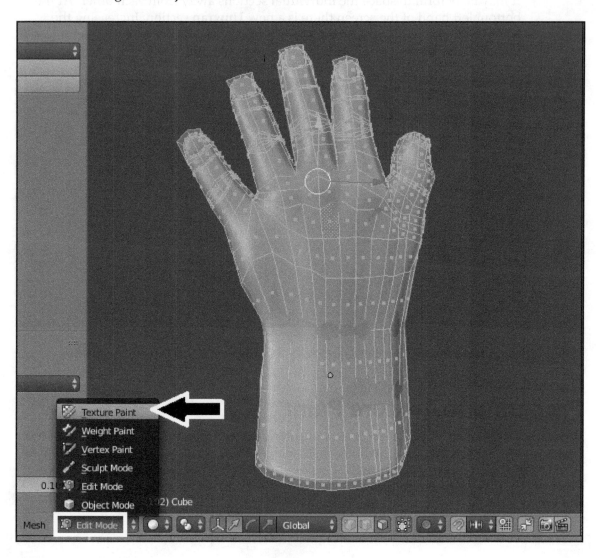

2. The hand turns bright white. In the **Tool Shelf** on the left side of the screen, there is a warning letting you know the object is missing a material. Click **Add Paint Slot**:

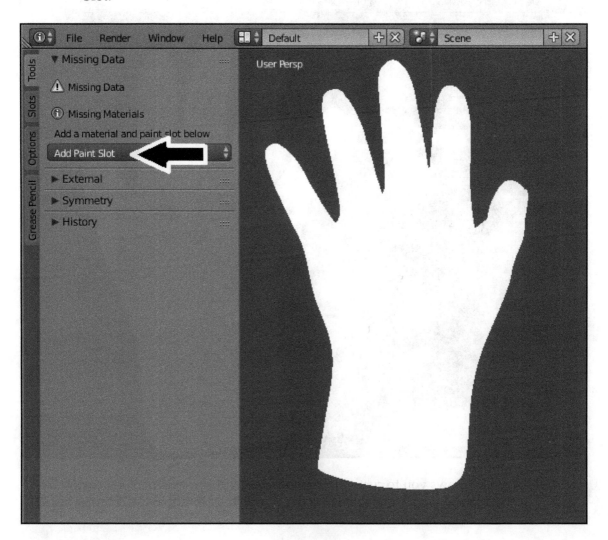

3. You can pick what type of **Paint Slot** to use. In my case, I select **Diffuse Color**:

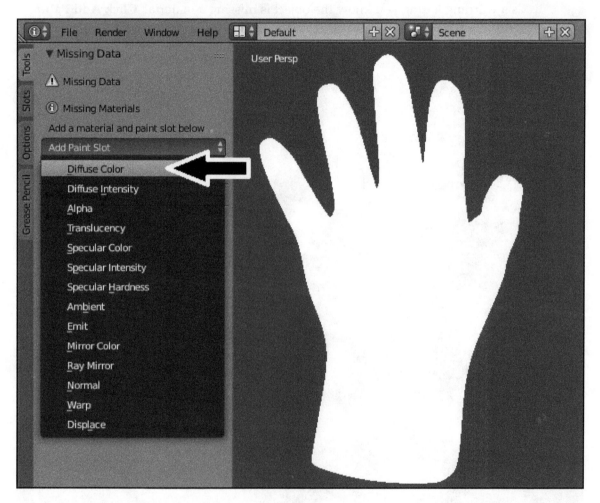

4. A menu allows you to customize options about the new Paint Slot. I customize the **Name** to HandColor and leave the **Width** and **Height** at the defaults. Hit **OK**:

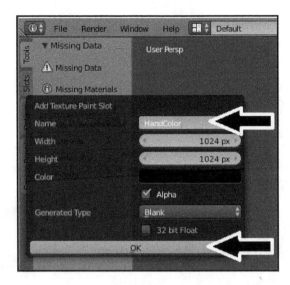

At this point, the hand turns black. The **Tool Shelf** changes to offer **Brush** options. If you take a detour to the **Properties Window** and look at the materials, you'll see a brand new material has been added:

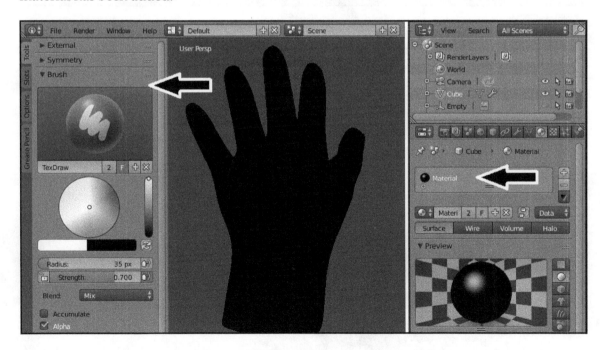

Once a Paint Slot has been added, Brush and Color options are available for use

There is one more thing we should do before beginning to paint. We need to define an image for Blender to save your work. The image will ultimately be uploaded with the model to the 3D Printing Service Bureau. The steps to set up the image are as follows:

1. In the **UV/Image Editor** panel, there is an image icon in the menu at the bottom of the screen. Click the **New** button to the right of that icon:

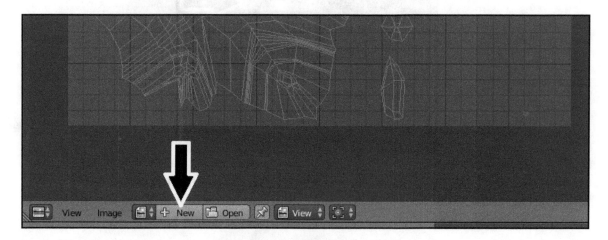

2. Blender will give you an opportunity to define information about the image. In my case, I customize the **Name**. I keep the default image size of 1024 by 1024 and hit **OK**:

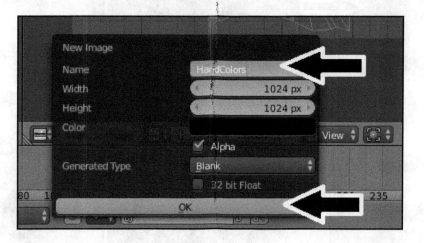

3. You will also want to tell Blender to physically save this work to an image file on your computer. Under the **Image** menu, select **Save as Image**. Customize the image name if desired and pick where to save it. I typically save my images in the same directory as the `.blend` file:

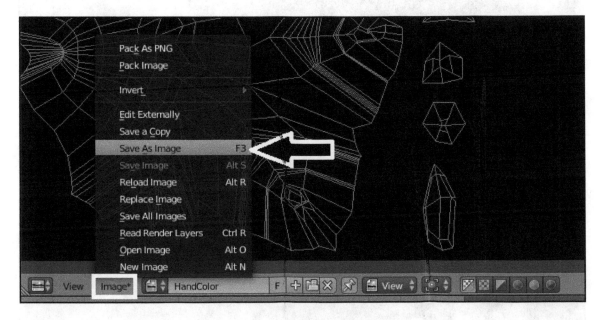

The background of your UV Map is now black as well, indicating we are ready to paint. In the Properties Window, there is a checkered box icon that allows you to access textures. Your image is listed there and can also be removed or changed if needed:

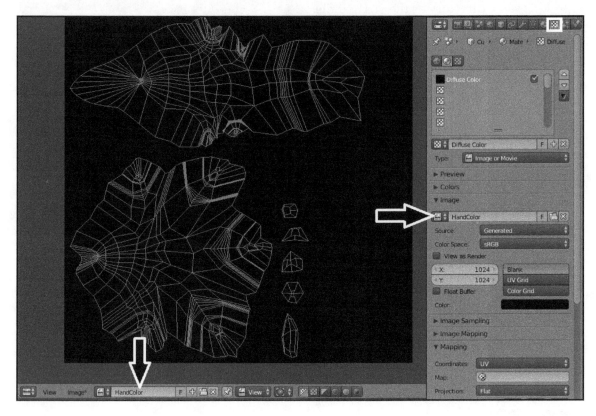

Image added, the background of the UV Map is black. The image is also listed in the Texture Properties

Painting in Blender

With a material and a texture image added, your mouse is now a paint brush. The default brush is simply Draw. In the Tool Shelf, you can pick the color you want to paint with. Like the earlier section, *Adding a Material to the Whole Object*, you can use a color wheel. In addition, if you click on the box with the color, a pop-up screen will let you type in specific **R**, **G**, **B** values:

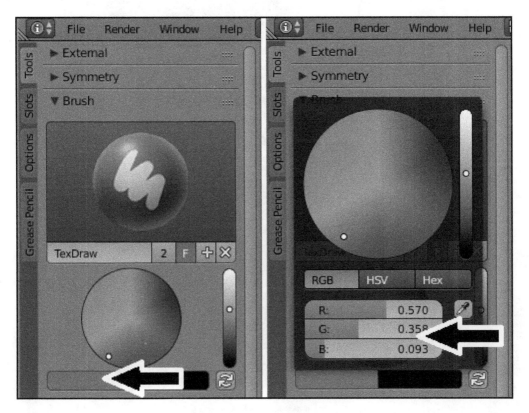

Colors can be picked in the Tool Shelf

You can also pick how big of a line the brush will make, the **Radius**, and how opaque it is, the **Strength** of the color. A high radius with a low strength will make a thick, transparent line. Thick strokes like this would be good for applying shading. A low radius with a high strength would make a very thin, solid line, one that is well suited for drawing details:

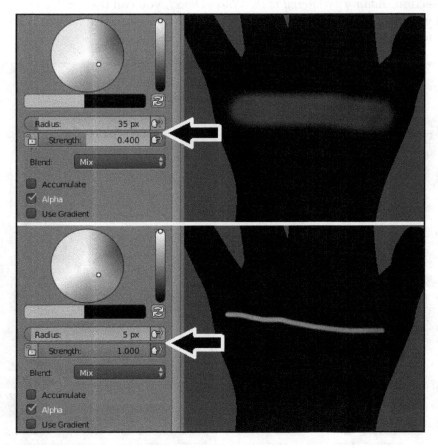

Impact of changing Radius and Strength

To start a line, click and hold the left mouse button, drag the mouse, and release the button when you are done. Both the **3D View** and the **UV/Image Editor** panels will give a view of your work:

Work is displayed in both panels

Using the Fill Brush

The **Fill Brush** is useful in setting up base colors for a piece. The steps to switching the **Brush** to **Fill** are:

1. In the **Tool Shelf** on the left side of the screen, look under the **Brushes** section and click the large sphere icon. A pop-up menu displays other options. Click on **F Fill**. Alternatively, you can go to the **Brush** menu at the bottom of the screen, select **Image Paint Tool**, and then pick **Fill**:

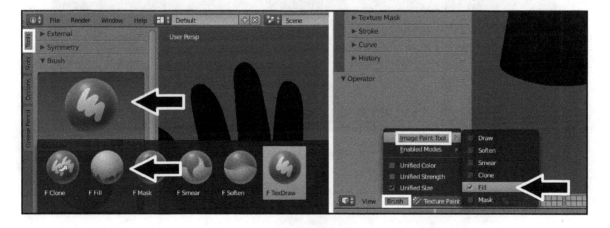

2. In the **Tool Shelf**, pick the color and the **Strength**:

3. Left-click your model in the **3D View** window to apply the color.

The entire model is painted with the selected color:

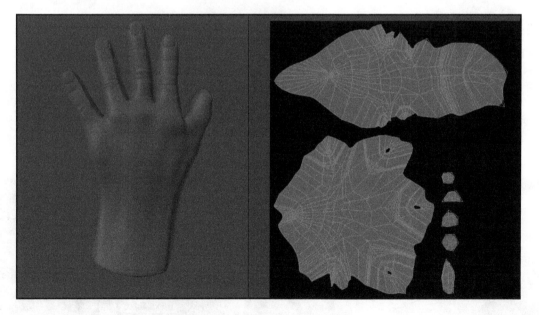

The 3D View and UV/Image Editor window reflects the fill color

Painting in the UV/Image Editor

You can also paint directly in the UV/Image Editor window. This is helpful if you want to confine something to the face islands, such as our fingernails that we have separated out in the UV Map. The steps to paint the fingernails are as follows:

1. In the **UV/Image Editor** window, there is a **Mode** drop-down menu in the bottom menu. Change that to **Paint**:

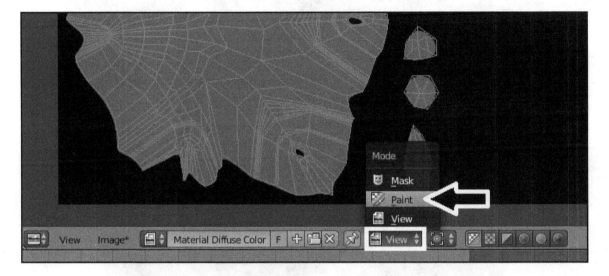

2. Pick the new color for the fingernails. I pick a much lighter color for contrast.
3. In the **UV/Image Editor** panel, click one of the fingernail islands to fill just that fingernail with the color:

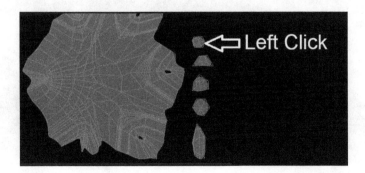

4. Repeat with the remaining nails.
5. When complete, be sure to save the changes to your image by going to the **Image** menu and clicking **Save Image**:

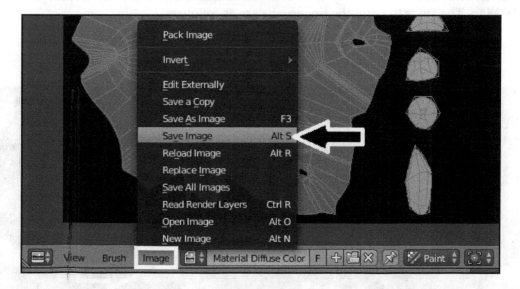

When I am done, each of the nails is set to a base color:

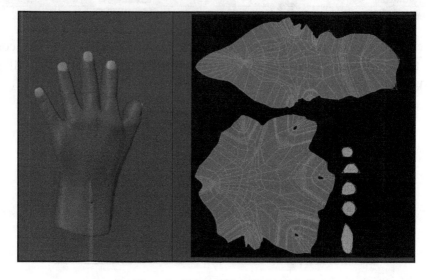

Two different colors for the base of the hand and the fingernails

You can switch back to the draw brush to add more details such as shadows and highlights. You can even draw in your own wrinkles if you want:

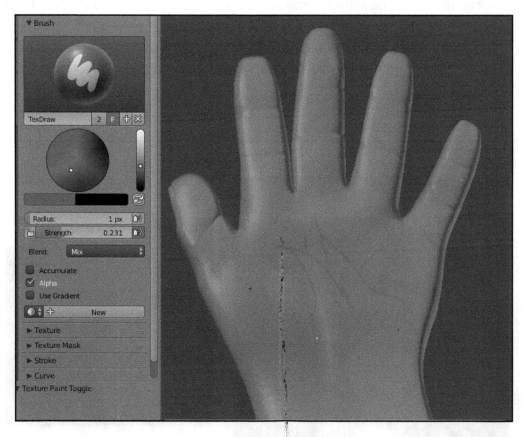

The draw brush can draw in extra detail lines

Editing images outside of Blender

If you have an image editing software you are already very comfortable with, you do have the ability to edit your image outside of Blender.

When you added your Paint Slot and New Image from before, you saved an image file on your computer. At any time in the process, you can edit that image with the following steps:

1. Open the image file in your software of choice, such as GIMP, Photoshop, or Paint:

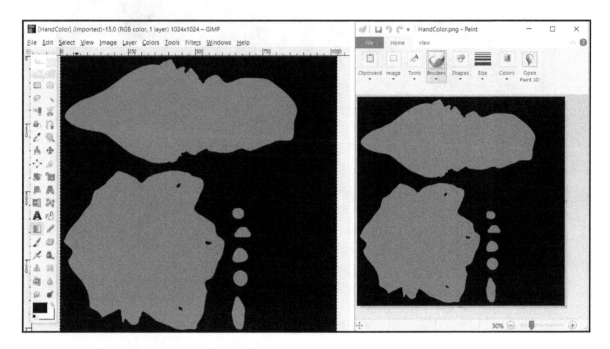

2. Make your edits in that program. As an example, I change my image to a gradient:

3. Save your changes to the original PNG file:

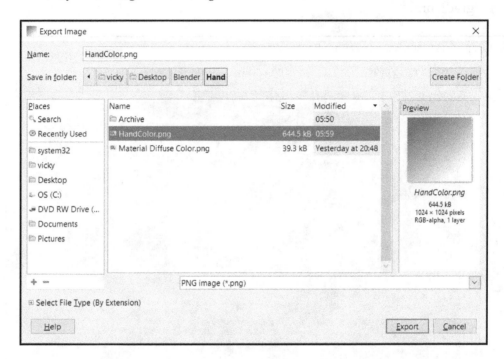

4. Back in Blender, in the **UV/Image Editor** window, click the **Image** menu and select **Reload Image**:

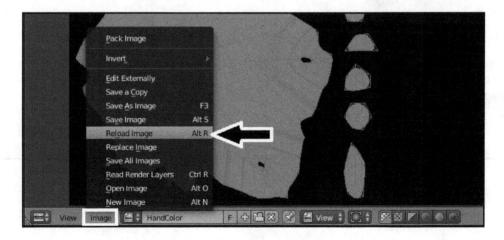

5. The model in the 3D View and the UV Map in the **UV/Image Editor** both reflect the new image:

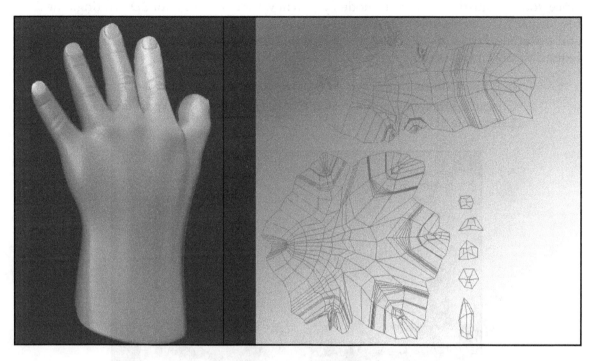

Outside edits to the image are now visible

Getting your UV Map for a background

Sometimes when working in an advanced image editing software, such as GIMP and Photoshop, it is helpful to have your UV Map as a background layer for reference. Blender can export such an image for you to use. Make sure your model is in **Edit Mode** and then go to the **UVs | Export UV Layout** menu option in the **UV/Image Editor** panel. This will make a PNG file that includes all the flattened edges and faces in your UV Map.

Exporting and uploading X3D files

Once you are satisfied with your model, you will want to export it for 3D printing. The .STL file format we have used for the other projects does not include information on the colors and materials. For a full-color project such as this one, we will want to use a format called Extensible 3D Graphics to make an X3D file. The steps are as follows:

1. In **Object Mode**, right-click your object to select it. In this case, I select my hand.
2. Go to the **File** menu at the very top of the screen. Click **Export** and pick **X3D Extensible 3D (.x3d)**:

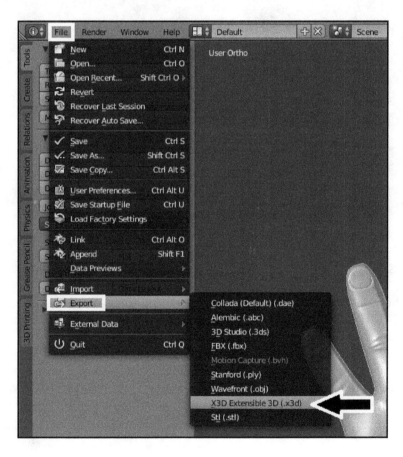

3. Customize the filename, if desired, and click the **Export X3D** button:

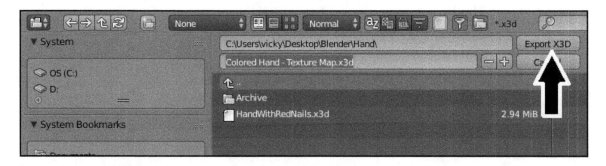

If you only colored your model with materials and did not use a UV Map or Texture Painting, then this X3D file is all you need for the 3D Printing Service Bureau. If you did use a UV Map, you'll have an extra step before uploading.

Zipping up the model and image files

Behind the scenes, the X3D file is just a text document with all the information about your model within. One part of that document lists any related image files:

```
Colored Hand - Texture Map.x3d - Notepad                    —    □    ×

File  Edit  Format  View  Help
  <Group DEF="group_ME_Cube">
          <Shape>
                  <Appearance>
                          <ImageTexture DEF="IM_Material_Diffuse_Color"
                                    url='"HandColor.png" "         icky/Desktop/Ble
                                    />
                          <TextureTransform
```

Inside the X3D file, the 3D Printing Service Bureau will find the images it needs to color your model

The 3D Printing Service Bureau is going to need that image to know how to color your model. As a result, instead of uploading STL file or X3D file, we will want to upload a ZIP that contains both the model (the X3D file) and the texture (the PNG file).

In Windows 10, the steps are as follows:

1. Open **File Explorer** and browse to the directory where you have your files saved
2. Holding down the *Ctrl* key left click to select both your X3D file and the related PNG file
3. Right-click one of the selected files and pick **Send to | Compressed (zipped) folder**:

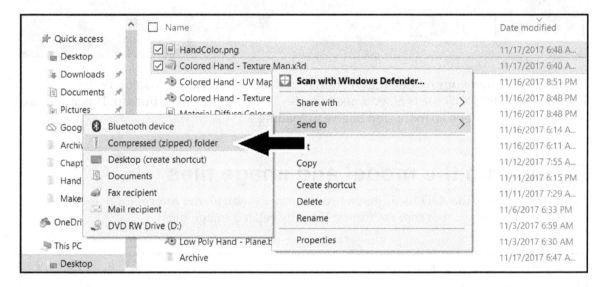

4. Upload the new ZIP file to the 3D Printing Service Bureau instead

Checking the renders for CMYK issues

Regardless of whether you upload just the X3D file or a ZIP file, I highly recommend you check the preview renders from the 3D Printing Service Bureau. Blender uses RGB colors, where the colors are defined by a combination of red, green, and blue values. The industrial 3D Printers use CMYK, a combination of cyan, magenta, yellow, and black. RGB is device-specific so what looks good on your screen may not look the same in a non-device specific, color scheme such as CMYK. If the preview looks off when you upload it, that is an indication your colors may need to be adjusted:

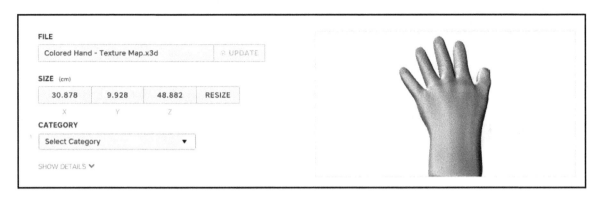

FILE

Colored Hand - Texture Map.x3d   ⟳ UPDATE

SIZE (cm)

30.878	9.928	48.882	RESIZE
X	Y	Z	

CATEGORY

Select Category   ▼

SHOW DETAILS ✔

Always check the colors in your previews from the 3D Printing Service Bureaus

Summary

In this chapter, you learned how to use the full-color capabilities of the 3D Printing Service Bureaus by exploring two ways of adding colors to your 3D model. First, you learned how you can add and assign materials to specific faces. Next, you learned how you can unwrap the surfaces of your model into a flat UV Map. You saw how UV Maps could be colored within Blender or outside of Blender in image editing software. You learned how to export your work into the X3D format that supports color information. Finally, you uploaded your work to a 3D Printing Service Bureau.

Sometimes 3D modeling for 3D printing can be a bumpy road. In `Chapter 15`, *Troubleshooting and Repairing Models,* you will learn how to troubleshoot and resolve common modeling issues.

15
Troubleshooting and Repairing Models

Blender is a very powerful application with capabilities that extend well beyond 3D printing. Because its goals are often grander, Blender is not always concerned with making clean, printable meshes. Sometimes your model will develop issues that will need to be repaired for better 3D printing. In this chapter, you will learn how to identify and resolve common issues. The skills include:

- Removing duplicate vertices
- Flipping bad face normals
- Locating and correcting non-manifold edges
- Enabling and using the 3D Print Toolbox add-on
- Using Windows 10's 3D Builder application to repair models

Removing duplicate vertices

Sometimes during modeling work, extra vertices are accidentally created. In `Chapter 7`, *Customizing with Text*, we talked about how setting the **Extrude** property for a text object before converting to a 3D mesh is likely to cause issues. The source of those issues is a large number of duplicate vertices.

Because they are in the exact same spot as other vertices, the duplicates are naturally camouflaged and hard to recognize. You may see subtle signs of their presence when you are multi-selecting with the *Shift* key. Normally, when you pick two vertices that are connected by an edge, that edge is also highlighted:

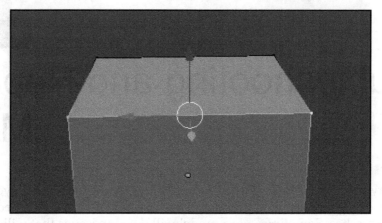

Normal behavior, selecting both vertices selects the related edge as well

If you select two vertices and the edge between them is not highlighted, there is something amiss. One of the vertices you selected is not part of that edge. There is a hidden vertex in the exact same spot that is:

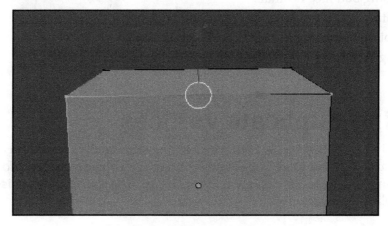

Both vertices are selected, but the edge in between is not

Although your object may look fine, duplicate vertices lead to other issues such as non-manifold edges and cause complications doing Boolean Modifiers. Luckily, they are very easy to fix. If you suspect an object has extra vertices, the steps to correct it are:

1. In **Edit Mode**, switch to **Vertex Select** mode and hit *A* to select all the vertices
2. Click the **Mesh** menu at the bottom of the screen, select **Vertices**, and then pick **Remove Doubles**:

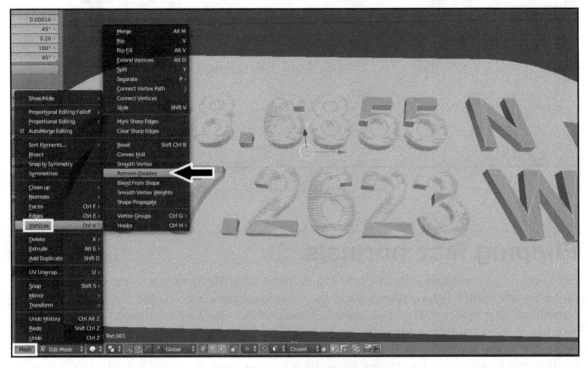

Using the Mesh menu to remove duplicate vertices

A small information box at the top of the 3D View panel will indicate how many duplicates were found and removed. If all is well, this box will read **Removed 0 vertices**. In the following example, 5710 duplicates were located and removed:

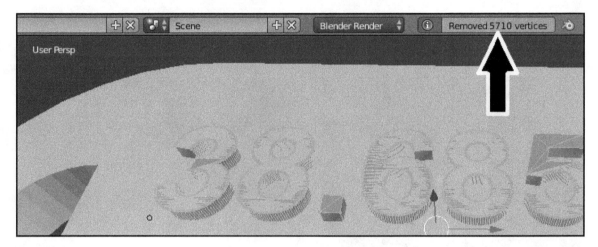

Blender reports back how many duplicates were removed

Flipping face normals

In Chapter 3, *Converting a Bezier Curve to a Properly Sized 3D Mesh*, you were introduced to face normals, which is how Blender and the slicer determine what is the inside and the outside of your object. A common issue is some of those normals are flipped so Blender would see the outside of your object as an inside. As illustrated in Chapter 3, *Converting a Bezier Curve to a Properly Sized 3D Mesh*, you can turn on a light blue line in the Properties Shelf to mark outside of your faces. For a normal cube, such as the cube on the left in the following image, each blue line is facing the outside. However, sometimes during your modeling process, particularly when you are making your own faces, one or more faces gets flipped. In the cube on the right, one face is missing a blue line. It is facing the wrong way and pointing to the inside of the cube instead:

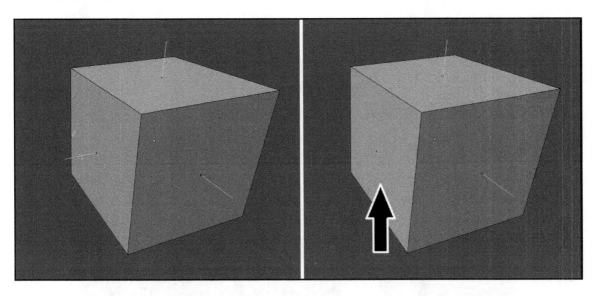

The cube on the left has appropriate face normals. The cube on the right has one flipped.

Sometimes bad face normals will become obvious when you are working with the Boolean Modifier. You may receive an error message or get some unexpected results. For example, if I were to do the Boolean Union on two good cubes, I would get the expected combination of both. The same Boolean Union, however, presents very different results when just one face is flipped:

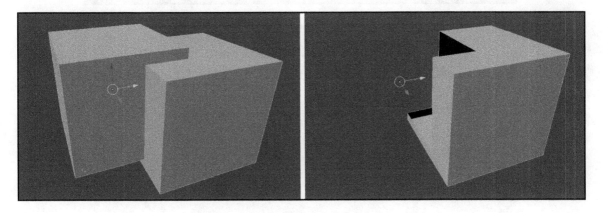

Unexpected Boolean Modifier results may be an indication of bad face normals

You may also notice bad face normals as you work with your object in **Edit Mode**. The insides of the faces are shaded slightly darker. Looking at a window from my house figurine, if I noticed some squares of glass were darker than the others, I would take a closer look at their normals:

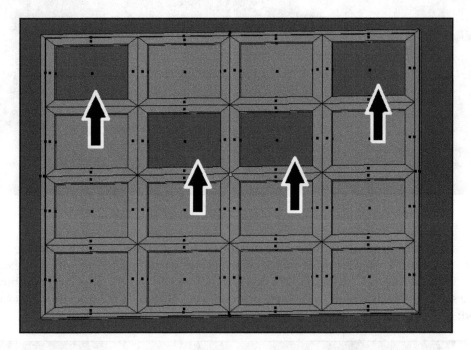

Darker faces in the window indicate discrepancies in the face normals

Similarly, when you are working in **Texture Paint** mode, Blender is painting the outside of your faces. If you are ever coloring your object and notice a black hole that does not correspond to your UV Map, that is another indication those faces are flipped:

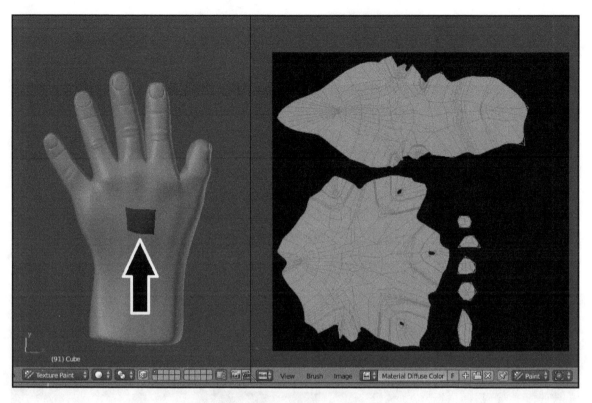

The black hole in the hand is due to faces being flipped

In most cases, you can correct these issues by having Blender recalculate the face normals for you. It'll take a fresh look at your object and decide what should be the outside. The steps are:

1. In **Edit Mode**, switch to **Face Select** mode. Click *A* to select all the faces.

2. Under the **Mesh** menu at the bottom of the screen, click **Normals**, and select **Recalculate Outside**. Alternatively, you can hit the *Ctrl + N* keys on the keyboard:

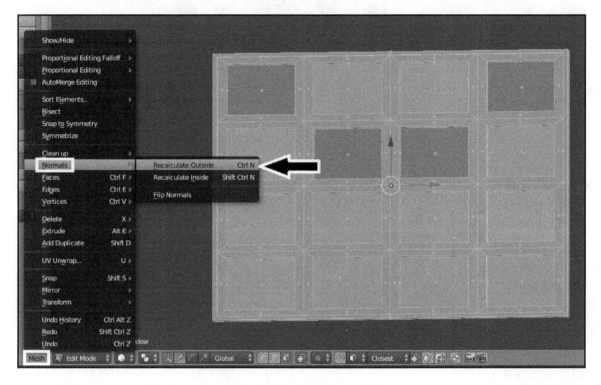

Asking Blender to recalculate face normals

In the event that that does not resolve the issue, you can also tell Blender to flip the normals for only specific faces of your choosing. The steps are:

1. In **Edit Mode**, switch to **Face Select** mode. Select the **Faces** you want to flip.
2. Under the **Mesh** menu at the bottom of the screen, click **Normals**, and select **Flip Normals**:

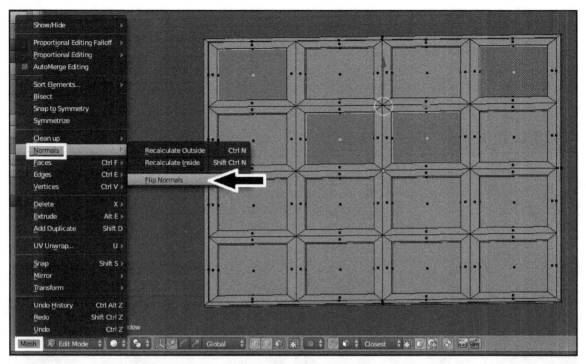

Flipping the face normals of specific faces

When done, the symptoms you saw earlier should be resolved.

Finding and fixing non-manifold edges

When I first started 3D printing, the non-manifold edge was an intimidating concept to grasp. For our purposes, you can think of manifold as something that can be manufactured and become a real-life object. Everything has an inside and an outside, is connected, has a thickness, and would make sense to the 3D printer. Non-manifold, on the other hand, would be a geometry that can't exist in real life.

Exploring examples of non-manifold edges

For a more concrete way of looking at it, all your edges should be connected to two faces with matching normals. Edges that don't meet that criteria will be flagged as non-manifold. Some examples are explained in the following sections:

Faces without thickness

A simple 2D plane is non-manifold. All four edges are only connected to one face. As a result, the object has no real-life thickness. Our profile pendant before extruding is also non-manifold. Once it is extruded, all edges are connected to two faces and our pendant has a thickness:

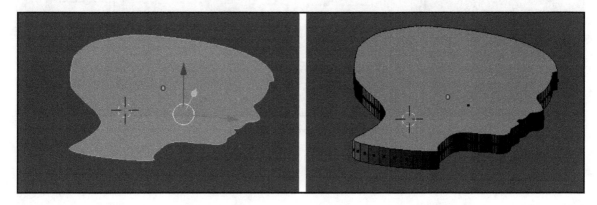

Any 2D object, such as a plane or profile, is non-manifold. It is missing a real-life thickness.

Missing faces or holes

Perhaps I decide I want to make the house figurine hollow to save on material cost. A misguided approach would be to delete the bottom faces of the house. The house looks hollow in Blender, but all the edges around the bottom are only connected to a single face and are therefore non-manifold. You can also think of it as the walls of the house no longer have a thickness. A better way to achieve my goal would be to insert and extrude in, which makes sure all edges have two connected faces and my walls have a thickness:

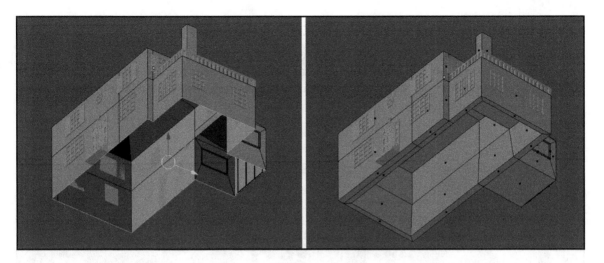

Deleting the faces at the bottom of the House Figurine would leave all the walls without a thickness and create non-manifold edges. Insetting and extruding faces would make sure my object stays printable.

Inconsistent face normals

The situation where a face normal is flipped will also cause non-manifold edges. The edge may be connected to two faces, but their normals are contradicting each other. One face is pointing in one direction and the other is pointing the opposite way. The sudden switch from the inside and outside of the object would not make sense in real life. Once that face normal is corrected, the edge is corrected as well:

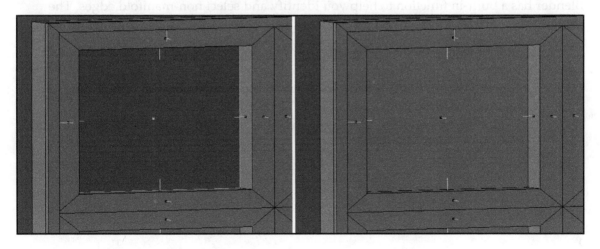

Edges connecting two faces with contradicting face normals are also considered non-manifold

Overlapping and unconnected geometry

Sometimes objects appear connected, but in reality, they are not. Take the case of duplicate vertices in the coordinate bracelet. The decimal point for my coordinate looks like an intact cube. When I select a corner point and move it, a gaping hole is revealed. The adjacent faces are not actually connected, leaving each edge affiliated with a single, independent face. In the correct geometry, when that single vertex is moved, the related faces adjust and no hole is revealed.

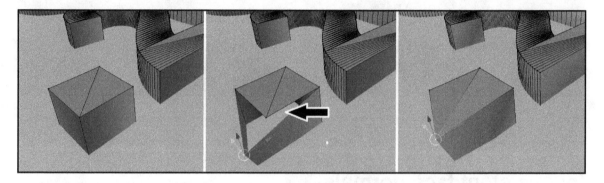

The decimal point looks normal, but when you move a vertex, a hole opens up in the object. The faces are not actually connected. When they are, vertices can be moved without creating holes.

Highlighting non-manifold edges

Blender has a built-in function to help you identify and select non-manifold edges. The steps are:

1. In **Edit Mode**, make sure you are either in **Vertex Select** mode or **Edge Select** mode
2. If you have anything already selected, hit the *A* key to deselect everything and start with a clean slate
3. Under the **Select** menu at the bottom of the screen, pick **Select All by Trait** and then select **Non Manifold**:

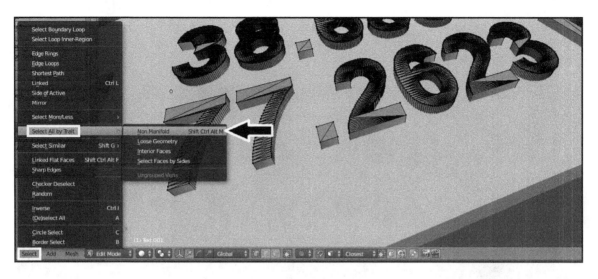

Blender can select all non-manifold edges for you

Blender will select and highlight all non-manifold edges for you. At the very top of the screen, Blender lists statistics. It'll show you how many edges are selected, as well as the total number of edges. Since we only have non-manifold edges selected, the first number is a count of issues. If that count reads zero, all edges are correct:

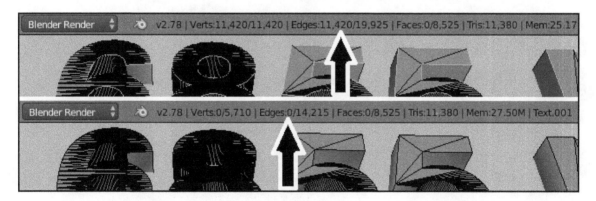

The selected edge count will give you a tally of non-manifold edges. When that count is zero, all the issues are resolved.

Sometimes the issues are extra geometry inside your object that would normally be hard to see. Switching the Limit selection to visible or switching to **Wireframe** view gives you better visibility of those problems:

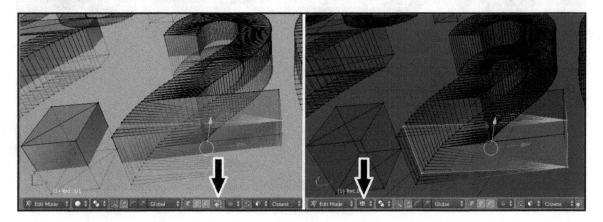

Toggling the Limit selection to visible and switching to Wireframe mode helps you see the troubled edges

Turning on and using 3D Print Toolbox

Blender also has a 3D Print Toolbox add-on that can help identify non-manifold and other 3D printing issues. It is not a necessity but can be helpful. You can turn it on simply by checking a box in Blender. The steps are:

1. In the **File** menu at the top of the screen, click **User Preferences**:

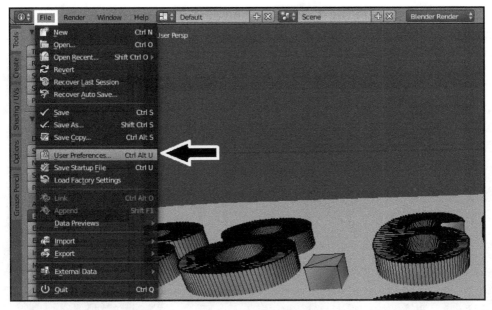

Getting to Blender's User Preferences

2. Click the **Add-ons** tab at the top. Under **Categories**, pick **Mesh**:

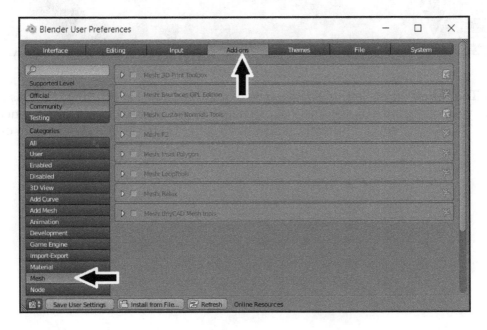

Exploring Add-ons

3. Check **Mesh: 3D Print Toolbox** and hit the **Save User Settings** button:

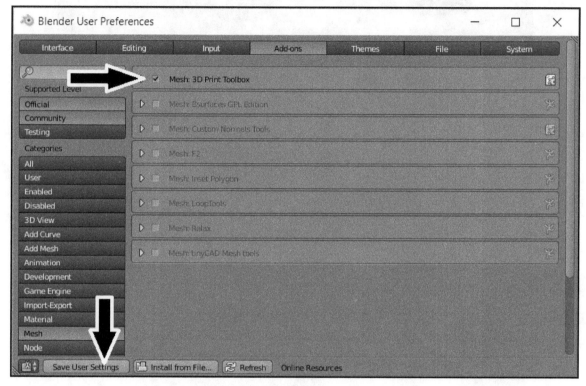

Checking the 3D Print Toolbox Add-on

In your **Tool Shelf** on the left side of the screen, there is a new **3D Printing** tab. This section can give you calculations on volume that can help you get a sense of your cost, particularly with the 3D Printing Service Bureaus. It also has a series of checks you can perform on your object.

Most commonly, I use it when looking for non-manifold edges. The steps are:

1. In the **Tool Shelf** on the left side of the screen, click the **3D Printing** tab. Under **Checks**, click **Solid**. You can run this check in both **Object Mode** and **Edit Mode**:

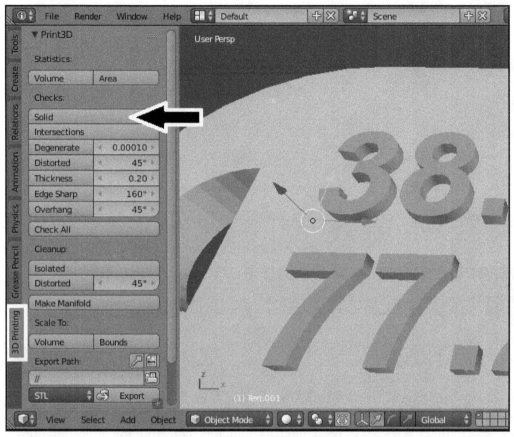

Performing a Solid check on the model

2. The **Output** section will list any issues, including a **Non Manifold Edge** count. If you have non-manifold edges and would like to select them, switch into **Edit Mode** and click the **Non Manifold Edge** button:

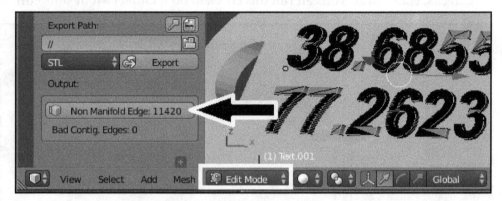

Clicking the Non Manifold Edge button will select all the bad edges

Like the **Select All by Trait** feature, all the troublesome edges are selected for review.

Correcting non-manifold edges

Your approach to fixing non-manifold edges will vary depending on the circumstances. As a general rule of thumb, my strategies are:

1. Are there other contributing issues? As we have seen, other problems in the model can lead to non-manifold edges. As the first plan of attack, remove doubles and check face normals.

2. Do you have missing faces? It is possible your non-manifold edges could be resolved by hitting *F* to create a missing face.

3. Are these extra edges or geometry? Sometimes deleting the offending non-manifold edges puts your model back intact.

If the model is still troublesome, you do have the option to delete and recreate offending edges and faces. That could be a tedious venture. Luckily, the 3D Printing Toolbox has a button to make model changes for you. The steps to use that are:

1. In **Object Mode**, right-click to select the troublesome object.
2. In the **Tool Shelf** on the left side of the screen, look under the **3D Printing** tab and click the **Make Manifold** button:

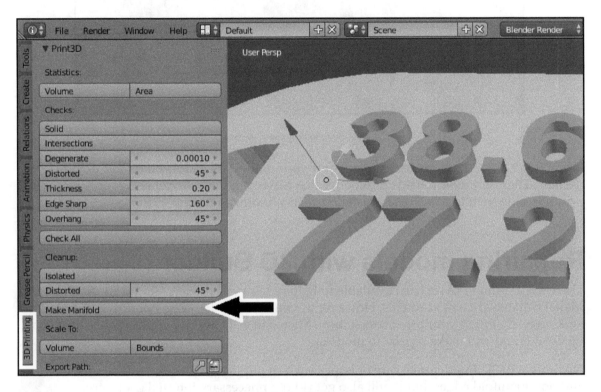

The 3D Print Toolbox has a Make Manifold function

An information section at the top of the screen will list the changes that were made to your model. This includes changing and making new faces:

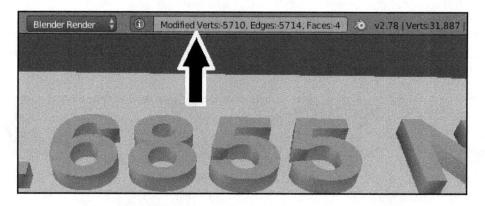

Model changes are listed in the top title bar

If you don't like the automated changes or if your model still gives you issues, do not despair. There are tools outside of Blender that can repair your model and prepare it for 3D printing. One such tool is already installed with Windows 10.

Repairing models with 3D Builder

There are a number of services available to help repair your models. Autodesk NetFabb and MakePrintable are two examples. However, if you are already using Windows 10, you need look no further than your own workstation. Microsoft's 3D Builder application is installed by default and will make repairs to models.

Not only will 3D Builder take care of issues such as duplicate vertices, bad face normals, and non-manifold edges, but it will also get rid of unnecessary internal geometry. In Chapter 4, *Flattening a Torus and Boolean Union*, we saw how overlapping separate objects (without doing a Boolean Modifier) would cause confusing internal geometry. 3D Builder will recognize and correct that issue as well.

To use 3D Builder in Windows 10, the steps are:

1. In Blender, go to **File | Export | Stl (.stl)** to save your model as an STL file. Don't forget to check the **Selection Only** box.
2. Open up **3D Builder** in Windows 10. You can type in 3D Builder in the Cortana search bar to find it:

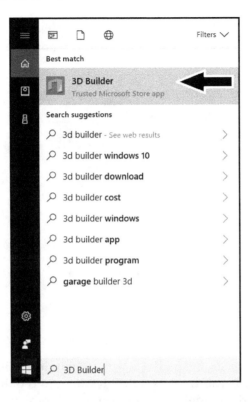

Finding 3D Builder with a Windows search

3. When 3D Builder comes up, click the **Open** button. On the next screen, click **Load Object**:

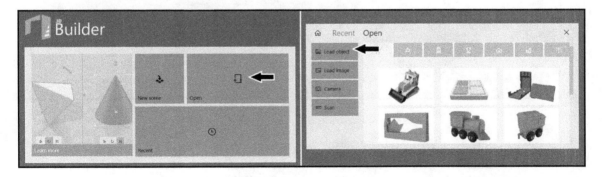

Loading an object into 3D Builder

4. Browse to and select the STL file you made in step one. Click **Open**.

5. A preview of your object appears. Click the **Import Model** button at the top of your screen:

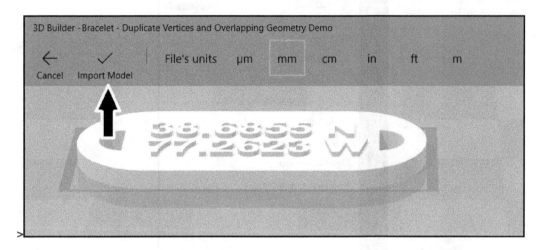

Importing the model and picking units

6. If there are issues with the model, a pop-up window will alert you that **One or more objects are invalidly defined. Click here to repair.** Click anywhere in the popup to repair the model. Another pop-up window will let you know the object is being repaired:

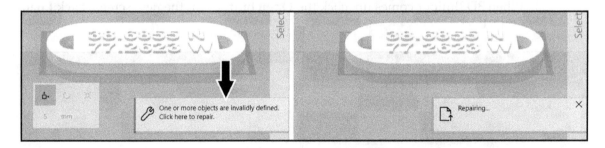

Model errors and repair status are in the lower right-hand corner of the screen

7. When the repair process is done, you need to save the fixed model back as an STL file. Click the three-line menu icon at the top left of the screen. Select **Save As**. Adjust the **Save as type** to **STL Format (*.stl)**. Name the file as you see fit. I often add a _fixed suffix to the original file name. Click **Save** to complete the process:

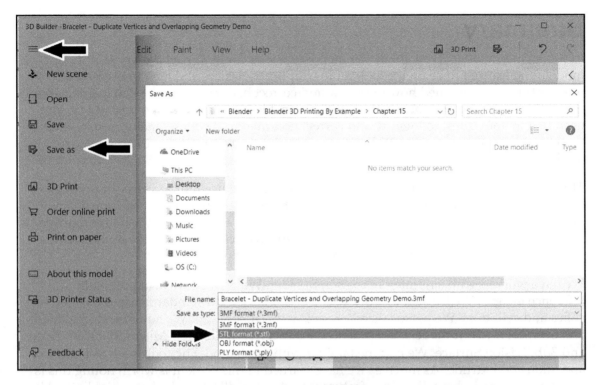

Saving the repaired file to a new STL

The repaired file will correct a myriad of issues. In this example, I had duplicate vertices and thousands of non-manifold edges. In addition, the coordinates did not sit flush on the bracelet plate. Instead, part of the text resided inside the bracelet itself. These issues presented challenges to the slicer and were putting me well on my way to a failed print.

However, the file saved from 3D Builder has all those issues corrected and gives me a much cleaner slice:

The unrepaired file on the left is quite troublesome. The repaired file on the right matches my vision.

Summary

In this chapter, you learned about common issues that could impact the printability of your model. You learned to be on the lookout for duplicate vertices and how to use Blender to remove them. You learned how to review and correct bad face normals. You learned about the tricky concept of non-manifold edges. You enabled the 3D Print Toolbox add-on and used that in your quest to identify and correct non-manifold edges. Finally, you learned how outside tools, such as the 3D Builder in Windows 10, can be used to repair your models.

Throughout this book, you have seen how Blender can be used for a variety of projects. Blender can help with jewelry projects, such as the profile pendant and the coordinate bracelet. Blender can accommodate architectural models, as seen with the house figurine. Finally, you are not limited to geometric, precisely-sized models. With the human hand, you got a taste of Blender's ability to make organic shapes.

We have worked with a number of tools in Blender. We learned ways of pulling in reference images. We learned to work with Bezier curves and standard shapes such as cubes and cylinders. We personalized projects with custom text. We added texture detailing and even color to our models. We practiced a battery of modifiers—Mirror, Boolean, Array, and Subdivision Surface. We became familiar with mesh modeling tools such as Loop Cut and Slide and Extrude. As much as we have learned in this book, it is worth noting this is just the tip of the iceberg. Blender's feature set extends well beyond what is highlighted in this book.

Blender is a very capable and flexible program. 3D printing is a very capable and flexible means of manufacturing. The combination of the two has helped me bring my ideas to life and make gifts for my friends and loved ones. I hope Blender and 3D printing help you to make the things you want to make.

Index

3

3D Builder
  used, for repairing models 402, 405
3D Cursor
  moving 34
3D mesh
  converting to 244
  rotating to 242, 244
  scaling to 242, 244
  text, converting to 150
3D Modeling Software 250
3D objects
  Extrude Region, using 54, 55
  face normal 52, 53
  face normal, viewing 52, 53
  making 52
3D Print Toolbox
  turning on 396, 400
  using 396, 400
3D printing
  model, exporting for 86

A

advanced mirror options 102
Array Modifier
  about 225
  adding 225
  combining with 245
  Fit Type, picking 225, 227
  impact of scale 227, 230
  nesting 232, 236
  Offset, setting 230, 232
  used, for making brickwork 224

B

background image
  adding 27
  adding, to Blender 29
  good photo, finding 29
  Orthographic View, switching to 31
base, jewelry project
  cube and cylinder combining 100
  making 100
  mirror axis 100
  Mirror Modifier, adding 107, 109
  Object's Origin, updating to specific vertex 102
Bezier curves
  3D Cursor, moving 34
  about 33
  adding 34
  control points 36
  control points, adding 39
  control points, moving 37, 38
  converting, into mesh 45, 49
  editing 35
  finalizing 42
  handle types, changing 41
  handles points 36
  Object Interaction Mode, modifying 35
  photograph, deviating 43
  shape, adjusting with handles 38, 39
  Toggle Cyclic feature 44
  tracing with 33
  work, checking 42
Blender
  about 250
  background image, adding to 29
  camera 26
  default cube 26
  Fill Brush, using 369, 370

images, editing outside of 374, 376, 377
lamp 26
painting in 367, 368
panel, adding 347, 349
using 26
UV/Image Editor, painting in 371, 372, 373
Boolean difference
  used, for making hole 130, 132
Boolean Intersection Modifier
  adding 273
  adjusting 276, 278
  applying 272, 278, 281
  placing 278, 281
  previewing 274
  Supporting Object, hiding 276
  Viewport Shading, switching to Wireframe 275, 276
Boolean Modifier 83
Boolean Union
  objects, combining 82, 85
border select tool 77
bracelet
  finalizing 153, 154
brickwork
  Array Modifier, adding 225
  Array Modifiers, nesting 232, 236
  making, with Array Modifier 224
built plate 8

C

CMYK issues
  renders, checking 380
colored materials
  adding, to faces 341, 343
  adding, to object 338, 340
  reusing 345, 346
  using 337
Constant Offset 231
control points 38
Ctrl key
  used, for multiselect 122, 124
cube
  default cube, resizing 90
  low-poly hand, modeling from 288
  working with 90

cylinder
  adding 92
  duplicating 112, 114
  moving, into place 97
  sizing 92, 112, 114
  working with 90

D

duplicate vertices
  about 151
  removing 383, 386

E

edge loops
  3D Cursor, rotating around 320, 323
  moving 315
  selecting 315
  sliding 317, 319
  using, for wrinkles 333
edges 46, 49
empties
  about 158
  adding 158, 160, 161
  adjusting, for differences in pictures 166, 168, 169, 170
  rotating 162, 163, 165
  scaling 166, 168, 169, 170
  transparency mode, setting 170, 172, 173
  using, for reference images 158
  X-Ray Mode, setting 170, 172, 173
exterior radius 66
extra edge loops
  adding 310
  base, flattening 313
  base, flattening with Loop Cut and Slide 314
  base, flattening with Mean Crease 314
  rounds, controlling 311
  shaping details 312
Extrude Region
  using 54, 55
Extrude tool
  using 152
Extrude
  used, for raising details of window 210, 211,

213, 215
using, fro fingernails 330
extrusion width 13

F

face normal
  about 52, 53
  viewing 52, 53
faces
  about 49
  colored materials, adding 341, 343
  creating 49, 51, 127, 129, 261
  filling 267, 269, 270, 271
  joining 261
  new edges, creating 267, 269, 270, 271
  normals, flipping 386, 388, 389, 391
  unnecessary edges, deleting 262, 264
  unnecessary faces, deleting 262, 264
  Vertex Coordinates, adjusting 265, 267
filament 8
fingernails
  Extrude, using for 329
  Inset, using for 329
  modeling 329
Fit Type 225
flat bases 283, 285
font filename
  finding 144
font settings
  font filename, finding 144, 146
  modifying 143
  new font, picking 146, 148
  size, adjusting 148
function
  sizing 22
Fused Deposition Modeling (FDM) printers 8
Fused Filament Fabrication (FFF) printers
  about 8
  detailing 11
  extrusion width 13
  flat bases 15
  layer height 11
  overhangs 8
  wall thickness 14

H

half cylinder
  Ctrl key, used for multiselect 122, 124
  faces, creating 127, 129
  making, with mesh modeling 121
  Shift key, used for multiselect 121, 122
  vertices, deleting 125, 126
handle types
  Automatic/Aligned handle type 41
  Free handle type 41
hole
  making, with Boolean difference 130, 132
  placing 115
  positioning, with reference cube 118, 120
  positioning, with ruler 118, 120
  positioning, with subtraction 116, 118
house base
  Extrude, using 178
  Loop Cut and Slide, using 186, 190
  modeling 174, 177
house
  exporting 281
  finalizing 281

I

Inkscape
  about 238
  URL 238
Inset
  about 204
  used, for finishing window panes 204
  using, for fingernails 329
interior radius 66
International System of Units 57

L

layer height 11
Loop Cut and Slide
  using 186, 190
low-poly hand
  face, rotation 294, 296
  fingers, extruding 297, 299
  fingers, scaling 297, 299
  Loop Cut and Slide, used for making fingers 289,

290
  manual adjustments, making 294, 296
  modeling, from cube 288
  modeling, from plane 299
  shaping, with Extrude 291, 293, 294
  shaping, with Scale 291, 293, 294
low-poly model
  about 286
  creating 286
  reference images, adding 286, 288

M

mesh modeling
  about 76
  used, for making half cylinder 121
mesh
  about 45
  Bezier curve, converting into 45, 49
  current dimensions, reading 58, 59
  metric system, converting to 57
  model, scaling by typing dimensions 59
  scale, reading 58, 59
  scale, updation by fixing proportions 61, 62
  scaling 56
  sizing 56
metric system
  converting to 57
model
  exporting, for 3D printing 86
  repairing, with 3D Builder 402, 405
modifier order
  used, for modifying object 132, 134
multiselect
  Ctrl key, using 122, 124
  Shift key, using 121, 122

N

non-manifold edges, examples
  about 392
  faces, missing 392
  faces, without thickness 392
  holes, missing 392
  inconsistent face normals 393
  overlapping geometry 394

  unconnected geometry 394
non-manifold edges
  3D Print Toolbox, turning on 396, 400
  3D Print Toolbox, using 396, 400
  about 151
  correcting 400, 402
  finding 391
  fixing 391
  highlighting 394, 396

O

Object Interaction Mode
  about 35
  edit mode 35
  modifying 35
  object mode 35
Object Origins
  cylinder, moving into place 97
  mirroring 95
  points 94
  positioning 96
  rotating 95
  scaling 95
  used, for lining objects 94
object
  colored materials, adding 338, 340
  combining, with Boolean Union 82, 85
  finding, with Outliner 241
  finding, with Properties Shelf 241
  joining, as shortcut 257, 260
  modifying, with modifier order 132, 134
  separating, as shortcut 257, 260
  unwrapping, into UV Maps 350, 352, 353
Orthographic View 32, 33
Outliner
  used, for finding objects 241
outlines 10
overhangs 8, 283, 285

P

peeling 16
Perspective View 31
Pinshape
  reference link 285

plane
low-poly hand, modeling from 299
position
setting, with Snap 220, 221
printer
sizing 21
printing processes
3D Printing Service Bureaus 17
about 7
Fused Filament Fabrication (FFF) printers 8
requisites, comparing 20
Selective Laser Sintering (SLS) printers 17
sizing 21
Stereolithography (SLA) printers 16
Properties Shelf
about 98
used, for finding objects 241

Q

quads 308

R

reference images
Empties, using 158
Relative Offset 230

S

Scalable Vector Graphics (.svg) file
3D mesh, converting to 242, 244
3D mesh, rotating to 242, 244
3D mesh, scaling to 242, 244
about 223
Array Modifier, combining with 245
importing, for stonework 237, 240
Outliner, used for finding objects 241
Properties Shelf, used for finding objects 241
Scale
used, for aligning vertices 79, 82
seams
clearing 354, 355, 359
creating 354, 355, 359
Selective Laser Sintering (SLS) printers
about 17
detailing 19

escape holes 20
overhangs 18
wall thickness 19
Shift key
used, for multiselect 121, 122
shortcuts keys 140
shutters
adding, to window with multi-cut Loop Cut and
Slide 196
slicer 8
Snap
used, for setting position 220, 221
Standard Triangle Language (STL) 86
Stereolithography (SLA) printers
about 16
detailing 17
drain holes 17
overhangs 17
wall thickness 17
stonework
Scalable Vector Graphics (.svg) file, importing
237, 240
Subdivide
used, for starting window panes 200
Subdivision Surface Modifier
adding 301, 302, 304
supported wall 15
supports 10

T

template shapes
faces, joining 261
faces, making 261
making 249
object, joining as shortcut 257, 260
objects, separating as shortcut 257, 260
vertices, duplicating 252, 256
vertices, separating 252, 256
text object
adding 137, 139
properties, using 150, 151
text, modifying 140, 141, 143
text
converting, to 3D mesh 150
Extrude tool, using 152

Texture Paint
  preparing to 359, 362, 366
texture painting 347
Thingiverse
  reference link 9, 10
thread width 13
Toggle Cyclic feature 44
torus
  about 65
  border select tool, using 76, 79
  bottom, flattening 75
  creating 65, 66
  laying out 65, 66
  object, adding 67, 69
  positioning 70, 72
  rotating, for Service Bureau Printing 72, 75
  Scale, used for aligning vertices 79, 82
  vertex visibility, toggling 76, 79
transparency mode
  setting 170, 172, 173
True Type Font 144

U

United States Customary System 57
unsupported wall 15
UV Maps
  Blender, painting in 367, 368
  coloring with 347
  images, editing outside Blender 374, 376, 377
  object, unwrapping into 350, 352, 353
  panel, adding to Blender 347, 349
  seams, clearing 354, 355, 359
  seams, creating 354, 355, 359
  Texture Paint, preparing to 359, 362, 366

V

vertices
  3D Cursor, rotating around 320, 323
  about 46, 49
  aligning, with Scale 79, 82

deleting, in cylinder 125, 126
duplicating 252, 256
moving 315
Proportional Editing, using 324, 326, 329
selecting 49, 51
separating 252, 256

W

wall thicknesses
  preserving 115
window pane
  exact thicknesses, applying 205, 208
  exact thicknesses, noting 205, 208
  finishing, with Inset 204
  number of cuts, controlling 201, 203
  starting, with subdivide 200
  subdividing edges 200
window
  copying 216, 218, 219
  creating, as separate object 195
  Extrude, used for raising details 210, 211, 213, 215
  modeling 193, 194
  renaming 216, 218, 219
  shutters, adding with multi-cut Loop Cut and Slide 196
wrinkles
  edge loops, using for 333
  modeling 329

X

X-Ray Mode
  about 170
  setting 170, 172, 173
X3D files
  exporting 378, 379
  image files, zipping 379, 380
  model files, zipping 379, 380
  renders, checking for CMYK issues 380
  uploading 378, 379